Mag

With Child

Also by Andy Martin

Reacher Said Nothing

With Child

Lee Child and the Readers of Jack Reacher

Andy Martin

polity

First published in 2019 by Polity Press

Polity Press
65 Bridge Street
Cambridge CB2 1UR, UK

Polity Press
101 Station Landing
Suite 300
Medford, MA 02155, USA

ISBN-13: 978-1-5095-3821-8
ISBN-13: 978-1-5095-3822-5 (pb)

A catalogue record for this book is available from the British Library.

Library of Congress Cataloging-in-Publication Data
Names: Martin, Andrew, 1952- author.
Title: With Child : Lee Child and the readers of Jack Reacher / Andy Martin.
Description: Cambridge ; Medford, MA : Polity, [2019] | Includes bibliographical references and index.
Identifiers: LCCN 2018059989 (print) | LCCN 2019007407 (ebook) | ISBN 9781509538232 (Epub) | ISBN 9781509538218 | ISBN 9781509538218(hardback) | ISBN 9781509538225(paperback)
Subjects: LCSH: Child, Lee. | Reacher, Jack (Fictitious character) | Authors and readers. | Fiction--Authorship.
Classification: LCC PS3553.H4838 (ebook) | LCC PS3553.H4838 Z77 2019 (print) | DDC 813/.54--dc23
LC record available at https://lccn.loc.gov/2018059989

Typeset in 10.75 on 14 Adobe Janson by
Servis Filmsetting Ltd, Stockport, Cheshire
Printed and bound in Great Britain by TJ International Limited

For further information on Polity, visit our website:
politybooks.com

Andy Martin (*right*) with Child
Photograph by Jessica Lehrman

Outside of a dog, a book is a man's best friend;
inside of a dog it's too dark to read.

Groucho Marx

FOREWORD

Andy Martin's extraordinary *Reacher Said Nothing* was a day-to-day account of the writing of my twentieth novel, *Make Me.* The idea was he should witness the first word, the last, and everything in between, and he did. Job done. But naturally we stayed in touch afterward, and he joined me for some of the launch events, six months after that last word was recorded. It seemed only fair – he had witnessed the long gestation, and he wanted to see the birth. Which meant he saw the book's early reception, and heard from its early readers.

Which led to another idea. We had talked a lot over the previous year, about the minutest minutiae of sentence construction, punctuation, word choice, and so on, but also about larger issues, one of which was my firm belief that writing and reading is a two-way street. First a book is written, then it is read, and only then does it exist. Readers create the story in their own heads, literally, at that point expending their own mental energy, burning their own calories. We agreed that the reader's sense of what the book is about is just as determinative as the writer's.

Andy was talking to the readers, listening to them, hearing their opinions. It struck both of us that *Reacher Said Nothing* was only half the story – the writer's half. We felt the readers' half should be recorded too. Hence this new addition. It completes the circle, and it tells me what the book I wrote is really about.

Lee Child
New York
2018

For all the seven billion potential readers.

BEFORE

'A LOT OF WRITERS ARE LIKE THAT, THEY START WITH DIALOGUE'

Three months later. New York.

CHILD: About a month after I finished *Make Me* I started writing 'Small Wars', the short story for the summer. I wrote the first line, 'In the spring of 1989 Caroline Crawford was promoted to the rank of lieutenant colonel,' and I turned around ... and you weren't there. Weird. I wanted to discuss the approach to setting the story in the past ... about how to let the reader know this isn't the present day. I felt it best to just announce, 'In the spring of 1989,' and have done with it. I'll have to get back in the habit of talking to myself. Instead of you.

MARTIN: It's like the end of a romance. There's one immigration guy convinced I was having an affair. Wanted to know why I kept coming back to New York. I said I wasn't working, it was just pleasure. How was it for you?

CHILD: The earth didn't move. Except when the subway went by under the building. I'm used to having a housekeeper knocking around the apartment. It's similar. And you had a knack of getting out just before I started to feel physically oppressed. I mean, I understood why you wanted to do it, but sometimes I thought, why me?

MARTIN: It could have been ... almost anyone. In theory. Maybe not Donna Tartt – too slow! But you were willing. I liked your economy of style – very degree zero. And you said, 'I'm starting Monday.' So naturally I hopped on a plane. I'm still trying to work out why you let me do it, though. I used to think it was

1

something to do with an ageing boxer wanting a spectator for his last big fight. Or maybe a magician who finally decided to twitch aside the curtain and say, 'OK, come back here and see how it's done.'

CHILD: Do you ever think there's something crazy about writing twenty books about the same guy?

MARTIN: Well, no crazier than nineteen, I suppose.

CHILD: That's why I did it. I thought it would make a change. I've been writing about Reacher for twenty years. I never had anyone watch me do it before. And it was a world first. A mad experiment. Literary criticism, but in real time. You were a wild card. What was the worst that could happen?

MARTIN: I was sitting about two yards behind you, reclining on a psychiatrist's couch, while you tapped away. Trying to keep quiet. I could actually make out a few of the words. 'Nothingness' I remember for some obscure reason. And 'waterbed'. And then I kept asking questions. I couldn't help myself. *How? Why? What the … ? Oh surely not!* A lot of people thought I would destroy the book. I was like the 'person from Porlock' who stopped 'Kubla Khan' in its tracks (according to Coleridge, anyway). 'You're killing Reacher, man!' as some guy said to me (after half a bottle of bourbon, but still).

CHILD: Here is the fundamental reality about the writing business. It's lonely. You spend all your time writing and then wondering whether what you just wrote is any good. You gave me instant feedback. If I write a nicely balanced four-word sentence with good rhythm and cadence, most critics will skip right over it. You not only notice it, you go and write a couple of chapters about it. I liked the chance to discuss stuff that most people never think about. It's weird and picayune, but obviously of burning interest to me. Previously only my daughter Ruth ever got it. Once we spent a whole drive to Philadelphia talking about a gerund we saw on a billboard.

MARTIN: And the way you care about commas – almost Flaubertian! I tried to be a kind of white-coated detached observer. But every observer impinges on the thing he is observing. Which would be you in this case. And I noticed that everything around you gets into your texts. You are an opportunistic writer. For example, one day the maid was bumping around in the kitchen and in the next line you used the word 'bucket'. Another time there was some construction work going on nearby and the next verb you used was 'nail'. We go to a bookstore and suddenly there is Reacher, more unexpectedly, in a bookstore. I couldn't help wondering, for example, if I influenced the 'home invasion' scene? Sneaking past your security downstairs, pen and notebook in hand.

CHILD: I don't know, to be honest. It was a logical development, for a thriller. It gave me a set-up for a set piece. But it could have been subconscious. I could have gone other ways. Or heard other things. Because you're right, that's my method. Like the thing with the bucket. In one ear, straight to the page. But not the name Wittgenstein [see page 398, *Make Me*]. That was a private joke.

MARTIN: The funny thing is you are clearly a frustrated academic. For starters, you have officially seen *Waiting for Godot* thirty-nine times. And you are good at the professorial analysis. Be it of Shakespeare's 'stony limit' (*Romeo and Juliet*) or your own onomatopoeia. All I had to do was quote you. It was like watching Lionel Messi running rings around the opposition and providing simultaneous commentary.

CHILD: I believe it was Kant who said something like, Newton knew what he was doing and could take you back through the steps logically, whereas Homer had no idea and couldn't possibly explain it either. I sort of thought: maybe I can explain it, I've been doing it long enough. Lots of readers ask me how I do this or that. I thought this was an opportunity to tell them. Or at least to figure it out for myself. Which was the main thing, to be honest. Normally I operate in a fog of instinct. I wondered if being required to explain as I went along might actually be more illuminating for me than for you.

MARTIN: That was the thing that drew me in: you never knew in advance what you were going to be writing about. You really were making it up as you went along. I can certify that. I remember what you said when we started off down this road: 'I have no plot and no title.'

CHILD: The beginning of a new book feels like stepping off a cliff into the abyss. A long free-fall. One of these days I'm going to end up flat on my face. Or not, as the case may be.

MARTIN: Sublime confidence. And no rules.

CHILD: Elmore Leonard had rules. Made to be broken. 'Never use an adverb.' Never *is* an adverb! If you want to start with, 'It was a dark and stormy night,' go for it. I mean, suppose it really was a dark and stormy night? What are we supposed to do? Lie?

MARTIN: Do you think you learned anything from watching me watch you for a year?

CHILD: Well, I learned that line about Kant and Newton and Homer, that was one of yours, so thanks to Cambridge for that. It was like having a coach in baseball or tennis – you're forced to reflect on what you're doing, and maybe therefore you do it better. And certainly I think *Make Me* came out well. After this I reckon every writer is going to want a meta-book to go with their book – a boxed set. What about you: did you learn anything of value over the last year?

MARTIN: I remember one of the first things you said to me. 'This isn't the first draft – it's the *only* draft!' Actually, you do finesse things a lot; 'churning', as you call it. But you trust your own voice. Maybe that's what I learned above all: don't try to sound like someone else. But, looking ahead, I know you're starting the next one on 1 September. The annual ritual. Any ideas?

CHILD: Pure *déjà-vu* for you. No title, no plot, nothing. Starting from zero.

MARTIN: How about *Remake Me*?

CHILD: That reminds me of my life in television. The endless sequels. *Make Me Again, Make Me One More Time* ... What about you? You going to watch Jonathan Franzen next?

MARTIN: I've done *Reacher Said Nothing*. I see a series. *Reacher Said Something*. Then maybe *Reacher Said a Load of Stuff, Reacher Said Way Too Much* ...

CHILD: You're not watching me again. So what are they going to be about?

MARTIN: No idea. Your influence. I thought I might steal your schedule. Start September 1st. Finish March or April. I had to learn something from the master. I'm like a sorcerer's apprentice. Begin at the beginning, go on to the end, and then stop. And drink a hell of a lot of black coffee in between.

FALL

1

THE GORGEOUS FEELING

It begins (whatever *it* is). Or it should do. 1 September 2015. New York. Twenty-one years to the day since he went out to buy the paper and the pencil he would use to write *Killing Floor*, his first Jack Reacher novel. Twenty novels later, it is time to begin the twenty-first, the successor to *Make Me*. 1 September: a date he cannot miss. Kick-off. Ignition. Genesis.

It is a ritual with him: a superstition, a good luck charm. So long as he starts a new book on the first day of September he knows that, infallibly and inevitably, he will complete it, some time around April, May at the outside, in the following year. It was a completely reliable system, like a chronometer, keeping the ship steady and heading in the right general direction rather than falling off the edge of the world. All he had to do was sit down at his desk in his office in his eleventh-floor apartment on Central Park West and switch on his computer and type. Pausing only to light another cigarette. 'It's not rocket science,' he would say. 'It's not curing cancer.' Writer's block was pure myth. He had nothing in his head, almost nothing, but something would come to him. It always did.

So long as he got going on 1 September. It was in the diary. What could go wrong?

Of course he had to have his traditional summer break, recharge the old batteries, hang with the family. He had spent a couple of weeks on a ship cruising around Norway; he loved all those fjords, and the bright sun at sea-level and then the snow-capped mountains right above. Crisp and clean. Cut off, remote from the world, no wi-fi. He was off the grid again, on the loose, roaming free, almost like Reacher. (Albeit with more stylish kit – and Reacher on a ship …? One way or another he'd probably have to sink it, after locking antlers with the captain, in reality a drug smuggler or people trafficker, and the second-in-command, and the third ... .)

As he looked up into those mountains – not so high after all, eminently climbable – and visualized himself up there, looking back at the ship a couple of thousand feet below, and peering out over the abyss, he couldn't help but recall the idea, which a friend had put to him in the Union Square Café, one year before, and that had fallen on fertile ground and grown and blossomed into *Make Me,* that when the time came for oblivion, all you had to do was climb up a mountain (did he say in Austria, specifically? or Switzerland? surely Norway would do – a couple of thousand feet would still kill you, it didn't have to be the north face of the Eiger) and fling yourself off, sailing down down into the void. A seductive idea, but he'd never given his friend's specific plan much credence.

All that climbing, the pure air, the ruggedly beautiful landscape below: you'd want to live! You'd never finish yourself off that way, unless you just accidentally fell off, exhausted by all the unaccustomed exercise. But the principle was sound enough: to choose one's own fate. With complete clarity of mind. And he knew the perfect little veterinary store down Mexico way with a more than adequate supply of horse tranquillizer, when the time was right. Pity about catalytic converters. Back in the day all you needed was a car exhaust and a hosepipe and it was off to dreamland. He loved the whiff of benzene.

But that time was not yet. There was at least one more novel to write. It said so in his three-book contract and he didn't want to let anyone down. Anyway, he could feel one coming on, even though he had no clear idea, no plot, and no title. That was the way he liked it. Inspiration would come, at the right time, in the right place. He didn't want to have to think about it too hard, in advance. Far better to relax and forget about it and let it happen. Just cruise ... on the cruise. He barely left his deckchair (got more reading done that way). An occasional lap of the deck – enough exercise and fresh air! Feet up again.

Back to Winston Churchill. *The Grand Alliance*, volume III of his history of the Second World War. The Brits declared war on

Japan faster than the Americans. Churchill only had to go through the cabinet; Roosevelt had to check it was OK with Congress. The British Prime Minister sent his letter to the Japanese ambassador, declaring war, the day after Pearl Harbor. Signed off with,

I have the honour to be, with high consideration,
Sir,
Your obedient servant,
Winston S. Churchill

'Some people did not like this ceremonial style,' he added in the history. 'But after all when you have to kill a man it costs nothing to be polite.' Reacher had a line just like that in *A Wanted Man* (Reacher 17). You don't have to be rude. Just do it. *After you, No, after you,* and then ... *pow*! The courteous killer. The executioner's etiquette. A gorilla with manners. He liked that, jotted the Churchill down on a scrap of paper and tucked it in his wallet. You never know when these things might come in handy. 90% of writing was reading anyway.

His muse had never been known to let him down before. She wouldn't this time either – always providing, of course, that he had it all lined up, everything in place, for 1 September. He had the flight booked for Monday morning, 31 August. From London. Not too early. But back to New York just a few hours later. Jet lag minimal. Down to it by the crack of noon the next day (coffee on, Camels out).

Got to London City Airport in plenty of time. So convenient. A brief pause at Shannon, on the west coast of Ireland, to refuel. Settled himself comfortably into his business-class seat, stretched out his long legs. (First-class? No thanks; they never left you alone for five minutes, 'Another glass of champagne, sir?' It was too much.) Felt sublimely, blissfully, confident. He'd had enough vacation, enough fjords, it was time to get down to business again. Reacher-time. And talking of time (he pulled out his phone and checked, he didn't have quite the same chronological omniscience as Reacher), wasn't this plane kind of late to take off?

2

THE DEARTH OF THE AUTHOR

I was barely on to my second cup of coffee that morning when I picked up the Leemail. By his standards it was almost long-winded.

```
Urgent — forget tomorrow — plane broke down,
stuck in Ireland for the night. Don't know when
I'll get home.
```

Which explains how it comes about that I am in New York, on 1 September, writing about Lee Child's newly published *Make Me* in the absence of Child himself. The author is not dead, he is only delayed, somewhere in Ireland. But he is AWOL. He has stood up the muse. Risky.

He should have known he was leaving it too late – the day before. Pure hubris and thoroughly deserving of a comeuppance. I had a kind of smug told-you-so feeling. Verging on *Schadenfreude*. I whipped off the following reply:

```
Looks like I'm going to have to start without
you. Maybe you should try writing in the airport
lounge?
```

I knew he hated writing in airport lounges. He had to be back in his cool, comfortable office space on the Upper West Side, or nothing. No loud rock music (unlike Stephen King, for one). No perching on stools in cafés. He needed that silver metal desk, the size of a steam engine or the wing of a Spitfire. The 27-inch monitor. The reference books and the bestseller listings on the wall. And – above all – the cigarettes. Maybe if you could smoke in airport lounges and Starbucks it would be a different story.

I wasn't too worried about him, to be honest. He would probably get over the bad start. Then again, maybe all his worst fears would come true and he would completely mess up the next book. Maybe it would never happen.

But it wasn't my concern. I had to prioritize. And my priority was the fate of *Make Me*.

I had watched over the slow, sometimes gruelling genesis and evolution of a book. I had borne witness, almost like a midwife, to its birth. In fact I was more involved than a midwife – I had been there, at the primal scene, overseeing the inception, the embryonic struggle for life, division and multiplication, the gradual formation of a text. And now it was out there, in the world, on its own, and somebody had to keep an eye on it. I had gone from midwife to nanny, or possibly minder.

Obviously, the author himself was useless, knocking back Guinness in a pub in the Emerald Isle, carousing with the spiritual descendants of James Joyce and Samuel Beckett. But even if he weren't, there wasn't a whole lot he could do, in any kind of practical way. He couldn't exactly write the reviews himself.

Months had passed since he had hit the *send* button. He had finessed, here and there, in response to his editor. She had one telling point: the bad guys in the home invasion scene would definitely refer to Chang's Chinese look (now that she was no longer 'Stashower'). He had proofread and eradicated error. Okayed the cover (had to change the colour scheme: silver came out grey online – that neon yellow ought to do it). And he would be present for the launch party at Union Square Barnes & Noble, he would go and converse with Stephen King in Cambridge (Mass.), he would give away enticing and intriguing snippets on talk shows, shrewdly summarize on breakfast TV, and try to sound like a serious and reputable writer on radio. He would sign a thousand copies (more!) as he trooped around the bookstores of North America and Europe. Not to mention a couple of high-security military bases. Maybe even a campus or two.

But the reality was that the book was on its own now. It was vulnerable. It was an orphan. The author was not dead, but he might as well be. It had been thrown in at the deep end of the world and now it had to sink or swim.

This is going to sound more ruthless than I intend, but the truth is, strictly from the point of view of the book itself, his premature demise would be no kind of disaster. *Au contraire.* 'FAMOUS AUTHOR DEAD' headlines would do it no harm at all. As far as *Make Me* was concerned, he could just go ahead and chuck himself off that mountain, fill up the tank with horse tranquillizer, or drink himself into oblivion in Ireland. It would not only be obscurely poetic, it would sell shedloads. A *posthumous* thriller – now that was thrilling. Look at Larsson, for example: finishes the 'Millennium trilogy', bids farewell to *The Girl with the Dragon Tattoo*, then promptly drops dead. Good timing, Stieg. 'The End', then *aaaagh.*

Better still, to come back to the case of Child, if some delusional obsessive should choose this moment to gun him down, *à la* Lennon, preferably on the doorstep of his apartment building, after all only a few blocks north of the Dakota, that would (personal regrets aside, and speaking purely on behalf of *Make Me*) be a great way to go. As I say, I am not advocating any such occurrence, only contemplating the kind of impact an author can have on his own work *after* it is finished. So far as I can work out, the worse for him, the better for *it.*

I happened to mention this scenario to Lee, some time later. He agreed. Didn't mind the harshness at all. Liked it, in fact. 'Seems to me I have three possibilities. The book comes out with zero participation from me. It does OK. It comes out *with* participation from me. Better. But, better still, a tragic feature – that would be best of all.' He was already using the word 'feature', as if it would make a good article, or a movie perhaps, seeing the creative, writerly possibilities inherent in a good death, even if it was his own. 'The best thing I could do would be to fall out of this window right now.' He had the window open, looking out over Central Park, and it was all of eleven storeys straight down. 98% guaranteed mortality he once told me. 'Or jump. An author dying tragically is a great sales booster. I'd be fine with the first second or so. I wonder what I'd be thinking about before the lights went out?'

14

'Headlines?'

'Thriller writer in mystery fall. Investigations continue. The police are looking for a white-haired guy in shorts and flip-flops. With a notebook.'

'Recreational drugs also suspected. Police analysing pipe found on premises.'

'Recreational? That's work!'

Short of actually pulling a Larsson, however, the author would be doing his utmost to sell the book.

Nevertheless, there was something beautiful and entirely appropriate in his absence from New York, the scene of the crime, as it were, where he had only written the book, and where it would now be read, many times over, quite independently and regardless of its author. But, surely, was he not father to the book? And therefore legitimately proprietorial? Deserving of respect? More – I thought – like a sperm donor, or a surrogate mother. He would have to let go, eventually. The readers now (quite literally) owned it. All the talk shows and the signings were just prolonging the agony. There was not a lot he could do about it. Nor could the publishers. All that immense apparatus, the network, the team, everybody beavering away, but fundamentally nobody really knew what they were doing. Why does *this* work, and not *that*? It was a mystery. 'You're trying to control the future,' Lee said. 'It's like picking a lock with a pipe-cleaner. Or pushing water. All you can do is put it out there and hope.'

Every reading was, potentially, an act of subversion. A form of deconstruction. Every reader (and especially reviewer) was an anarchist, mounting a coup, refuting the authority of the author. Reading was tantamount to revenge. Stephen King's story of the fan-turned-sadist-and-tyrant (*Misery*) is only a dramatization of the truth that every writer acknowledges and fears. The fate of the book is in the hands of the reader (always assuming there is one), not the writer. As Lee says, it's the reader who gets to decide whether or not a book is any good.

On the other hand, there were those 'Reacher Creatures': addicted to the works of Lee Child, desperate for their next fix, all in the grip, to a greater or lesser degree, of a specific form of lexomania. All of them relying on the author to get the job done.

The writer needed his readers, but those readers definitely needed the writer. They were accomplices in a perfect dialectic.

```
from: LeeChild
to: andymartinink
subject: Reacher said nothing
Will be back late tonight. Determined to get the
first sentence down before midnight.
```

3

BEFORE MIDNIGHT

The plane had been leaking fuel apparently. Just as well they didn't try to make it over the Atlantic (at least as far as the *next* book was concerned).

Lee and the other eleven passengers (a small United plane) had been shuttled off to the Strand hotel in Limerick, only a short ride away, where he spent a comfortable night, other than panicking. There had been a tacit consensus not to talk about what anyone did for a living. If anyone had asked, Lee was planning to say 'drug dealer' – maybe it wasn't that far from the truth, metaphorically speaking. Anything other than writer (he feared the dread follow-up question: *And have any of your books been made into a movie?*). A Jamaican guy had been wondering whether to retire to Edinburgh or Honolulu, and the odd thing was that he was only in his thirties. Suspicious. But, on the other hand, maybe not everyone was a criminal. The jury was out. Anyway, they got shuttled back again to Shannon the next morning, the plane had been repaired, and they took off. Legs stretched out again. Newark by 8, hopped in a cab, back safely in the apartment by 10, still on the first day of September. He was almost relaxed. The idea had come to him on the flight over. Dropped right into his lap. And a title. Manna from heaven, as usual.

Fuelled up on coffee again, he went into the office, sat down at the desk, cranked up the computer, and opened up a fresh file. 'NIGHT SCHOOL'. It was only a provisional title – it might not stick, but he liked it. Where had it even come from? No idea. Re-education. Everybody needed it. Especially Reacher. And the word 'Night', that was promising. *School*? Was that too ... Jack Reacher and the Philosopher's Stone? *Fuck Rowling!* She can't Hogwarts everything! He lit a cigarette and inhaled deeply. Got the first sentence down, no problem. Nice. Now he was on a roll. Got half the next sentence down ... then he got stuck. A medal ... Hmm, what kind of medal, exactly? He'd have to think about that. It couldn't just be 'a medal' – or could it? Oh well, that would do for one day's work. Flaubert only managed an adjective some days. Just a very, very good adjective. One-and-a-half sentences. A grand total of twenty-two words. It was a start. *Before* midnight, that was the crucial thing. Mission accomplished, job done. He had stayed true to the good old tradition that had never yet let him down. Big sigh of relief. The gods had been appeased. As far as the new one was concerned.

More importantly, as regards the *last* one, there was another development. I hit it first online, but went out to buy an actual paper copy of *The New York Times*. Now it felt real. I opened the newspaper, Tuesday, 1 September, around the same time Lee was sitting down to work on the next one. It was exactly one year to the day (as Lee himself reminded me, in his chronocentric way) since he tapped out, 'Moving a guy as big as Keever wasn't easy' and I watched him doing it (all I could make out from my position was the '-ing'). And now it was all over the front page of *The New York Times*.

Maybe 'all over' is a slight exaggeration. It was all over page C4, to be precise, in the Arts section, but it had its own dedicated box on the front page, previewing what was on the inside ('"Make Me", Lee Child's latest novel, hints at change for Jack Reacher'). Lee Child nestled naturally alongside 'Hope Running Out, Iraqis Rally', 'Crisis Tests European Core Value', 'Obama Aids US Workers In Late Push', and especially 'MURDER RATES RISE SHARPLY IN MANY CITIES'. I flipped through, passing over the tempting 'New Cache of Clinton Emails'. The full review of *Make Me*. By Janet Maslin. Under the heading, 'Tough Guy Protagonist Adds Another Layer'. Huge. Two whole columns running right down the page (with just a little box on the *New York Times* Wine Club right at the bottom).

It was a great review, because it insisted the author was still getting better. The closing lines were: '... the big guy's definitely on the upswing. The guy who writes about him is too.' As if to prove the point, the article carried a classic hard man author photo, Lee in the leather jacket with all the zips, a taller, thinner-looking Marlon Brando. Taken straight off the back cover of the book itself.

'It's kind of gnomic,' Lee said, the following day, around noon, uptown. 'You never quite know what she means.' He was looking stubbly, a bit Desperate Dan, but not too bad considering. His apartment's air-conditioning was a mess and there were guys making holes in walls, or mainly standing around and scratching their heads.

By anyone's standards, it was a rave. She had certainly not given too much of the plot away. Only hinted at the 'horror', as if it was the end of *Apocalypse Now*. But she also threw in how Reacher was learning more than he ever wanted to know. 'Yeah,' Lee said, rubbing his chin. 'Normally he not only wins, he likes to show the other guy that he really has lost. Rub his face in it. It's not like that this time. The whole thing is too big. He can't really defeat the evil. All he can do is staunch the flow, for a moment. It goes beyond him.'

'Does that explain the romantic enjambment? A kind of consolation?'

'It's funny, I only have him not answering a question directly. Everyone takes that for a yes.'

'Come on!' I was attached to Chang, the ex-FBI agent formerly known as Stashower. 'Let Reacher have some fun for a change. Apparently some advance readers have already been bitching about how it's too dark and they had to avert the gaze.'

'That's the world. It's not all pleasant.'

I was thinking, as I walked away from Lee's place, that maybe there was something in this sense of even Reacher, wise old bird that he was, discovering something new and utterly beyond his power to master that inspired the 'Night School' idea. There was at least a certain continuum there, even though the new novel was a prequel, the young Reacher back in the army again (as he was in *The Enemy*, *The Affair*, and the short story, 'Small Wars', the one Lee had dashed off back in July).

I knew I was focusing on *Make Me*. But it all came from the same place. And just as I had fallen for that opening sentence about Keever, the big guy, and the moving, and how hard it was, so too I couldn't help but think about the new opening sentence too. This was all hush hush. I had to keep it under wraps for now. But the first sentence he'd written was this:

In the morning they gave Reacher a medal, and in the afternoon they sent him back to school.

4

LIKE A COCKROACH

I knew it was serious when he offered to pour me a mug of black coffee. We wandered into the kitchen and he refilled the coffee machine.

'For the first time, I'm actually worried.'

'About?'

'Sales, obviously. We've got the new Stieg and the new Franzen coming out at the same time. It's going to be tough.'

Lee had written a very fair and balanced review of *The Girl in the Spider's Web* (by David Lagercrantz) – the Stieg Larsson sequel – for *The New York Times* (and kindly sent me a preview). Thoughtful. Shrewd. Pros and cons. 'I thought your review was very fair and balanced,' I said.

'What I really wanted to do was to kill it. Stomp on it. Like a cockroach. It's competition. I had to grit my teeth not to trash it totally.'

I sort of wondered what he thought of Jonathan Franzen. His name came up from time to time but I realized I didn't know what he thought of his writing as opposed to the myth and the hype. And I wasn't about to find out either, because he raised another question entirely.

'And then Harper Lee is still selling.' *Go Set a Watchman*, the new old one.

'Oh come on!' I spluttered, having read that phony non-novel over the summer. 'That is crap!' And then added, 'Sorry,' feeling that my one-word review was perhaps a little unfair, but also that the other Lee was not even in the running. Unless it was fixed. (Need I add, I know nothing. When I finally get around to opening the 'Bestsellers' page of *The New York Times*, dated Sunday, 30 August, guess what I find? Yep. Fiction. 1. GO SET A WATCHMAN.)

Lee smiled. Oh well, one down. 'What they did for Larsson makes me wonder ... Is there anyone else out there who could carry on the Reacher series?'

I scratched my head, like the aircon engineers, trying to think of someone. 'Like the James Bond franchise. Of course, unlike Larsson, unlike Fleming, you're not dead yet. You're not planning to retire young like that Jamaican guy you met on the plane are you?'

'I can't! There's no one to take over the store.'

'You must have had offers.'

'There's a number of people hinting at it. Ghost-writers.'

'Almost like writing your will and there are all these relatives poised to swoop. Vultures. "Hey, Lee, you know, when you're dead and all, I wonder what happens to good old Reacher ... Got any plans?"'

'Yeah, that kind of thing.'

'Anyone?'

'Nah, not really.'

'Carl Cederström – he'd do a good job. He's Swedish.'

'Yeah, he's got the umlauts.' Lee liked Scandi names, thought they would have an edge. 'And he's tall.'

'What about Big Blue?'

Lee had recently visited the IBM artificial intelligence research lab (invited there by our friend Quiller). I assumed they had stolen some part of his brain to incorporate into their electronic neocortex.

He was generous. 'There is a madness to Reacher. Big Blue could hit maybe 90% of it. But it's the off-the-wall stuff it can't do.'

'*Make Me*, for example.'

'Come on, who else is going to come up with Reacher reciting the Gettysburg Address in the bath? Would anyone else do that? Who is going to go there?'

'Or the name "Mother's Rest"? That is so idiosyncratic. Almost absurd.'

'I guess I'd better keep going then.'

'I know, what about ...?' I mentioned a couple of names, one man and one woman. Maybe they could do it?

'Them!' he exploded. 'In their self-published world, they just make me feel that whatever it is I do is the *Real Thing* by comparison!' He wasn't scornful, just conscious of a differendum. I think it was why he liked academics so much. It reminded me of something he had said when I told him I was off to go to work in Starbucks. The kind of thing he refused to do. It wasn't just the cigarettes, he argued. 'They're all writing novels in Starbucks! Who isn't writing a novel with a latte in one hand?' He spat out the word *latte* with a particular disgust. Coffee was coffee and milk was milk and never the twain shall meet. 'Starbucks should have a competition – the Best Novels Written in Starbucks.' He made the kind of derisive noise that suggested he wouldn't feel worried by that kind of competition. He was going to be head judge – and executioner. They were bound to be frothy, latte-lite books. But he was worried about Franzen and Lagercrantz. Big guns. Not just black but double espressos.

I'd always liked that self-confident line of Reacher's: 'There are only five or six guys in the world who are maybe as good as I am.' By *good* he meant *good at killing*. 'What are the chances that your guy is going to be one of them?' (When I checked back with Lee about which novel that line came from he said, '*The Visitor*? [*Running Blind* in the UK]. Hmm, could be any one of them really.') What were the chances that Franzen and Lagercrantz could be bigger and better?

Lee was up against it. In fact, he was (as Sartre would say) doomed to fail. I had only just realized. All the time I had been watching him write *Make Me*, the whole of the previous twelve months, I had been convinced that I was watching the Numero Uno. Something like Socrates and Schwarzenegger all rolled into one. The Napoleon of literature. Beyond compare (we had agreed to leave J. K. Rowling out of it). And, it was true, he was writing beautiful sentences and an epic book. But, coming out again into the real world beyond the precincts of that hushed, orderly library that was Lee's fortress on Central Park West, Child Tower, it was obvious: he was just one guy, up against hordes. The mob. The book would do OK for a while. But, as the economist John Maynard Keynes shrewdly pointed out, 'In the long run, we're all dead.' Lee would live or die by the numbers. And the fact was, even if you got to be a bestseller, you couldn't be a bestseller for ever. Not unless you were the Bible or Shakespeare. The other guys were Lilliputians, but there were a lot of them. Even if you got to No. 1, all it meant was that there was a long line of contenders waiting to knock you off your pedestal.

Even Napoleon had Waterloo and St Helena on his CV. Dead aged fifty-one. Lee was nearly a decade older.

5

THE ZIPLESS FUCK

'It came out good. I keep wondering – was there a cause and effect?'

'You mean, with having me around keeping an eye on you?'

'Did it make a difference?'

'Well, the couple of times I suggested anything you went in the opposite direction.'

'You probably stopped me goofing off all the time.'

'There's that last sentence, for example. Look at it.'

He had just given me a copy of *Make Me*. The book itself, the hardcover, freshly minted, was a thing of beauty. Glossy. Acid-free paper. Real cuts in the cover. I was a bit choked up, to be honest. He had inscribed it, 'Andy, thanks for a fun year.'

Obviously I was going to have to be cooler and more objective and more detached than ever if this stood any chance of coming out right, whatever *this* was. I flipped to the last page. 'It's sixty-seven words long! I'd been concentrating on the four-worders. So I'm guessing you did that deliberately, just to show you could do Proust if you felt like it.'

'It felt right, at the time. Wanted to end with a flourish.'

'*Needle*. Final word. My first thought was: something sadistic. But there are all sorts of positive connotations. It has a *point*. Old record player. Sewing – I think Georges Perec's old crew, Oulipo, were into that – the '*Ouvroir* de la littérature potentielle'. And then, a camel through the eye of. Rich man? Miracle? Transcendence?'

'It's one fucking word.'

'It's polysemic.'

'It's a wonder you didn't completely screw me up, now I think of it.'

It was Labor Day and he was doing a breakfast TV show. Good slot. Great snacks and inexplicably beautiful women hanging about. But there was one other temptation on his mind. He was concerned lest, like some reality TV star, driven to madness and verbal diarrhoea by the camera lens, he might blurt out, accidentally, under interrogation, half the secrets of the book, in one spontaneous ill-thought-through sentence. He was working out how not to give it all away. 'I'm thinking I ought to concentrate on the beginning. That should be safe enough.'

'Famous last words,' I said. *Safe enough*, straight out of the mouth of the bad guys in *Make Me*, signifying typical over-confidence ...

'Reacher is attempting to *not* get involved. That is the crux of it. Keep out of it. Spectator. Detached observer. But then there is a woman at the train station. Keeps looking out for a guy on the train. Who isn't there. How could he not get involved?'

'And then Mother's Rest. Nowheresville. Hick town of all time. Nothing happens there, obviously.'

'It's the set-up. That's what I need to focus on.'

'You know one thing you're good at.'

'What?'

'I've only ever known two people who were good at this. The other one was ...' I mentioned the name of a former Provost of King's College, Cambridge. 'He was a bastard, of course, dead now, but he had this skill. You've got it. Of taking dumb questions and kind of reconstructing them in some way so that the answer comes out interesting and the guy asking the question thinks that was a pretty clever question in the first place.'

He said nothing. Grinned.

'And you're pretty quick. Remember that idiot question when that woman was asking you about the time – you were only seventeen – when you were auditioning strippers. Incredible.'

'Oh yeah,' he recalled. 'Were you a breast man or a butt man? That one?'

'"I liked the one with snakes!" Come on, that was genius, the old Provost of King's would never have thought of that.'

I guess it was thinking about Cambridge that made me mention how terrible I used to be at interviews. 'I managed to combine terror and arrogance,' I said. 'I'm not recommending it. Until I discovered the trick.'

'Which was?'

I showed him. It's not very complicated. I sat there with my hands on my knees for once. Not something I did very often with Lee. I happened to be sitting in one of his armchairs at the time, which made it easier. 'Look, if I lean forwards, it's "Oh my god, maniac! Too keen, he wants it too much, he'll be unbearable." If I lean back,' I leaned back, 'it's more, "Lazy bastard! he'll never do any work." But hands-on-knees … aha! a man of learning and moderation, so so reasonable, he'll do …'

'It's all about the body-language,' Lee said. He showed me *his* trick. He always used it in television interviews. 'This is how I normally come across.' He sprawled all over the couch. He was already sprawling, but he somehow seemed to sprawl a little more, like the ever-expanding *favela* around some Brazilian city. 'This is how I fix it.' He sat up some more. 'Well, I can't at the moment. But if I had a jacket on, I could. I actually sit on the tail of my jacket.'

'Isn't that a bit awkward?'

'Serves two purposes. First, it stops the collar of your jacket riding up around your neck. The village idiot look. Secondly, it keeps me reasonably upright. It's like having a leash on. But I still like to lean forwards a bit. Makes you look engaged, you know, interested in whatever pisspoor comments the interviewer is coming out with.'

Of course, it all depended on wearing a jacket in the first place. September in New York – strictly shirt-sleeves most of the time. But TV studios were over-air-conditioned anyway, so a jacket was fine. He had this Brooks Brothers charcoal two-button he pulled out regularly for the purpose. And he was really into what he called 'forward movement'.

'You're just sitting there. You've got to have forward movement. You've got to have something going on. Of course,' he said, reflectively (I sometimes forget – he used to be in television), 'it's possible to overdo it. Look at all these BBC guys. They've obviously received a memo.'

We had been talking about how the baristas in Starbucks tend to overdo the 'Have a great day!' I had estimated that one young woman serving had been saying it at least once a minute all the time I was there. She had *received a memo* (and she kept it up with the same even-handed enthusiasm too; it was impressive).

'You stick them in front of the Houses of Parliament or the latest terrorist outrage and watch their hands. They're all doing it.' He came out with lots of different very plausible hand movements that instantly put me in mind of a BBC presenter. He was a great mimic. 'It's like watching the Karate Kid. It's supposed to draw you in, humanize the talking head. Comes out like some kind of nervous disorder. Utterly ridiculous. I don't want to do that.'

I wanted to know if he'd ever thrown a fit and stormed off the set. 'It's always so embarrassing when they forget to take off the microphone,' he said, impersonating someone trying to storm off and then getting dragged back by a wire around his neck. Almost strangled. The closest he'd ever come to it was at the Cheltenham Literary Festival one year. Ian McEwan had one of his novels coming out on the same day and the BBC tried to set it up as a class struggle between the bourgeoisie (McEwan) and the proletariat (Child). A showdown, an *agon*. They were trying to wind him up. 'I was fairly categorical and blunt. You know, forceful, verging on aggro. But it's a win-win for me. I can't lose if I answer like Reacher. They expect that, it's what they want.'

'They would love it if you head butted someone.'

'It's got to happen one of these days.'

'Yeah, the Provost of King's was a bit like that too. Attack-dog.'

'You know the new Erica Jong is coming out on the same day?'

He had always had a soft spot for Erica Jong. Had quoted her phrase about the 'zipless fuck' from time to time. In other words, he liked the idea that at least some women, some of the time, had the Reacher mentality when it came to romance. *Un amour sans lendemain*, as Camus and Gainsbourg would say. *Je t'aime moi non plus*. No suitcase, no attachments. In military terms, the brief skirmish rather than the long-drawn-out war. It was part of his evenly egalitarian outlook: if guys could think like that, then so could women. He was a feminist too, loved to have strong women characters in his books. And he thought that if one part of feminism was the right to say No, then the other part of it was certainly the right to say Yes, in certain circumstances, to the right guy (or gal), without you necessarily having to sign up to a long-term contract. Short and sweet. You drop into a relationship, and you drop out again. It wasn't going to suit everyone, but it was there.

Turned out he wasn't quite so worried about Jong's *Fear of Dying* as he was about Lagercrantz. Of course, neither of us had actually read it. 'Bad title,' he said. 'Who's afraid of dying? It's the living too long we're afraid of.'

6

MYSTERIOUS

I bought a couple of books: Pierre Lemaître's *Camille* – diminutive hero, five-footer (his Ma smoked too much when pregnant), opposite of Reacher – why didn't they get Tom for that part? I thought. And, of course, a copy of *The Girl in the Spider's Web*. I felt a bit of a traitor, to be honest. But I had to keep up the detachment. This was research. On the other hand, I had to go and wave it in Lee's face. 'Can't wait to get stuck into this baby!' I said, cheerfully.

He looked up from behind several tall piles of *Make Me*s, like a Swiss yodeller calling out across the valleys. 'Week before mine. He has seven days to rampage and maraud ... before it gets *crushed*!' He was nervous, though, I could tell. Trying to be confident, but edgy.

We were in Otto's Mysterious Bookshop in Tribeca. Lee was doing a spot of pre-signing. I counted 350 books, roughly. Only took him about an hour or so. It was all part of the job. And some of those dedications were long and specific. 'This one's an essay!' he gasped. But he ploughed on anyway. Readers had given instructions telling Lee Child what to write. He was now in their hands (literally, or at least literarily). Like an amiable genie, theirs to command.

This was not public, just Lee and a Mysterious guy. But even so a nice couple from Boston popped up and had their photo taken with him. 'Could you make it out to Richard, please? He's ninety now. But he loves your books. We are a bit worried about the mental side.' It wasn't clear if there was a connection between the early stages of dementia and an addiction to Reacher. 'He's always asking, "When's the next one coming out!?"' If he was asking that all year long, that could drive anyone up the wall. Maybe he'd give it a rest for a couple of days.

Lee wrote: 'Hang in there, the next one is coming right up!'

Which was true. In a way.

'How's the second sentence going?' I asked.

'We're getting there,' he said. 'Might have a shot at the third tomorrow.'

He wasn't exactly sprinting straight out of the blocks. His mind was at least half still on *Make Me*. 'I've got to work out what to say about it on Monday. Without giving it all away.' He was still worrying about that.

I was just sitting there, on the sofa, flicking idly through *The Girl in the Spider's Web* while Lee kept on signing *Make Me*. The piles were gradually getting whittled away. 'Lagercrantz and I have something in common,' I pointed out. 'He was shortlisted for the William Hill Sports Book of the Year. Cool.'

'I'm with Eva Gabrielsson,' he said. 'If she had had her way, it would never have been published. Quite right too. It's not good enough.' Gabrielsson was Larsson's partner, but unmarried. Larsson left no will. Finished the trilogy then promptly dropped dead. Gabrielsson was left with nothing. The family got it all. Tough.

'Swedish laws seem incredibly harsh,' he went on. 'She gets nothing? Andy, make your will now. You might be worth something one day.'

'I think it was the self-destructive writer's diet. Too many burgers while he was working. Sugar Puffs probably. Look at him, you can see he was overweight. Heart attack waiting to happen.'

'Ran up the stairs, conked out. And he'd been accepted for publication.'

'Should've worked out more.'

The Mysterious guy piped up. 'I think he used to smoke too much. Very heavy smoker.'

Lee coughed. Heavy smoker's cough. At least he was thin. 'One thing I noticed. Blomkvist is reading an Elizabeth George novel. American, but sets her books in England. They're fine but everything is just slightly off. I wanted to say something about that in my review, but then I thought, whoa, I'm doing the same in reverse, so I'm just convicting myself out of my own mouth.'

'Fantasy America,' I said. 'That's all anyone wants. Cowboys and injuns. Larry McMurtry without the horses. *Shane! Come back, Shane!*' Lee had had to write a whole article pointing out the differences between Reacher and Shane and also stressing that the kid in the original Shane story never says that – it's only in the movie. Come back, Alan Ladd. I was pretending I hadn't read it.

I realized what I was doing: I was adopting the persona of the Bad Reader. Maybe it wasn't even a persona. At the core of every Good Reader (Umberto Eco speaks of the 'Model' or 'Ideal' Reader) there is a Bad Reader just waiting to rear his ugly head. Jekyll and Hyde. Lee was doing his best to pre-empt all the potential Hydes out there. The monsters and the moaners and the bitchy reviewers.

We were paying for our books. 'How's *The Girl in the Spider's Web* doing?' I said to the guy at the till. I regretted it almost immediately. 'It's a hot one, all right,' he says. Entirely oblivious of Lee standing there. Maybe didn't know who he was. It was like hearing an ardent Republican raving about Donald Trump or Sarah Palin, not noticing that Obama was within earshot. 'Very positive feedback. Everyone says it's a worthy successor to the Millennium series.'

'Sounds great,' I said, trying to keep my voice down, looking over my shoulder, guiltily.

'Oh yeah,' enthused the guy. Upping the volume. And the inappropriate elation. 'It's flying off the shelves!'

7

THE PRESSURE KEEPS BUILDING

This is a story about Jean Cocteau, not Lee Child. But I wondered if something similar could apply. It was just after the Nazis had invaded Paris. They were marching up and down the Champs Elysées, having photographs taken in front of the Eiffel Tower, rounding up anyone they didn't like the look of. Maybe Cocteau would be next? In any case, Hitler had taken Paris. *Merde*. A friend finds Cocteau in his apartment, in a distraught state. On the sofa, sobbing, moaning. 'There, there, Jean,' he says, with a dash of de Gaullian Resistance spirit. Hand on the shoulder. 'We will overcome, in the end. We will never let the Boches win.'

'I don't know what you're talking about,' says Cocteau, batting away the hand, picking up that morning's newspaper, open at the Arts section. 'Look at this review. They've completely trashed my novel!' Or latest play. Or exhibition.

'Writers – we have to get our priorities right,' Lee said, sympathetically. 'Everything else is secondary.'

We were having lunch in Le Pain Quotidien. I had automatically picked up the small pot of milk they had put on the table and was on the verge of pouring some into my coffee. Lee gave me a look. 'Of course,' he said, like some Grand Inquisitor keeping a stern eye on the heretics, 'if you're going to be the kind of person who puts milk in perfectly fine coffee ...' I put the pot down again.

I genuinely wanted to know how Lee reacted to reviews. Even though his book wasn't technically *out* yet, they were starting to appear. *The New York Times* weighing in, then the *Star-Telegram* (Fort Worth) and the *Oregonian*. And the *Huffington Post*. All positive, by and large. 'A brilliantly crafted mystery and one of Child's best,' said the *Huff Post*. He wouldn't have to start reaching for the 'Neglected Work of Genius' defence just yet (my personal favourite, when it came to my own stuff, was 'succès d'estime' or perhaps, at a stretch, 'cult classic').

Only a boxed quote in the *Star-Telegram* struck a slightly regrettable note:

EVEN THOUGH THE MISCAST TOM CRUISE SEEMS
DETERMINED TO RUIN THIS CHARACTER ON
THE BIG SCREEN, THE LITERARY VERSION OF
JACK REACHER IS FASCINATING
– David Martindale

Lee had a degree of clinical detachment where reviews were concerned. Didn't ignore them, took them seriously, but didn't take them to heart. Didn't go all prima donna when they were good or throw a Cocteau-like tantrum when they were bad. 'There's a subjective element to reviews, of course,' he said. 'But there's an objective element too. And you can quarrel with it objectively. I know if it's well paced or not. I don't need someone else to tell me.'

I once vowed to go and have a word with Dirk Bogarde after he misconstrued, in a review for the (London) *Times*, my description in *Waiting for Bardot* of hitching a lift in a Ford 'Consul' car (back in the sixties) as having something to do with the British Consul in France. And then there was that Dutch translator who just flat out omitted my classic 'porridge' metaphor in *Walking on Water*. I was booking the flight to Holland when I heard from another Dutch friend he was already dead. Lee was sympathetic to President Truman, who wanted to go and give a black eye to some reviewer who had slated the latest by his daughter Margaret. But he took a broadly utilitarian line towards what people wrote about him – *What difference would it make to sales?*

Apart from occasional references to telephone-number advances, we had spent most of the time when he was writing *Make Me* speaking about *art* or possibly *craft*. Now it was time to revert to the bottom line. Unlike most writers, Lee was not embarrassed by talk of money. He embraced the cash-nexus, the idea that, fundamentally, writing was a *job*. I had once worked night shifts at the Ford factory in Dagenham, England, around the time he was interviewing strippers. Lee liked the 'car' metaphor for books. 'There's an apocryphal story, about a kid who becomes an apprentice at Ford and one of the senior managers takes him to one side and says, "Do you know what we make here, son?" "Cars?" says the kid. "Nope," says the old-timer. "Money."' For Lee, art and commerce were all one, there was no contradiction. Build a better car and people will buy it.

'The pressure keeps building,' Lee was saying. It was something Roger Federer had said. Winning so much can be a monkey on your back. People expected you to keep on winning. 'I recognize the syndrome,' said Lee. 'You're never satisfied. Not unless you can be No. 1 for fifty-two weeks of the year. Which is practically impossible. You have to get over it.'

He assumed failure was normal, failure would be in some sense liberating. Success is only failure postponed. 'I'm just trying to postpone it as long as possible.'

I mentioned a writer character in Franzen's *Purity* who writes something 'bloated' and gets slaughtered in *The New York Times*. Classic writer's nightmare. 'I wish I could do *bloated*,' said Lee. 'I'm getting too economical. There's minimalist and then there's …'

'*Child said nothing*. Two-sentence novel. They'll be wanting their money back.'

'If I could only work out in advance which one is going to be the stinker. Then I'd stop at the previous one. Get out on top. I'd like to retire on a high.'

I think I had worked out why he kept up his quasi-religious schedule. The double-barrel approach. Worrying about the next book spared him from worrying too much about the last one. It was like that little gizmo you could use to attenuate muscle pain by delivering regular electric shocks. The cure for pain was another kind of pain.

Over time Lee had learned to live with the anxiety factor. It was like walking around with a bullseye on your back. He had been touring one of his books around the UK a few years ago. He was in a chauffeur-driven car, sitting in the rear with his agent. They're discussing figures. He'd come out at No. 5 that year.

His agent says, 'No. 4 would have been better.' The driver turns around for a moment. 'Why don't you wake up and smell the roses?' he says. Point duly taken. He was doing nothing but drive all day for a living. At least they got to be driven around, whether at No. 4 or 5 or whatever. Whereas he, the old driver, was down around No. zillion.

'Yep,' Lee said. 'Could be worse.'

Dedicated fan that he was, he had been following the England vs San Marino game on his phone in Le Pain Quotidien. 'Rooney scored,' Lee said. 'Penalty. That means he's equalled Bobby Charlton's record [for the number of goals scored for England – forty-nine]. Seems bizarre, I know.' Neither of us were great Rooney lovers. 'But you can't argue with the numbers. Rooney's coming out on top.'

If they were dogs, Lee would be a greyhound (red setter possibly) and Rooney would be a bulldog (or maybe pitbull), but there were clearly points of comparison. For practically the whole of the previous year, I'd been hymning the artistry and the poetry and the music and all of that as Lee actually wrote the book, but it was finally coming down to sheer *numbers*. It was all about the stats. What was the *score*? Who was *winning*?

The publishers loved his *style*, they loved *him*, but if his books sucked in sales, then he would pretty soon be *persona non grata*. 'Lee who? Oh him, yes, he used to be quite good, but he went out of fashion. Yesterday's man. It's all Lagercrantz now. He's working on the twentieth in the series.'

Jack Reacher (6'5", 250 lbs of solid muscle, direct, technophobe) vs Lisbeth Salander (4'11", 90 lbs, thin, tattooed, savvy, techno-anarch). Literarily speaking, they were both in the pirate class. Swashbuckling outsiders, unmoored from the main. Adept at killing. They had a lot in common. But they were sworn enemies.

The game was afoot.

8

I'M NOT AN AUTHOR

'Well,' I said, whipping out my copy of *Purity*, and flourishing it, like a white rabbit pulled out of a hat. 'I don't think you'll have to lose too much sleep over this one.'

'You read it?'

I'd been reading it on the subway. I was up to page 323. I thought it was funny and well written and not even too heavy. Big on screwed-up relationships. With a few bad sex scenes that will stay with me, alas. 'We could try an experiment – remove the spine, throw all the pages up in the air, let them land where they may, stick them back together again at random, and see if anyone can tell the difference. In fact, I have a feeling Franzen may have already done something like that.'

'I told you to go and look over his shoulder,' Lee said. 'We need to know.'

'He wouldn't be doing *this*, would he? If he turns down Oprah ...'

We were in a limo heading for the CBS studios on 57th. Breakfast TV show. Labor Day. 5 a.m. wake-up call. Sharon the publicist had a clipboard in her hand with lists of names. The big city was quiet, still slumbering.

'You got the front page!' I was referring to his review of Lagercrantz on the front page of the Book Review section of *The New York Times*. 'Was that a subtle demolition job?'

'I honestly don't know how they let me get away with it!' He was chuckling to himself like Professor Moriarty after hatching some fiendish plot. 'They took out my umlauts. Took me bloody ages to work out how to do them. Then, "We don't do umlauts." Typical *Times*.'

I'd been rereading his review and would now like to delete my previous 'fair' and 'balanced' remarks. It was scholarly, informed and informative, but overall a put-down. He'd even invoked a passing reference in the book to Stephen King's *Pet Sematary* to suggest that too much time had gone by to resurrect Lisbeth Salander decently and that she should have been allowed to fade peacefully away. The reborn Salander, Lee implied, was a zombie, a freak, only half-alive, better off dead and buried.

'They asked me if I knew Lagercrantz. They should have asked me if I had a book coming out the same week.'

The CBS studios are like a dream: everyone is perfect there, men and women, the coffee and the croissant and the bagel. The archetype of melon slices. The quintessence of pineapple. The excitable girl with the freckles on her nose. They would all look good in swimsuits.

One guy was prepping Lee in the green room. Maybe he, for one, got it slightly wrong. He'd overdone the make-up and come out looking orange. 'You're probably only here for a couple of weeks, right? That's what most people think. On the Riviera the rest of the time?'

'I only had two weeks off this year!'

There was no stopping the orange guy. 'At every airport in the land, it's just you and Patterson, right? It's like – which one am I going to choose?'

I had to straighten him out. 'The difference is, Lee actually wrote *Make Me*. On his own. I saw him do it. Patterson is just shuffling pieces of paper around. In a factory. Lee's a serious writer. In the grand tradition.'

'I guess thriller writers have all these filing cards on the wall. The plot is all carefully mapped out, like a movie script. I've seen how it's done.'

Lee was being polite, sprawled on the sofa, coffee in hand. I happened to be just standing there, stuffing in a banana. Like his bodyguard or stunt double. Sent in to bat for Child. I'd often see myself as Stendhal to his Napoleon, Tonto to his Lone Ranger, Sancho Panza to his Don Quixote. Now I realized what I had truly become: henchman to his Don Corleone.

'Look,' I said, 'I just read a review in which the reviewer said by page 200 he still had no idea what was going on. Mystified. And the funny thing is Lee was just the same. By page 200 he still had no idea what was coming.'

Mr Orange was struck by that. 'Really?'

'I prefer it that way,' said Lee. 'It keeps me interested. I get bored otherwise. It's just like being alive – you never quite know what is going to happen next.'

He goes in. Cameras all over him. He's sitting coolly on the tail of his jacket. Charcoal with some kind of t-shirt underneath. No hunchback effect. Not too much hand movement. *Make Me* is different, he's explaining: 'Reacher really likes a woman. That makes him vulnerable. He gets hit in the head. He gets hit in the head a lot, but this time it really hurts.'

'Why is Reacher so popular?'

'You ever had a mortgage? He doesn't. And he does the right thing. You can't do it in real life any more. You'll only get fired.'

But Tom Cruise was doing most of the hard work for him. Tom wasn't there in person. The interview had turned into a trailer. Clips from *Jack Reacher* the movie, talk about the next one. A stream of free association. Book cover, Lee, Reacher, Tom – it was all a blur. CBS owned Paramount Studios, or Paramount owned CBS, or Hollywood owned Random House, one or all of the above, all complicit in some hallucinatory conspiracy, the literary-industrial complex, infiltrated, hacked, seduced, usurped, perverted, shrunk by Hollywood. *Cruise-control.*

'I'm not an author. I think of myself as an entertainer.'

'Thank you, Lee Child! *Make Me* goes on sale tomorrow.'

'It's Labor Day!' he said, lighting up outside, defensively.

I was muttering something like, 'Entertainer, huh!' With a degree of why-do-I-even-bother bitterness.

'Come on, you boring bastard, no one wants Franzen with their cornflakes, you said so yourself. The book has to feel like a vacation.'

Sharon shoved us back in the car. She had kids to go and take care of. And a husband, a journalist *with integrity* (she pointed out, for some reason).

The CBS people had quoted *Forbes* magazine, 'The strongest

brand in literature', and a nice line from the *Washington Post*, the kind of line any writer would die for. 'Reacher is the stuff of myth ... One of this century's most original tantalizing pop-fiction heroes.' I couldn't help wondering, on the road back, what was the worst thing anyone had ever said about his writing? I wasn't trying to be mean or get my own back. I just wanted to know is all.

'"Brain-dead". The *Kirkus Review*. My second book. I thought that was pretty harsh.'

'Mostly it's that snooty Harold Pinter/Edward Docx line, "I say, old bean, one simply cannot understand what people see in this fellow Child."'

Lee was regretful but philosophical about it. 'So stupid. It's a refusal to understand. It's like a footballer saying, "I don't really understand *passing* . . . I don't *understand* this goal-scoring business." I quite like something someone said. Online somewhere. "I hated this book so much, I wish I could *unread* it." Nightmares. That is a real badge of honour. I think that was *Persuader* oddly enough. Can't imagine what the objection was.'

'It failed to persuade.'

He was flying to Boston the next day, going to the Red Sox game with Stephen King. 'Don't worry,' he said, getting out of the car, heading for a shower to take off all the make-up. Become an author again. 'I'm pressing on with *Night School*.' He knew it had to be as different as he could make it. *Make Me* was a hard act to follow, which is why he had had to come up with a prequel. He had worked out the second sentence, just hadn't got it down yet. 'I've got the first chapter in my head, though. The new cycle has started, the new season. The year. It's all about time.'

Lee had it in for farmers. All that farming was obviously a front for something (as it was in *Make Me*). Sinister silos. Grain! Ha! What was really concealed within? Then again, he often spoke like a farmer, cyclically, in terms of 'planting' and the harvest. The annual schedule. He had sown and he would reap. Unless ...

'After anaesthetists, it's farmers, you know. Statistically. Who commit suicide most often. It's easy for them. Like pressing a button. They have a lot of shotguns.'

9

HAVING AN ORGASM, STANDING UP

It occurred to me, once or twice, that Lee looked quite a bit like a younger Bill Clinton. (Not everyone can see the resemblance, granted.)

His daughter Ruth had met Clinton once, in England. She had been working over there and she went along to the Hay Literary Festival for a laugh. Bill was giving a talk, pushing one of his books. *When I Ruled the World* or *Me & My Zipper Problem* or something. She went up to him afterwards. Pushed through the scrum. Said Hi. He said Hi. Moved on. She called out, above the hubbub, 'My Dad writes Reacher!' Sudden silence. He stops in his tracks. Turns.

'Hold everything! This lady's father is Lee Child, the greatest writer on the planet. Come on over here!' She was in.

Turned out the President was a fan, had read them all. (Ruth confirmed the charisma. Irresistible, apparently.) I saw a photo of him reading *Make Me* too, on a plane, flying off to some international conference somewhere and needing to revise his ruthless, relentless vigilante strategy.

Another time Lee was talking to this cop. A woman. Mid-forties. Worked traffic in New Jersey mostly. Tough job, tough cop, hard as nails. Hardcore Republican too. Loved Reagan, Bush (father and son), Palin, all that crew. Had no time for Clinton at all. Except she had had to provide crowd control one time when he passed through New Jersey on the campaign trail.

The crowd took a lot of controlling, they were all cheering and stomping. The cop thought it was ridiculous and no way was she voting for this guy, no matter what.

Then afterwards he comes up to her, personally thanks her for

41

everything she has done to make his day in New Jersey go so well. Shakes her by the hand. She melts. Totally.

'I was actually having an orgasm, standing up,' she said. 'Never happened to me before.'

Sometimes the myth is real.

This is the kind of research Lee Child does. Cops open up to him. As I say, a little like Bill Clinton.

I checked: no, Obama is not a fan, as such. Lee was invited to some Obama function. The President comes up to him and says straight out, 'I haven't read Reacher, sorry!' Lee liked that: straight shooting, no smoke in your eyes. And he appreciated that the guy probably had other things on his mind. But still. 'And that's despite the cigarette!' Lee had once given him a cigarette, when they were standing together outside some lonely hotel somewhere between speeches. He remains confident that Obama will swing around in the end. One day. 'Maybe when he retires and he needs the excitement.' Lee kind of hates it when it turns out someone is *not* a reader. Yes, the cop was. Didn't mention if she'd had the orgasm reading Reacher too.

10

STEPHEN KING IS SHOCKED

9 September 2015.

It was like being at a Cup Final. Or a rock festival. Or a riot. There was a kind of hysteria in the air. Tribal passions. When the mob stood up and cheered I had to stand up with them, for fear of getting my teeth kicked in. (*What is wrong with you, man?!*) I didn't want anybody to think I was rooting for the *other side*.

Which is odd, really. Because it was just a couple of guys speaking at Harvard. You'd think it would be reasonably civilized. Hushed. Orderly. But not when the two guys are Stephen King and Lee Child. To some extent you can blame Jonathan Franzen for the fervour. Even though he wasn't there. Or Professor Harold Bloom at Yale. *The opposition.*

Lee and King were sitting up on stage together, in armchairs, to talk about books. Specifically one book, *Make Me*. But they were also fomenting revolt. They were overthrowing an intellectual empire in a way that reminded me of the old Revolutionary war: wild colonial boys versus the masters. Now it is pop fiction versus the literary *ancien régime*. Were this crowd applauding words? No, not really. They were baying for blood, they wanted heads on pikes, the massacre of the literati. What I was witnessing was a full-blown Readers' Revolt. It felt a little like watching Danton and Robespierre having a conversation in front of the pro-guillotine Committee of Public Safety.

In the midst of all this inarticulate frenzy, I almost missed the headline news: King announced that he – the implacable author of fifty-odd novels, many of them almost physically unbearable – had been 'shocked' by the surprise ending of *Make Me*. Then he added, just in case anyone should misunderstand, 'The new one is absolutely fuckin' fantastic.' I think it's fair to say that King is a fan. In his novel *Mr Mercedes*, the bad guy pulls a Lee Child book out of his backpack; in another, *Under the Dome*, Major Reacher, 'the toughest goddam Army cop that ever served', provides a character reference.

Stephen King had just received the National Medal of Arts. Quite a big deal. It's like being appointed Secretary of State; you have to be vetted to make sure nothing too embarrassing is going to come out later. Previous recipients include John Updike, Philip Roth, Maya Angelou. The next day King was flying down to DC to have the medal – hilariously massive – hung around his neck, like an Olympic champion, by President Obama. Lee nicely said it was 'the crowning achievement of his administration'. Only a day or so before, Lee had been writing the sentence about giving Jack Reacher a medal. A strange synchronicity between two writers. A *medal* for writing. For services to the *nation*. (I checked: Lee didn't know anything about it when he started writing *Night School*; yet somehow, mysteriously, it still leaked into the Reacher story.)

The Sanders Theater auditorium is massive, on three separate levels, with room for a thousand. And it was packed. More people than I have ever seen at a book signing in my life. The actual queue of readers lining up to get their copy of *Make Me* autographed by the author was not just long: it had strata, like a millefeuille. People at the back must have been in line for hours. They may still be there. I don't know because I left to catch the last train back to New York (and I missed the train too). That queue was like a giant boa constrictor that wanted to *eat* Lee.

Altogether mysterious, and if I was Jack Reacher I would suspect there was some terrible conspiracy going on behind the scenes. Turns out there was. Except it was out in the open now. Call it *The Revenge of the Reader*. Or *The Reader Strikes Back*. What is Stephen King? A writer of horror stories, thrillers, science fiction? No. He is first and foremost a patriot. Like a latter-day Mark Twain or Walt Whitman, he sings the Song of America. From 'I Was a Teenage Grave-Robber' (his first published story) to *Finders Keepers*, at the core of even his most terrifying works there is (buried in there somewhere, like one of his bodies that just won't lie down in *Pet Sematary*) a celebration of ordinary, everyday life in the United States. Secretly, every one of his books is a utopia. A hymn to a brave new world. (Or at least it could be if not for mad axemen, zombies, aliens, serial killers, man-eating cars, etc., etc.) Think of *The Green Mile*, for example. Even Death Row is a place of wonders. It seems appropriate that he likes to write while listening to loud rock music (notably Metallica and Guns 'n' Roses).

'You're British,' said King. (This got a big cheer by the way.) 'But you really *know* America – I mean, in a loving sort of way.' Which is true. Lee fell in love with America aged five when he came across a book at the public library in Birmingham called *My Home in America*. He married an American girl. He lives in Manhattan. He said that the thing that inspired him was something Brian Epstein had once said to the Beatles, in Paris, following some transatlantic phone-call, back in the sixties: 'YOU'RE NUMBER ONE IN AMERICA!' Lee said. 'My plan A was to become one of the Beatles. But this is the next best thing.' He's an adopted Child.

Jack Reacher drops out of the army to become a drifter vigilante hero. But the key thing is that he criss-crosses the whole of the United States, like an old troubadour roaming around Occitania. He loves it good or bad. In fact bad is good as far as he's concerned. It gives him something to do. He might just get bored otherwise. But Lee also loves the 'nothingness', what Jean Baudrillard called 'the desert of the real'. 'I was driving through west Texas,' he said. 'It's *uninhabited* according to the official census. Fewer than five people to the square mile, it's "uninhabited". I drove for 80 miles without seeing a single construction. Eventually I spoke to one woman on a farm. She said she had to drive five hours to buy anything she hadn't grown or killed herself. And five hours back again.'

Reacher has to be huge (6'5" and 250 lbs) because he encompasses a continent. He loves the weirdness of America. He embraces it. I overheard a guy in the row in front of me trying to sum up the works of Lee Child for another guy, a Reacher virgin. I thought he nailed it: 'Reacher is, like, so totally …'

Not so, Jonathan Franzen and Harold Bloom. They are the opposite of *so totally*. They have a European slant to their writing. Elitist. They think most Americans are stupid. Franzen refuses to go on the *Oprah* show because it's too down-market for his taste. He bad-mouths tweeters and social media. Harold Bloom, self-appointed guardian of the 'western canon', has gone on record as saying that awarding anything to Stephen King, a writer of 'penny dreadfuls', is nothing but 'a testimony to [the] idiocy' of the awarding committee. He didn't flat out say King was an idiot and all his readers were idiots too, but he might as well have done.

Bloom and Franzen, to be fair to them, are fighting a rearguard action on behalf of what can loosely be called the *Untranslatable*. They want to preserve Anything That Cannot Be Made into a Movie (especially one starring Tom Cruise). King and Lee, on the other hand, are modern mythologians. Lee is a serious writer, even if he denies it publicly, in a line-by-line way (try reading one of his books *slowly* – yes, put it down, come back to it, savour those sentences, short though they may be). But Lee's and King's stories and characters, like the ancient myths, don't belong to any particular form. They are essentially oral and translate into any medium. ('I'm in!' said that other guy, by the way, in response to the 'So totally ...' 'Can't wait to see the movie!') Try making *Purity* into a movie. It would be worse than that Thomas Pynchon film, *Inherent Vice*. (What do I know? It's now slated to become a television series, starring Daniel Craig.) Whereas *Stand By Me* and *The Shawshank Redemption*, both based on King novellas, are modern masterpieces.

But readers have had enough of traditionalists, Ph.D. patricians like Bloom and Franzen aristocratically pissing on them from atop their ivory towers. And the internet enables them to band together and show their muscle. Child and King are the opium of the people; and the people were definitely high at Harvard. God Save the King! Long live the Child!

11

A FRUSTRATINGLY ONE-WAY TELEPHONE CONVERSATION (EXCEPT JUST AT THE END)

We are in a car going downtown. 10 September 2015, around 6 p.m. (EST). Heading to Union Square, Barnes & Noble. The official New York launch. Lee's phone buzzes. He looks to see who is calling. Turns to me. Raises eyebrows. Whispers, 'Hollywood.' Presses *Accept*.

HOLLYWOOD: ...

LEE: Yeah, you can say that again.

HOLLYWOOD: ...

LEE: Is that hardcore enough for you?

HOLLYWOOD: ...

LEE: Has Tom seen it?

HOLLYWOOD: ...

LEE: Seriously?

HOLLYWOOD: ...

LEE: Sounds good to me.

HOLLYWOOD: ...

LEE: [*sarcastic*] I have a dream that one day it will be made into a movie.

HOLLYWOOD: ...

LEE: [*checking his email*] OK, yeah, I'm getting it now.

HOLLYWOOD: ...

LEE: You'll be the first to know.

He presses the off button.

'You want to know how that conversation started?'

'What do you think?'

'He said, "I've just finished *Make Me* and you are *one sick bastard*."'

'Good call, Hollywood.'

'They said if this one takes off then we get another three. A series. A franchise. Cool or what?'

The producer had just emailed him the script for *Never Go Back*. That was what was coming through. He promised to have a look at it. They needn't have sent it. The contract gave him no editorial rights. Nor did he want any. Still, they respected him too much not to at least show him the current draft.

Maybe it served him right that the very first question (I kid you not) at the Q & A was, 'What do you think about Tom Cruise playing Reacher?'

What I remember of his answer struck the right note: 'I am the least worried guy on the planet.' The great thing for him was that he had absolutely no responsibility. 'If you don't like the movie, stick to the book.'

12

ATTEMPT AT AN EXHAUSTIVE DESCRIPTION OF PEOPLE AT BARNES & NOBLE WHO WERE HAVING THEIR PHOTOGRAPHS TAKEN WITH LEE CHILD

Husband and wife. Sixty-plus. Well preserved. Good hair. Cosmetic surgery? The wife goes around the table to stand right next to Lee. The husband takes the shot. 'We've come all the way from ...' She is going to email Lee her address.

Hawaiian shirt. Big guy. Shorts. It's a look.

Balding man in yellow shirt.

Her t-shirt says 'Levi's' on the front.

Yoga girl.

Two women. Older, CEO type. Younger, tight pants. 'My co-worker'. Older woman, glasses and blue top. Three copies of *Make Me*. 'We're going to see the movie.' (Lee: 'They make it more violent than the book!')

Short denim shorts, frayed. Red blouse. Twenty-something. 'I love the young Reacher stories.' (Lee: 'So do I.')

Woman, black hair, jeans, fitting. Asian? Native American? Jewellery. Black shirt. Tight.

Twenties. Blonde. Purple top, shorts, trainers. Nice legs.

White button-down, Levis, glasses. Scholarly sort of guy. Artist/web entrepreneur.

Guy. Check shirt, helmet of prematurely grey hair. Thirty-something.

Woman, red hair, long black coat. The red and the black.

Baseball cap. The right way round. Latino-Californian. Aims camera right in Lee's face. 'Ten seconds on *Make Me*. Starting now …' (And Lee gave him precisely ten seconds.)

Black guy, blue shirt, tan shoes, gold glasses.

Young Vikram Seth.

Woman with page-boy cut. And telescoped umbrella. Goes for the over-the-shoulder pose.

Black woman with big suitcase on wheels. Goes around to Lee's side. Moves well. Dancer?

Balding. 'Who Wants Pie?' on the t-shirt. Cut-offs, green back-pack. Goes around. Looks like the answer to his question is, 'I do.'

Retired Columbia professor. Good hair. Blue shirt. Leonard Bernstein-lookalike.

Woman with glossy dark blue hair. (Lee: 'I love the hair – awesome!') Goes around.

Very tall woman with red hair. 'Good to see you again.' A regular.

Twenty-something. Screenwriter. Woman. 'This is for my Mom. She told me to read Reacher.' (Lee: 'Always listen to your Mom'.)

Young (male) writer. White t-shirt. Tall, slim with broad shoulders. (Lee: 'My advice is ignore all my advice. Do what you want to do and see what happens.')

('Hello, ladies.') Blue and pink. They go both sides. Lee sandwich. ('Did you get me?')

Big guy. Zip-up black leather jacket. Black jeans. Salomon trainers. Goes the other side.

Woman all in black. Short skirt. Muscular. Lisbeth Salander type.

Tom Selleck moustache. 'Midtown North' t-shirt. On the back: 'New York City. THE WORLD COMES TO US.'

Woman who loves *The Affair* (Reacher 16). Thirties. Art nouveau motif on dress. Voluptuous. Boyfriend Adrian. (Lee: 'Has he got life insurance?')

Cop. Yes, doughnuts, but in fair shape. Hair grey, but it's there. 'I try to be like Reacher.' (Lee: 'Thanks for keeping us safe.') Five copies of *Make Me*! Goes around.

Man and wife. Dotty blouse, striped shirt. 'We both love Reacher.'

Blue tattoos. Blue t-shirt, legend: 'SOMETIMES YOU FEEL LIKE A NUT. Almond Joy.'

Girl, ginger hair. Nose ring. Sleeveless top.

Woman in elegant black dress. *New York Times* journalist now working for *Serial*. Leaves with guy. White hair and crumpled khaki jacket. They go and have dinner at Peace Food Café on 11th.

I was that guy, so I have to stop there.

There is no 'type' of reader. Everyone is different. Then again …

I almost forgot to mention the deranged, obsessive fan (other than me).

13

THE DERANGED, OBSESSIVE FAN

I couldn't help but notice, at the very end of *Finders Keepers*, Stephen King had written a message to the reader. The last lines in the book. 'And you, CONSTANT READER. Thank God you're still there after all these years. If you're having fun, I am, too.' Heartfelt, of course, sincere, but at the same time it sounded a little bit desperate. Perhaps apologetic. Because the rest of the book was all about Fear of the Fan.

Which was not surprising. He'd already written *Misery*, a couple of decades back. Annie Wilkes holds the author hostage. Nurse. Fan. But she has an axe to grind. Literally. Chop chop. That is what I call editing.

In *Finders Keepers* (no spoilers here, this happens near the beginning), Morris Bellamy shoots and kills John Rothstein, the great Rothstein (a hybrid of Philip Roth and J. D. Salinger), 'reclusive genius'. Partly to get his hands on all those unpublished notebooks. Partly because he feels betrayed: the author allowed his favourite character, Jimmy Gold, to go into … advertising! The writer had, in effect, sold out.

Another dissatisfied reader.

Young Pete, who also loves Rothstein, realizes (at the point where Bellamy is threatening to kill his little sister and has already offed any number of other people) that the 'marker of true, deep insanity' in Bellamy is that fictional characters are more real for him than actual human beings. Type on the page engaged his feelings and sympathy more than any being of flesh and blood ever could.

Bellamy was a bad, bad man. But, really, was that so insane? The love of unreal people, I mean. Odysseus, Don Quixote, Emma Bovary, Anna Karenina, the Lone Ranger, Jack Reacher:

don't I care for them more than the anonymous hordes passing me by on the street? (And yes, I do feel obscurely betrayed by Flaubert and Tolstoy – I imagine Morris Bellamy or Annie Wilkes would have hunted them down too, given the chance.)

And the equally mad idea that 'the writing was more important than the writer'? Roland Barthes set it out coolly, with structuralist rigour, in his essay on 'The Death of the Author'. The author is dead (especially if you shoot him yourself), long live the text!

Something like this was in Lee's mind. He'd written twenty Reachers, not to mention numerous short stories. Didn't he want to try his hand at something else? He had 'ten or twenty' different ideas, but ... He had a responsibility to the Reacher fans. He was 'locked in'. They would only be disappointed if he wrote something else. It was bound to end badly. He didn't want vengeful readers coming after him en masse. He had had enough trouble with the Tom Cruise objectors. And then there were the Tea Party guys who complained and mailed him white feathers and suchlike when Reacher started sounding too anti-war ... ('I was only quoting word for word messages from serving soldiers!')

That *locked in* put me in mind of *Misery*. It was as if he really was being held hostage. By his millions of readers. They wouldn't let him out of his room until he had written another Reacher. Fans could be demanding.

I was one of them.

There was another at Barnes & Noble, Union Square. Except he had to be restrained. (I mostly succeed in restraining myself, apart from the occasional, 'Come on, Lee, stop goofing off!') Security guys were all over him, they had him cordoned off, like some kind of dangerous animal, concerned that he might want to take home a piece of Lee Child. Or something like that. So I didn't get a chance to speak to him.

He was probably harmless. Just over-enthusiastic. Big and unshaven and unkempt. Lennie in *Of Mice and Men*. Maybe John Coffey in *The Green Mile*.

On the other hand, I can't help thinking of my friend Michael Scott Moore. Doing research on Somali pirates. They liked what he had written. In *The New York Times* and elsewhere. Kidnapped him and held him hostage for a couple of years. They thought his writing was worth a lot of money. The better his work, the higher his ransom. Lee Child was probably not going to Somalia on this tour. But he knew that all readers were, potentially, pirates, that they wanted to kidnap him and take him home with them. Most of them would make do with one of his books.

For now.

14

LUNCH WITH LYDIA LAIR

Lee was having a 'charity lunch' in New York. It was only later I heard he was having lunch with Lydia Lair. Which is going to sound strange to readers of *Make Me*. Possibly even insane.

Lydia Lair, readers will recall, is the victim, or one of the victims, of the home invasion scene (chapter 39). She is married to a doctor by the name of Evan Lair. Her older brother is Peter McCann (also known as 'Maloney'), who goes missing. It could have been different. Lee liked the name Lydia Lair. It reminded him of Lois Lane and Lana Lang in *Superman*. Back in February 2015, in the midst of writing *Make Me*, he toyed with the idea of giving the name to his main woman character, now known as 'Chang' (formerly 'Stashower'). But, appealing though the name was, on so many levels, he decided in the end that he didn't want 'Lair said' too often. Thus Lydia Lair became the Lydia Lair of the novel, as we have it.

And she could have died. She was certainly threatened with death. Which is to say that Lee was threatening her with death. With a degree of sadistic satisfaction. (It has to be remembered that Lee Child is every bad guy he ever dreamed up as well as Jack Reacher, über good guy.) 'I don't know if Lydia is going to get through the day,' he would say. 'There are going to be bullets flying every which way.' Or, 'Lydia is looking like a goner.' 'Let's put her out of her misery.' And so on. I like to think that I had a hand in saving Lydia. Not Reacher: me. 'Oh come on, give her a chance!' I would say. Or, 'You can't do that! She's paid thousands of dollars to be in the book. To a good cause as well ...'

That was the unvarnished truth. Lydia Lair, the real Lydia Lair, who lived in San Antonio, Texas, had bought the right to have her name in the book at a black-tie charity auction, the

'Heart Ball', back in February 2015, in Hilton Head, South Carolina. She, Lydia Lair, would be immortalized – providing his books lived on! – by the author Lee Child. She was already a fan of his work, had read all his novels, was half in love with the character of Jack Reacher. Fantasized about him, the way one does. Therefore stuck her hand up when it came to the auction of CHARACTER'S NAME IN THE NEXT LEE CHILD JACK REACHER NOVEL. Who knows, maybe she would get to hang out with Reacher. Maybe she would fight Reacher or make love to him. None of that was a given; the novel hadn't been written yet. It was maybe half-written. Lee Child knew nothing of the existence of Lydia Lair. But, if she put her hand up often enough, he would. It was a popular ticket. Went up in substantial increments.

Finally she saw that it was down to her and one other woman. The price was getting ridiculous. She'd never intended to donate this much money. It was crazy. She and her husband, art lovers and collectors, had been to many charitable functions over the years, but this was the first time they had gone out on a limb. They tended to favour 'silent auction items' (no bidding wars). The Lairs looked at one another. 'One more bid,' she said. She stuck her hand up one last time. This was the maximum. She assumed it was game over and she would be outbid. But the other woman (merely mortal name unknown) surrendered. Lydia Lair had won. She was *in*.

Her name was duly communicated to Lee. It registered in his mind, he typed it out, it appeared on his computer screen, he started playing around with it in Bermuda, it ended up in the book.

Obviously, I had to go and have lunch with her. It was the closest I was going to get to having lunch with Reacher himself. I would be breaking bread with a real live fictional character. To my way of thinking, it was like having a date with Anna Karenina or Emma Bovary.

But first of all Lydia emailed me. Imagine if Anna or Emma were to email you. emma.Bovary@gmail.com. This was on a par. And this was the key thing: Emma Bovary had now finally read *Madame Bovary*. Lydia Lair had read *Make Me*. Lee had given her a copy – it was all part of the deal. Emma had had her photograph taken with Gustave. And now she had read the book.

But here is the truly extraordinary part of her story. Which shocked her, Lee, and me. Lydia Lair really did have an 'Evan' in her life; and she had had a brother who died. 'Other than family members and close friends back in 1968, no one has ever known about Evan. You can imagine how shocked I was to read the name in the book as my husband.' Evan – fiancé; car crash (long ago). Brother – 'tragic accident' (recent) on his farm.

So reading the book was both pleasure and trauma for her. She was excited whenever she came up against her own name. *Hey, look, it's me! I'm talking to Jack Reacher.* And then every time she read the word 'Evan', or the word 'brother', her heart skipped a beat. It was almost unbearable for her. But at the same time a form of catharsis or exorcism, the tragic mix of pity and terror. She was reliving her own life, mediated through the writing of Lee Child. And feeling ripped apart.

There were further parallels. She had been brought up 'on a small wheat farm in a dusty town in western Kansas', rather similar to Mother's Rest. In *Make Me*, Lydia Lair is hosting a party for her daughter, who is getting married. In the world beyond the novel, Lydia Lair was mother to the groom: her son was due to get married in Colorado on 26 September.

But here was the great mystery: how did *Lee* know? There was no way he could know. He only had the name 'Lydia Lair' to work with. That is all he had. That is all he was given. He knew nothing of the woman Lydia Lair herself, her life and loves. She was a closed book to him, not even a book, nothing but a few syllables. He liked the *sound* of the name, blissfully unaware of the individual the name was attached to. Which was fine as far as he was concerned. I had asked him when he was writing. 'Who is she, Lydia Lair? Where does she come from?' 'She is whoever I say she is,' he would reply. 'She is someone who wrote out a big fat cheque to have *her* name in *my* book.' I wanted him to try to find out who she really was, but he couldn't be bothered. After all, he had to write. The deadline was only a couple of months away.

He wrote *Make Me* in the third person, using point of view some of the time, and some of the time the more detached omniscient narrator, who sees all and knows all. (Think of Balzac or Tom Clancy, the way they claim to know everything, '*All is true!*') But the strange thing was, in Lee's case, it wasn't a metaphor: he really did seem to have attained some measure of omniscience. He knew stuff he had no right to know.

Lydia confessed, in her email, to being mystified.

```
Lee is a brilliant writer who always amazes me
with facts, quotations, experiences so detailed
and in depth that I think it must be personal,
and then the next year, I read a totally differ-
ent book in a different location, etc. ...   Of
all his books I've read, this was clearly the one
for a character with my name ... who would ever
have known?
```

Sceptics would keep saying to me, 'You're making this up.' I would say, 'You can't make this up.' On the other hand, Lee was making it up, wasn't he? Or maybe he wasn't making it up at all. I had to see if Lydia Lair was real.

I had read about Lydia Lair. I had received emails with her name on. But I had to have more, I had to have lunch with her too. The final proof.

15

ON TOUR WITH LEE CHILD: PUBLISHER'S SCHEDULE

Friday, 11 September

7.55 p.m.	Lee arrives at London Heathrow, BA 178, eta 19:55 at Terminal 5
	Brad to meet Lee
Overnight	The Langham Hilton Hotel
	1C Portland Place, Regent St, London W1B 1JA

Saturday, 12 September/Sunday, 13 September

Overnight	The Langham Hilton Hotel

Monday, 14 September

7.30 a.m.	Crawfords car collecting Lee from the Langham Hilton, picking Patsy up from home
	Rcf: 630350
9.55–11.05 a.m.	BA Flight 1326 from Heathrow to Newcastle
	Brad to meet Lee and Patsy at Newcastle Airport
12.30–1.30 p.m.	WHS
	36 Northumberland St, Newcastle upon Tyne NE1 7DE
	Contact: Carol

So far I've got a sentence and a half written. It's a start.

Newcastle to Harrogate – 1½ hours

3 p.m.   Research chat for BBC BREAKFAST –
               calling me on my mobile

'She should be hot!' No, she shouldn't.

3.30–4.30 p.m.   WHS
               Victoria Shopping Centre, Cambridge
               Street, Harrogate HG1 1TU
               Signing session
               Contact: Ruth/Judith
               Harrogate to Manchester – 1¼ hours

*It's a bit like being a movie stuntman. You have to jump off a
tall building. You hope that it's going to be a soft landing.*

6 p.m. arrive   PHIL WILLIAMS SHOW
               1st Floor, Quay House, MediaCityUK,
               Salford Quays M50 2QII

*The job doesn't need a lot of physical prowess. As long as you
can sit in a chair …*

6.30–7 p.m.   Recorded interview, Tuesday 15th @
               11.30 p.m.
               Hannah, Planning Producer, 5live Lates,
               BBC Radio 5 Live

The movie is always going to be worse.

7.30 p.m.   WATERSTONES
               91 Deansgate, Manchester M3 2BW
               Evening speaking event + signing
               Contact: Charlie
               Events.manchester@waterstones.com
               Sales rep: Martin

A lot of it is memory. I used to rule the schoolyard. I was big for my age. Then they started catching up with me.

9.30 p.m.	Dinner at Hawksmoor, 184–186 Deansgate, Manchester M3 3WB Attending: Lee Child Patsy Irwin Tom Chicken Phil Henderson, Buying Manager, Asda Nathan Mills, Books and Entertainment Category Director, Asda Bradley Rose

It's better than digging a ditch.

Overnight	Holiday Inn, Waterfront Quay, Salford Quays M50 3XW

Tuesday, 15 September

8.15–9.15 a.m.	BBC BREAKFAST 2nd Floor, Quay House, MediaCityUK, Salford Quays M50 2QH E-mail: tiffanysweeney Tweet: @TiffanySweeneyX

I see this big guy lumbering towards me. It's late. It's dark. I think, oh shit. But I'm not going to cross the street. It would be too weak. But I'm panicking. And then ... he crosses the street. I think, well, I guess the old magic is still working.

11–12 noon	WHS Store 5, Arndale Centre, Manchester M4 3AD Contact: Karen

The story happens in the reader's head.

	Manchester to Chester – 1 hour
1.30–3 p.m.	WHS
	5/7 Foregate Street, Chester CH1 1HH
	Contact: Damian
	On the day: Margaret

I was a 'featured extra'. $1,300 for the day. I still get residuals.

	Chester to London – just under 4 hours
7 p.m.	Publication dinner at The Wine Room,
	The Gaucho Grill, 25 Swallow St, London
	W1B 4QR

Attending:
Lee Child
Darley Anderson
Tom Weldon
Larry Finlay
Marianne Velmans
Patsy Irwin
Tom Chicken
Chris Wyatt
Lucy Keech
Louise Jones
Janine Giovanni
Elspeth Dougall
Christina Ellicott
Sam Pettit, Assistant Buyer, Tesco

I was getting interviewed about New York back in the eighties. I said, 'I never had a moment's trouble.' She said, 'Yeah, but you're 6'4" and look like an axe murderer.' I've always liked that.

| Overnight | The Langham Hilton Hotel |

Wednesday, 16 September

10.45–11.15 a.m.   Asda – recording for in-store tannoy +
social media – at the Langham Hilton –
awaiting details from Christina

DEDICATED ASDA EDITION (WITH BONUS SHORT
STORY)

It's great to be here in my favourite supermarket.

*He doesn't want to get involved. But there is a woman.
Waiting for someone to get off the train.*

*The reader doesn't know what is going to happen because the
writer doesn't know either.*

*Nearly everyone gets a movie deal. They buy everything.
Almost none of it ever gets made.*

If I hadn't done the writing, I'd be a warehouseman in Kendal.

[Asda: 'It's been a pleasure. Speaking to a real writer. I normally only get to speak to reality TV stars who have written their
autobiography. And you know what – they can't even pronounce
"autobiography".']

11.30 a.m.–12 noon   THE STEVE WRIGHT SHOW
BBC Western House, 99 Great Portland
Street, London W1A 1AA
Contact: John Dutton

*Never forgive, never forget. I still bear a grudge. I'm still angry.
After twenty years.*

*He either had a mental illness, or he was ex-military. So I made
him ex-military.*

1–2 p.m.	WATERSTONES
	1–3 Whittington Avenue, Leadenhall
	Market, London EC3V 1PJ
	Signing session
	Contact: Robert
	Or Manager: Tom
	Sales rep: Amanda

It's entirely autobiographical. I've just toned down the sex and violence a bit.

3.30 p.m.	OPEN BOOK, BBC RADIO 4
	Interview with Lee and Andy about
	Reacher Said Nothing
	Interviewer: Nicola Holloway
	Go to Old Reception, Broadcasting
	House

He kept on sending me these books. One was about surfing. I didn't read that, because I hate anything resembling healthy exercise. The one about Sartre and Camus was OK, though.

It made me think about what I was doing. I was quite interested. I don't know if anyone else will be.

4.30 p.m.	GOLDSBORO
	23–27 Cecil Court, London WC2 4EZ
	Stock signing

5.30 p.m.	Interview with Simon Toyne for Bookd –
	to be confirmed
	@ 1 London Bridge St, London SE1 9GF
	Contact: Jaime Frost

Nothing prevents him from doing it. He's a 6'5" psycho.

6.30 p.m.	Arrive at The Sun HQ, The News Building, 1 London Bridge St, London SE1 9GF Ask for Amy or Cate
7 p.m.	THE SUN event Natasha Harding interviewing Lee Contact: Claire Gribben, Head of Sun
Perks	
	Contact: Robert (as above) 5 × tickets reserved for Transworld – attending Patsy, Janine

COLLAGE OF SUN HEADLINES ON THE WALL BEHIND HIM: 'GOTCHA!'. 'UNION BOYCOTTS WAR'. 'ELTON TAKES DAVID UP THE AISLE'.

I used to look after my younger brother. He had big sticky-out ears. I used to love the head-butt. It got it all over quickly. Then I could go and play football.

Buying Villa would be an extravagance. I'm holding on to some shreds of sanity, so I probably won't be doing that any time soon.

[Audience: 'I have a copy of *Make Me*. I can't bear to start it, though. Because then I'll finish it. And I know it's going to be a year till the next one.']

Overnight	The Langham Hilton Hotel

Thursday, 17 September

	London to Colchester – 1 hour 44 minutes
12.30–1.30 p.m.	WATERSTONES 12–13 High St, Colchester CO1 1DA Contact: Clive

'How comes you're so thin?'

I got into this food group thing early on. I combined two groups.

'What two groups?'

Caffeine and nicotine.

Colchester to Norwich – 1½ hours

4–5 p.m.   JARROLD
                    1–11 London St, Norwich NR2 1JF
                    Unticketed signing session
                    Contact: Chris

I liked Connelly's work. So naturally I had to do the opposite. He had a hero with a complicated name, Hieronymus Bosch. So I kept mine simple. His guy was based in LA. Mine was based nowhere. His guy was normal. So my guy was anything but. He had a house and a daughter. I had nothing.

5 p.m.   MUSTARD TV
                    Interview at Jarrold
                    Contact: Jessica Hewson

My whole philosophy has been – I'm going to have more fun in sixty years than you are in ninety. The only problem is now I've hit sixty. So I'm living on borrowed time.

We can sort it out behind the bike sheds.

6.30 p.m.   JARROLD
                    The Pantry Restaurant, Floor 3
                    Contact: Chris
                    Sales rep: Neil

My bills are paid for the next thousand years. So it's all about an emotional contract with the reader.

Danny Craig? – ha! he's smaller than Tom. I was on a plane with him one time. I went to the bathroom – and I tripped over him! Hugh Jackman – small. Clint Eastwood – not big. I put Eastwood's tweed jacket on once – the one he wore in Dirty Harry. *The sleeves came about half-way up my arms. All actors are small. It's cheaper fitting them on the screen.*

Overnight	St Giles House Hotel
	41–45 St Giles St, Norwich NR2 1JR

Friday, 18 September

9.45 a.m.	Arrive at University of East Anglia's
	Campus Registry
	Meet Henry
	Five-minute video interview for Creative
	Writing MA. Signing at Waterstones.

'You've sold out!'
Not you too!
'I mean, your books are all sold.'
That's a relief.

10–12 noon	UNIVERSITY OF EAST ANGLIA
	CREATIVE WRITING (CRIME
	FICTION MA MASTERCLASS)

He lies and cheats and shoots people in the back. And people seemed to like him.

How would I feel if they phoned me up and told me how to do it?

I don't like sidekicks.

I'll read anything. I read a book about rust. It was good. Another one about air-conditioning. Called Cool. *How many of you can sit there for four or five hours at a stretch, just reading?*

Third person is so much easier for writing a thriller. It enables you to write 'Meanwhile, back at the ranch ...'

The scene that came into my head, towards the end of August, was a backhoe, a hole, burying a guy. A big guy. Who was this? Why were they burying him?

I don't have any spare opening scenes sitting around the house. I use them all up. I always finish. I'd rather hang myself than waste any of 'em.

The idea of a bestseller, selling millions, will be outdated. There will be niche audiences. Vampire zombie detectives. I hear sister-in-law zombie porn is doing good business.

Norwich to Milton Keynes – 2½ hours

3–4 p.m.   WATERSTONES
72 Midsummer Place, Milton Keynes,
Bucks MK9 3GA
Signing session
Contact: Julie

On any working day I smoke a packet of cigarettes and drink way too much coffee ... if I were to write more than four or five days in a row I'd have a stroke.

Milton Keynes to Reading – 1½ hours

6.30 p.m.   WATERSTONES
United Reform Building, 89A Broad St,
Reading RG1 2AP
Evening speaking event
Contact: Cheryl
Sales rep: Kate

Travel

- I have got a permit for you to park in our service yard
- Cars must not be left unattended without a permit as they may get clamped
- For sat navs the church postcode is RG1 2HX
- I attach photos of the road to our service yard which is to the left of the church as you look at it
- See the Google map on the link below – it is the turning shown to the left of the Minster Church of St Mary the Virgin, bear left and you will be in our service yard. You will need to park right next to the back door of Waterstones. Our store is shown on this map as Broad Street Independent Chapel

I made him thirty-six in the first book. It was a tribute to Dick Francis – his heroes are always thirty-six. I reckon he's late forties now.

He's an analogue guy in a digital world.

I don't want character development. How would you feel if he became a vegan pacifist?

Overnight   The Langham Hilton Hotel

Sunday, 20 September
Tbc   Signing at Heathrow Airport? PI to discuss with Lee

                             Lee flies to NY (To be arranged)

Monday, 21 September
POLITICS AND PROSE BOOKSTORE
5015 Connecticut Ave NW, Washington
DC 2008
Interview with Laura Lippman

I love women. All my friends are women. I'm not the kind of guy who goes to a bar with the boys. I would hate that.

He doesn't kill anyone in that book. It's rather shocking. And nobody noticed!

You have to trust your voice. It's all you have.

That was a homage to John D. MacDonald. Travis McGee taught me so much. He was like a blueprint. He wrote twenty-one novels. He had to stop there, though, on account of being dead. So I said I'd write twenty-one, like him. But I'm on the twenty-first now. So what am I going to do?

I goof off in the fall. There's no point denying it. I might as well embrace it.

16

COMMENT ON THAT 'GRUELLING' PUBLICITY SCHEDULE

STUDENT AT UEA: Isn't that a rather gruelling schedule?

LEE: I've met around five thousand people in the past week. Every one of them comes up to me and says, 'I love your work!' They wouldn't come up to me if they didn't. How hard can it be? It's like lying in a warm bath.

ME: [*still chuffed because one guy at UEA said he liked my work. One. Thank you, Henry*] Five thousand? As in you're 'feeding the five thousand'?

LEE: It's intoxicating. A publicity tour is designed to give you a Messiah complex. I'll get over it. You need to get over it too. That was all a long time ago. Did you put that guy up to it?

17

A NOVEL WITHOUT REACHER

Readers can't get enough Reachers. Can't you write faster? At the same time, they often ask: Are you planning to write any non-Reacher novels? Lee's answer is always something like: *I have five or ten ideas a day for books that don't involve Reacher, but I know my publishers won't publish them, so I never get around to typing them out.* And readers will be expecting Reacher to turn up at any moment, so it's lose-lose for him. Nobody would be satisfied.

In some way, Lee was the captive of his readers' demands. Was he kidding about all those *other* ideas? I don't think so. This is something he and Stephen King shared in common: they had almost too many ideas. Their problem was what to leave alone: in Lee's case, forget everything that doesn't include Reacher; in King's, it was pure graphomania, there was no turning off the tap – he'd even tried retiring completely once, and found that, like a Sinatra of literature, or an old boxer feeling the pull of the gloves and the ring, he had to make a comeback.

Just once, in my experience, in front of students at UEA, Lee sketched out one of his hypothetical novels, one that he would like to write, but just had never quite got around to, and maybe never would.

The time is now. Britain. A guy is killed. Chapter 1. Let's call him Bob. Nothing too sinister or suspicious about it. A car accident. Rather like Stephen King, he is strolling along a lonely road and a drunk driver smashes into him from behind. Drives away leaving our hero dying or dead. A last sigh perhaps. Regrets, he's had a few; sins, nothing too horrendous. Hey, he was getting on a bit anyway. He probably smoked as well. The end. Except ... Chapter 2. He comes back. What!? Yes, reincarnation is real. But weird. Bob returns, but in the guise of a four-and-a-half-year-old boy. Himself, but young again, *Bobby*, with his parents and whole family, several decades back in time, but – and this is the key point – he has all the knowledge he had at the point at which he was killed, in 2015.

In the classical version of rebirth, the souls line up to be reborn, but they have to take a dip in the river Lethe first, which cleanses them of all memories, wipes their hard disk, so they are born knowing next to nothing. Innocent again. Bob, *au contraire*, remembers everything. No purification in Lethe. No age of innocence. But he is a kid. A kid with a kind of omniscience. He knows what is coming – the Beatles, 9/11, 7/7, all the wars, assassinations, financial crashes and crises, the internet, Wendy, whom he is liable to get pregnant if he tears another condom in his haste, and so on. All at the advanced age of four and a half. All that knowledge inside the mind of a little boy. An almost unbearable burden.

Bob tries to slot back in to being Bobby. He doesn't have to *pretend* to be a kid. He enjoys climbing trees and kicking a ball about and playing with the other kids. But he knows things. So the first uncanny thing he does: he tells his grandfather to put £10 on Foinavon. 'A 100–1 shot? You have gotta be kidding me, young Bobby!' Somehow Bobby persuades him. 'Oh, OK, it's not as if I know any better. What the hell! Let's take a punt, eh?' As it was, so it must be: Foinavon romps home. It's the 1967 Grand National. All the other horses either fall or are snookered in a massive pile-up. The grandfather is £1,000 richer. A tidy sum in those days. 'Out of the mouth of babes and sucklings,' says he, chuckling and expelling a rich, dense cloud of celebratory cigar smoke. But, more to the point, Bob (no longer Bobby, henceforth to be treated with respect) is a phenomenon. His family gradually start to realize that he *knows* stuff. Not just how to play marbles. He is like an ancient oracle. A bearded prophet. Now aged five. He is not Superman, he is not huge like Reacher, but he has a prophetic soul. Quietly, they all get rich on account of his 'predictions' (of course, they aren't predictions, they're *recollections*, it's pure Plato). Who is going to win the Cup Final? The election? *Ask Bob!*

Time rolls on. Word starts to get out. But, if he can forecast the future (in this regard like one of the 'pre-cogs' in Philip K. Dick's *Minority Report*), then Bob becomes a valuable commodity, even irresistible. Maybe a threat. He can see 9/11 coming? He knows that Apple shares are going to go through the roof? *That* boy band? Unbelievable. Soon everybody wants a piece of him. Maybe somebody wants to kill him, all over again. Or kidnap him, like a golden goose. Could he, on the other hand, do anything to stop planes crashing into the Twin Towers? Maybe he could even write a very successful series of books – how about a schoolboy wizard? Or what about an XXL, ex-military vigilante who would always win a fight, no matter the odds …

That's all folks!

If you could sit Lee Child down for long enough, he would be able to type it all out, and come up with a resolution too. He likes plots to have a dénouement. Feels that readers are just being cheated otherwise. I couldn't help thinking that there could be a rash of novels, coming out of UEA, to do with very knowledgeable four-year-olds. And I guess Lee would be fairly relaxed about it. It was a gift. Generous. Gratis. Here, have a bestseller.

But this is the thing that occurred to me: wasn't Bob another alter ego of Lee Child? He was a kid inside the body of a sixty-year-old man. But a kid equipped with supreme knowledge. Omniscient narrator again. Sitting in Kirkby Lonsdale, in Cumbria, in the north-west of England, he could write about Georgia, for example (in *Killing Floor*), in the southern United States, without ever having been there. Mysteriously, mystically, without quite knowing how, he just *knew*. (He finally rectified the omission in 2017. He said, 'It looked exactly the way I imagined it.')

18

LEE CHILD'S ULTIMATE NIGHTMARE

Lee has a recurrent nightmare in which he is being pursued by innumerable nameless bad guys and ends up being chased over a cliff and plummeting down down into the abyss. Which is when he wakes up.

This was a bit like that. Except it was all real. I'd just got off the plane. First thing I did was stop at the JFK Hudson News stand and buy a copy of *The New York Times*, Sunday edition. Huge and heavy, just what I didn't need, but I had to check the bestseller charts at the back of the Book Review section, come what may. It was the definitive barometer of sales. I turned eagerly, expectantly, to the back pages. All vicarious thrills, but still.

I had been bumping into Lee here and there back in England. We had a coffee in the lobby of the Langham Hilton one morning. Another time I was in the back of a car with him in Norwich. The first time his publicist was telling me how *Make Me* had become an instant No. 1 in the UK. The second time she was saying how it was the same story in the US. The figures had just come in apparently. 'Crushing victory,' said Lee. Not exactly triumphantly, but not exactly not triumphantly either. 'Lagercrantz a distant second. Stick that in your Scandi pipe,' he added with schoolboyish glee, 'with extra umlauts, Lager pants!'

In short, it was like he had put all his money on a single lucky number, the wheel had spun around, and lo! there it was, his number had come up. Jackpot. Records broken. Competition officially wiped out.

So it was that when I opened the newspaper and scanned the Book Review lists, a chill Scandinavian darkness seemed to fall. Was *that* all a dream or was *this*? There it was at No. 1. Sunday, 20 September. **Fiction.**

1 THE GIRL IN THE SPIDER'S WEB, by David Lagercrantz

I couldn't believe it. Maybe something had gone wrong with the *New York Times* computer or something. I scrolled down the page.

2 PURITY, by Jonathan Franzen

Insult added to injury. Lee didn't even make No. 2. Lagercrantz *and* Franzen. His two big rivals. *Bêtes noires* plural. Lee was nowhere. Unless, of course, you counted this, on the next line down. The other Lee.

3 GO SET A WATCHMAN, by Harper Lee

They were all after him. He had been chased off the cliff, plunging to his doom. Instant oblivion. The book had dive-bombed. Total annihilation. Didn't even register on the radar over here.

Then I noticed the crucial further information, in the small print, to the right-hand side of the list. 'WEEKLY SALES PERIOD OF AUGUST 30–SEPTEMBER 5'. It was the pre-Lee period. Maybe he hadn't even joined the race yet. No one was pursuing him. He was pursuing them. But he was still on the starting line, limbering up.

It was like just getting off the plane: he was in a different time zone. He hadn't had a chance to recover from jet lag yet. Give it time.

And one other thing occurred to me then, seeing Lagercrantz in the Book Review. Lee's review, nuanced but negative when you looked at it closely, on the front page of the very same section, two weeks before, had failed to land a glove on Lisbeth Salander after all. Despite his best efforts to sabotage and scupper. His article had, if anything, backfired. One tweeter noted,

```
@andymartinink FWIW the review left me eager
to read *The Girl in the Spider's Web*. (But
the ending of *Make Me* is true vigilante
horror.)
```

Front page, Lee Child: it was all gravy to Lagercrantz. Who cared about a few minor, pedantic quibbles? All it had done was give it extra prominence and trumpet its arrival on the scene.

At No. 1. *Ja!*

PS: Later that day I picked up the following email:

```
Wait till next week. #1 throughout the English-
speaking world.
```

19

INSIDE FORT Z

I'm not making it up. It exists. I'm just not allowed to say what it's really called. I don't think anyone is actually going to kill me if I do, but there's no point taking chances. And I can't say where it is either, a few miles outside one of the major cities, out in the sticks a bit. But it is huge. The size of a small city in itself in fact. Fifty thousand people live there, all of them either in or associated with the military.

Fort Z functions more or less the way a city functions. And it looks kind of like a city looks. It has roads, junctions, stop lights. It has parking lots, with a greater preponderance of Humvees than one would normally find elsewhere. And a lot of pick-ups too. But it has miraculously meticulous ground-keeping. People tend not to drop litter here. There are no Subway wrappers and Big Mac boxes listlessly rustling in the breeze. No visual chaos. Everything is neatly squared away. Geometrical, pressed, and creased. Spit and polish on the scale of a city. No one is pissing against a lamppost.

And there are no billboards either. No advertising. No one is selling anything.

Except in the PX (or 'Post Exchange'). The PX is vast, an everything emporium, Walmart-style. You name it, it has it, one way or another. Nothing too luxurious perhaps. Food, clothing, domestic appliances. Again, relatively abnormal, different kinds of military uniform for sale (yep, they have to buy their own). But also books. And a large number of the works of Lee Child, including stacks (neat, geometrical, dust-free stacks) of freshly minted volumes of *Make Me*.

The author is visiting Fort Z. They ran checks to see if he had too much of a criminal record. They had to. They turned a blind eye to the self-confessed recreational drug-taking. It's a wonder they let him in at all. But the creator of Reacher is awarded Special Privileges.

In a way it's like any other signing routine: we have the table, the chair, the piles of books, a massive poster of the cover behind him. One woman (her name is 'Marty') critiques one or two of his works that seem to her inferior. But in a polite, rather formal way. An unusually high proportion of people address him as 'sir'. He, in return, is cordial and courteous. He always is. Never hurries anyone. There are authors who don't even look up. *Next!* Not Lee Child. He gives readers a fair crack of the whip. His full attention and a serious exchange. He respects the reader. Particularly because in this case the reader is Reacher.

The author is practically surrounded by Reachers. Reachers who are also readers. The Military Police. He has been invited to Fort Z specifically by a regional Commander who has responsibility for some vast swathe of the country. Funnily enough, the Commander himself is not monumental, more wiry. Superfit of course. But he has a warrant officer in attendance called (I am not making this up), 'Battleman', or possibly 'Battelman'. He is more on the Reacher scale. Tall and broad and muscular. Lee Child is presented to a whole platoon, a battalion of MPs. They actually salute him. *Ten-shun!* He sort of waves back at them in a hazy gesture. Doesn't want to fake anything.

The reason they love him: he makes them feel like heroes. He has upgraded their status. Now they boast about being better than the FBI. They didn't use to feel that way. They used to think they were just heavy-handed party poopers (which is how they were once depicted in the movies). Now they have a legend to live up to. The author wanted to know if this unit was anything like Reacher's old unit, the 110th MP. The Commander didn't think this one was, but he was fairly confident that there must be a unit somewhere that corresponded fairly closely. The mimetic presumption. But it was justified: Lee had succeeded in spawning a generation of Reachers in the real world. They were springing up out of the ground like Greek myths.

Another guy had spent years designing the perfect stockade. In other words, a military prison. He had come up with unbreakable toilets, for example. A breakthrough in prison technology. And mirrors made out of stainless steel or aluminium. But a few years later the Marines, on the look-out for a new base, had taken it over for themselves. It had good plumbing and good wiring and decent accommodation. Weird, but OK. And then he is reading one of the Reachers and what does he find: a stockade that is taken over as a barracks for the regular troops. How the hell … ? Where did he get that from? The author said nothing, just smiled, enigmatically. He thought he had made it up. Turned out it was impossible to make anything up that hadn't already been done.

There was that other time. In *A Wanted Man* (Reacher 17). He'd come up with the idea of that FBI installation in the middle of the country, a kind of high-security motel, where they could park innocent witnesses who had seen more than they should and were at risk of cracking open some undercover op. Till the whole thing blew over. Nothing too totalitarian but just what was necessary. And then later on he had started to worry … was that too far-fetched? So he'd called up one of his old FBI contacts. Told the guy what he'd just dreamed up. 'Hold on,' says the retired G-man, 'Where did you get this from? That was supposed to be top secret. No one is supposed to know about it.'

One of the real Reachers said that, contrary to what the author maintained in one of his novels, not all military prisoners went to Leavenworth. Some went here, others there, it was just, OK, the majority of prisoners went to Leavenworth. The author thanked the guy for the info. Later on (back in the land of billboards and litter of every stripe) he turns to me and says, 'Sometimes you have to get it wrong to get it right. People believe that they all go to Leavenworth. If you say otherwise, they will never believe you. You destroy your own credibility. It would be like describing London without bobbies and red telephone boxes. *C'mon*, people will say, *where are all those nice policemen?* I've just come back from London. All the police I saw had automatic weapons. Not a single helmet in sight. Or a telephone box either.'

Another thing we were laughing at: the guy who built the stockade ('I didn't build it, I designed it') said that Lee ought to get his 'team of fact-checkers' to work on some of these things. Nelson DeMille could get these things right, why not Lee Child?

But Lee didn't have a team of fact-checkers. He didn't even have one. He didn't have his own personal army at his command. He was a solo operator. Almost a drop-out. A drifter. Lee 'Anomie' Child. Which reminded me of a conversation we had once had. Why don't you set up your own production company and make your own movies? I asked him one day. He had enough cash surely. He said, 'I would, but I don't know if I can get on with that many people every day. I'm too used to working on my own now. Just a guy in the back garden shed working away. With the tools at his disposal.'

He was old school, a nineteenth-century poet at heart, scribbling away in his garret. It's just that his garret happened to be an apartment in Manhattan high over Central Park.

20

IN THE FOUR SEASONS, WASHINGTON DC

Lee was having a pizza. As a result of poor parenting, he always leaves the crusts. Followed by some kind of fudge pudding with chocolate ice cream. And coffee. Black. Room service. Silver platters and linen napkins. You wouldn't get that in the Skyline (where I was staying). No big deal, but you have to take note of these small things. I was being Reacher, putting up in grimy motels. He was in the presidential suite. I was sitting there drinking coffee from his silver coffee pot. And helping myself to some of his fries on the side.

ME: And you have a gym.

LEE: I, for one, won't be making use of it. You use it. Go and do whatever it is you do in there.

ME: What about the pool?

LEE: Nah, can't be arsed.

He used to be a swimmer, long-distance, international level, with that long reach of his, but dropped out (or climbed out and never dived back in).

The luxury was wasted on him. He basically had to stay in cool places, on account of being so huge. Physically, and commercially.

And lo, his forecast had come true. With extra marmalade on top. *Make Me* was No. 1 in all the English-speaking countries. Without regard to category. It was the bestselling book in the western world. Bar none. Lager pants, Franzen, the other Lee, all comprehensively trounced.

'For that week at least,' he pointed out. 'Maybe not longer. It's cool for you. You were there when I started the first sentence. And now it's ...'

'Top gun. *Numero uno*. Everywhere. Oddly enough, I know I didn't write it, but I still feel a kind of semi-paternal pride. It's groovy. You deserve it, man.' I really meant it, by the way. I was drinking his coffee after all. I didn't actually get up and slap him on the back, but it was close. 'How do you feel about it? I know that is very BBC, "How do you feel about winning the World Cup?", but how are you feeling right now?'

'Mmm, good pizza,' he said. 'But hold on, let me think … It's a relief, to be honest. *Said he, heaving a sigh.*'

'A relief?'

'I wasn't always a bestseller, you know. I did OK, but it didn't take off till about 7 or 8. Maybe 11 or 12 over here. Then you set these standards.'

'The bar keeps going up. Like a high jump. Or pole vault.'

'There are expectations.'

'Like Federer said, Winning can be a monkey on your back.'

'*Can you do what you did the last time?*' Lee said.

'Can you?'

'It's gone way past. Broken records. *They*'re happy anyway. I'm still growing.'

'I heard from someone at Waterstones. You're the only one. Graph still going up.'

'Double-digit in the UK. More modest here. I can't compare myself to Chelsea any more. [Having won the season before, they had got off to a bad start and were in the doldrums.] Or Villa of course. Maybe Leicester – they're doing OK.'

'West Ham. They're right up there.'

'Can you keep it going though? I doubt it.'

'Hammers fans have the most melancholy song. "I'm Forever Blowing Bubbles". The bubbles nearly reach the sky. But then they fade and die.'

It didn't seem fair to compare him to a gloriously precarious football team. Fading and dying. Wrong note! I added quickly, 'You said it was *intoxicating*?'

'Yes, intoxicating. Funny, isn't it. I'm quite shy really. Now I have to perform like a stand-up comedian. It's a lot of running around. It's exhausting. But it is intoxicating.'

The reviews were coming in from the UK. They were all 'overwhelmingly positive', even if the *Mail on Sunday* reviewer reckoned the dénouement 'strained credulity'. 'Do you think it strained credulity?' he asked.

'Didn't strain mine. They must mean that it was too shocking and they had to look away. You know, the manacles and all that.'

Some lone reader had been kicking up a fuss too. Had emailed Lee. 'Why did you call it *Make Me*? Doesn't make sense. It doesn't even come up on a word search. I checked.'

'She must have it on Kindle. Does she have a point? Should the title have to correspond to the text?'

I'd run a word search on 'make me' too. It comes up often enough in other works: *Personal*, for example, the previous work ('I said, "Make me."'), so *Make Me* can be seen as a continuation of a grand tradition. 'It can be oblique,' I said. 'Look at the Bible. *Ta biblia*. Tells you nothing. It's a book! Or books. *The Seven Pillars of Wisdom*? That's just ridiculous. Where are those pillars? I was expecting a map.'

'Am I playing fair? Is it reasonable? Does it matter?'

'The title is just a selling point,' I mumbled. I was having difficulty speaking at the time. Not emotional. I had pinched a caramel from the bowl sitting on the table. My teeth were all glued up. 'You're not supposed to say everything on the front cover otherwise what's the point of reading the book? Say you were to call it *The [Giving-it-all-away title]*. You'd just give the whole damn plot away.'

There was something Lee used to say about living in New York. He said the great thing was, whatever you did, you could always find a lot of people doing it better than you, and a lot of people doing it worse. You were always somewhere in the middle. And how he liked that feeling. But now there wasn't anyone doing it better. Lee was the top top writer in the world right then. Not just New York. He was the Mr Big of literature. He still cared about that lone reader though.

Lee liked to quote from a book of David Mamet's, *Bambi vs Godzilla*. When the hero comes on the screen for the first time, he mustn't have this 'I want you to like me look'. He has to not care. 'I don't care what you think of me,' he has to be saying (without actually saying it). I think Lee tried to be like that: stoncy and indifferent. But at some level he wanted everyone to like him. To love him. He was concerned, perturbed, when they didn't. ('What is wrong with France?!' he used to groan, where his sales were laughably negligible.)

I went back to the Georgetown Starbucks. In the rain. There were still a few bewildered-looking guys wandering the streets in shorts and flip-flops, but summer was over.

I was thinking about Lee's 'thought experiment'. Imagine, he said, that you had seven billion pre-orders for your book. The marketing was so good that everyone on the planet wanted a copy. Had to have it. Then, obviously, you'd be No. 1 for the week that it was published. Hurrah! But then everyone would have their copy. So, in the second week, you'd be gone. Being No. 1 was nothing (well …) – the real trick was staying there. 'It's like a great start to the season. You always fear it's going to fall apart.'

21

WHERE DID YOU GET THE FOLDING TOOTHBRUSH FROM?

It was a good question. Asked by that girl in Washington. Maybe seventeen or eighteen. She said, 'I started reading your books when I was aged fourteen. They made me feel intelligent. So thank you for that!' Reacher as source of wisdom. Not so much the thuggish head-butt, more the subtly intellectual brain-massage. It was an unusual but entirely plausible take on the works of Lee Child.

But what she really wanted to know about (like so many) was the folding toothbrush. Where did he get that from? It was one of those questions with an easy enough answer. 'I got it from owning one. Which I got from a CVS pharmacy. I think it's a wonderful invention. I also own a folding hairbrush. I don't think Reacher will be using one any time soon, but I do.' The folding toothbrush was Lee's concession to personal hygiene. Reacher liked to take showers too, from time to time, but he could go for long periods without washing if he had to. Scrambling around in the dirt. On the other hand, you have to look after the teeth. He probably wouldn't be getting them knocked out in a fight, but they weren't immune to decay, in certain circumstances. Hence the toothbrush. But it has to be folding, so he can carry it around with him easily, in a pocket. I guess he just improvises where the toothpaste is concerned.

So how did Lee know a little folding toothbrush could be such a big deal? He 'intuited' it, he would say, in the way that he 'intuited' the character of Lydia Lair. You couldn't 'manufacture' these things. It had to be 'organic'. He was concerned, for example, that J. K. Rowling, masquerading as Robert Galbraith, was overdoing it with her hero detective. 'So he is missing a leg. Fair enough. But did he have to have bad hair too?' It seemed a little forced to him, artificial, in a way that the folding toothbrush was not. You couldn't go about just adding things on, for the sake of it. It had to be burned in, not bolted on. He adhered, if anything, to a principle of non-invention. It was something Jules Verne had said, in a critical vein, of H. G. Wells: 'Mais, il invente!' You couldn't just whistle up anti-gravity paint: if you were going to shoot at the moon you had to use real technology (Verne preferred a giant gun). Stephen King had said something similar to him at Harvard: 'You make shit up!'

But did he?

Maybe everything is a fiction. The *Matrix* view of the world. The universe (including everything in this book) is a hoax. The desert of the real. Everything is phoney. It's a reasonable attitude. Everybody is lying about everything all the time. You'd be an idiot to believe anything. Ever.

But what if, on the contrary, nothing is invented? There is no shit being made up by whomever. No fiction. Everything is truth. (Lying is not impossible, but it is only a minor variant of truth.) What then? This was more in accord with Lee's aesthetic: 'My editor says to me, *Wouldn't it be better if this happened after that?* Probably, I say. But it didn't!'

And it was a philosophy espoused by the British empiricists John Locke and David Hume. For them there was no out-and-out fantasy or 'fancy'. Your wildest dreams, your most outlandish nightmares, your most fabulous creations, what were they, after all, but permutations and combinations of lived experiences? And the drug-fuelled hallucination? Nought but a variation on actual percepts. The prophetic vision? An extrapolation from the facts. Every imaginary monster is a chimera, joining together real parts. No one could invent anything, because there never was anything in your head to begin with. Nothing innate. You begin with a clean slate: the *tabula rasa*. The mind, like a blank sheet of paper, like a virgin field of snow, bore no traces, no imprint, at the outset, and would only gradually accumulate 'impressions' and 'ideas' as the years went by. There was nothing in the brain that had not been put there ('imprinted') in the course of your life, and you could therefore only – in your imaginings, in your novels or movies – reorganize, rearticulate the original sense-data.

But in Lee Child's epistemology, the *tabula rasa* was the greatest fiction of all. The 'clean sheet'. The Rousseauist state of nature, the golden age, the wu-shin, the blessed state of innocence, the Garden of Eden, a degree zero of knowing, it was all nonsense. We were always already fallen. Every brain of every newborn bore the traces of at least seven million years of human history, and then some. *We* were already, from Day 1, a permutation of everything that had preceded us, randomly spun together, like candy floss. In there, somewhere, were traces of geology, geography, history, cosmology, syntax, if you could only drill down deep enough: amoeba, bacteria, jellyfish, ape, all our palaeontological incarnations were preserved, could never be fully expunged and erased from the DNA record. Nothing was lost. Which was why we were still vicious killers, when we had to be, or when we just felt like it. All that bloodthirsty tribalism – how could we ever transcend it? For how could we transcend ourselves?

Perhaps the absence of the mythical *tabula rasa* explained why Lee never worried about writer's block. He was not haunted by the dread blank page, there was no blank page, it had already been written on many times by his precursors, his text was no more than a palimpsest. But even if there was no *tabula rasa*, maybe it was still true that we invented nothing. It was just a matter of knowing everything. Attaining 'Bob'-like omniscience. Was he making Reacher up? Or was Reacher real? All Lee had to do was 'read' Reacher. It went back to the origins of his name. Lee Child, a 'reacher' in a supermarket because he could stretch out his long limbs and reach out for a can of soup for an old lady. But what if he could reach out beyond the can, beyond the supermarket shelf, reach out and dip into the minds of others? It was another explanation of what he was doing when he went into the trance-like state, the zone, of writing. He wasn't writing, he was *mind-reading*.

Reacher, in *Without Fail* (Reacher 6), to a couple of tough guys: 'I can read minds.' Maybe he wasn't joking.

22

PRECURSORS OF REACHER

Honourable hunter-gatherer
Hercules
Goliath
Jesus
Lancelot
Robin Hood
Popeye (post-spinach)
King Kong (but with less body hair)
Desperate Dan (*The Dandy*)
Superman (without kryptonite)
Shane (but taller)
Godzilla
Ronin
Travis McGee
Rambo (*First Blood*)
Bruce Willis (*Die Hard*)
Hieronymus 'Harry' Bosch (antithesis)

Descendants
Tom Cruise
A lot of military policemen
A lot of would-be bestseller writers
At least one New York cop
Me (attitude only, retd)

23

HOW TO SAY 'SAID'

Even when you write 'Reacher said nothing,' you still have to say 'said'.

I remember an old newspaper editor of mine saying, 'There's nothing wrong with "said".' (I had presumably just written 'he jested', 'she quipped', or some such extravagance.) But it's not quite as easy as he liked to make out. Every now and then, unless he is to become entirely mute, Reacher has to say something. The occasional furious diatribe, but by and large one-liners. He remains economical, even parsimonious with his speech-acts. But then other people are forever mouthing off. The question is: how, in what order? In the Child oeuvre, there are at least three phases.

1 From *Killing Floor* (Reacher 1) to *The Hard Way* (Reacher 10).

Back-end. 'Said' as sequel. Taking the form, 'X,' he said. 'Y,' she said.

It was satisfactory, it did the job, it was conventional. Every line of dialogue had to be attributed. It was only fair.

2 From *Bad Luck and Trouble* (Reacher 11) to *61 Hours* (Reacher 14).

It was inevitable. He had already eliminated quipped, jested, riposted, guffawed, coughed, snorted, boasted, growled, muttered, croaked. It only remained to delete 'said'. Like the last man standing – it had to go. There was a drawback: loss of intelligibility. But there was a tremendous gain in economy. *Said* was dead.

Well, not quite, maybe. But it was hanging by a thread. It could be sacrificed in favour of rhythm. Or just a pause.

3 From *Worth Dying For* (Reacher 15) to *Make Me* (Reacher 20).

Front-end. Compromise. A rapprochement with the reader.

Said makes a comeback, is reborn, as prequel. Thus, taking the form, 'He said, "X." She said, "Y."'

'I've never seen it done that way before,' said one reader.

But it was logical enough. He'd tried it out on an ad hoc basis; now it had become a system. Lee said: 'Why would you read a line and then ask who said it?'

The only problem was the audio recording. It sounded 'clunky', he thought. Too many 'he said's and 'she said's. It had to work orally. 'There has to be some other way!' Which suggested a phase four.

To be continued ... he said.

24

IS *MAKE ME* FUNNY?

That was Laura Lippman's reading: '*Make Me* is a *funny* book. It really is. Isn't it? It surprised me that way.' She actually laughed while reading it. 'I don't think I have a sick sense of humour,' she added, just in case anybody thought otherwise. This in a book with more than 200 deaths in it. Part-voluntary, part-involuntary. Maybe that was the fundamental joke: *You want to commit suicide? Fine, we'll help. What? You don't like dying that way? What is your problem exactly?* The heartless killers of Mother's Rest almost had a point when they argued that their victims had relinquished all rights when they checked in at the Last Supper hotel. Death would take a little longer, but in the great scheme of things, it was a minor delay. *C'mon, don't take it personally!* One can imagine them laughing their heads off, enjoying their work.

I had a favourite line, which made me laugh out loud the first time I heard it. Reacher has already shot a guy, blasting a huge chunk out of his neck. He ought to be dead, but he is still hanging on. So Reacher decides to put him out of his misery, squeezing the arteries feeding his brain. Chang has moral qualms. Reacher reminds her that only a few minutes before this very same guy was threatening to kill and rape en masse. OK, well how long will it take? 'Not long,' replies Reacher. 'He wasn't well to begin with.' Graveyard humour a speciality.

Lee liked to quote the line in *Personal* (Reacher 19) where a guy Reacher has beaten to a pulp is dying in the back of the car. His sidekick, Casey Nice, notes that the guy is not breathing and suggests Reacher really should do something about it, and Reacher snaps back, 'What am I, a doctor?' More like an anti-surgeon, perhaps, forensic pathologist, taking bodies apart.

There was that scene towards the end of *The Enemy* (Reacher 8) where Reacher pays a visit to the home of the evil General. He has a gun trained on him. 'I meant well,' says the General. 'I understand that,' says Reacher, lowering the gun. 'I'm going to let you live.' The General breathes a sigh of relief and gets a grip. 'Nah, just kidding,' says Reacher and shoots him dead. Good joke. Almost hilarious, unless you're the General of course.

Not forgetting the bathroom scene in *Echo Burning* (Reacher 5). The dumb racist trucker says, 'You some kind of smart guy?' Reacher says: 'Well, I'm smarter than you, that's for damn sure. But then, that's not saying much. This roll of paper towels is smarter than you. A lot smarter. Each sheet on its own is practically a genius, compared to you. They could stroll into Harvard, one by one, full scholarships for each of them, while you're still struggling with your GED.' Then, for good measure, adds, 'The bacteria on this floor are smarter than you.'

Is killing funny? It certainly isn't played for laughs. Reacher generally scorns the wisecrack à la Philip Marlowe. But there is a fundamental congruence between killing and humour. Henri Bergson was the first philosopher to draw attention to it. Why do we laugh? he asks (in *Le Rire*). Consider the classic, cartoonish scenes: a man walks into a lamppost and breaks his nose; another puts his foot on a banana skin, slips up, and lands on his backside. Why would anyone laugh at that? These two sad souls have just endured pain and embarrassment, perhaps they are seriously injured. What is funny about that? The answer, says Bergson, is that they have both deviated from a protocol. A set of rules. The rule in this case is: *Look where you are going! (Don't, for example, go bumping into lampposts or treading on banana skins.)* Or take Don Quixote, mistaking windmills for knights. Thus offending against a fundamental rule that says, *Don't confuse one thing with another*. We laugh at anyone who deviates from the rules.

Laughter is a form of revenge: the revenge of the collective on the deviant individual.

Reacher takes revenge, on behalf of others, for deviations from goodness.

Therefore, Reacher is right to laugh. Reacher is funny.

25

REACHER THE READER

Reacher with a book in his hand. It doesn't happen that often, but it came up in *Personal*, almost. In fact it's concealed within the multilateral title itself. The whole plot kicks off because Reacher reads an ad in the personal column of the *Army Times*. And someone expected him to read it. It was a reasonable way of getting in touch with this elusive, grid-free drifter. So not really a book at all, but you could always count on him picking up a newspaper along the way.

Reacher novels always assume some basic level of literacy. They assume readers. *Make Me*, too, recruits a journalist, Westwood, in the investigation, with a hint that the whole text could be an extended report, a series of articles perhaps, by Westwood, recounting his adventures with Reacher. There is a note, too, from the deceased Keever, a posthumous message from beyond, with important information. Finally, the hero even picks up a book.

Reacher is not often to be found in bookstores. It sounds as improbable as the legendary bull (or, in certain languages, elephant) in a china shop. He might have gone into one, had there been one, in Mother's Rest. This is one of the counts against this soulless town, one might almost say *necropolis*. Lots of rubber, but books, no. Reacher will read just about anything, generally acquiring books by chance on his travels: 'Battered paperbacks mostly, all curled and furry, found in waiting rooms or on buses, or on the porches of out-of-the-way motels, read and enjoyed and left somewhere else for the next guy' (*Make Me*, page 320). At a loose end, in Menlo Park, outside San Francisco, he enters a real bookstore. He has a slight preference for fiction over non-fiction on the grounds that so often non-fiction is not quite 'non-' enough for him. But the question of genre doesn't detain him for long. 'He wasn't strict about genre. Either shit happened, or it didn't' (page 321). In this scene, no actual shit happens. It is an interlude, a postponement of the climax. Reacher doesn't pause to pass comment on King or Baldacci (surely the latest Lee Child should have caught his attention?), nor does he buy anything (unlike Lee Child himself, who never goes into a bookstore without buying *something* – feels it would be bad karma).

But in a way Reacher never stops reading. He even reads a few pages of Proust at one point (*Without Fail*, page 339). Admittedly the book, *Du côté de chez Swann*, the first volume of *À la recherche du temps perdu*, belongs to his brother Joe. 'He could manage the language, but the content passed over his head.' (He does better with Dostoevsky's *Crime and Punishment*, which he had bought in Paris and given to Joe – it may be the only time he actually *buys* a book.) But so many of the plots he unravels hinge on some small point of language. For example, in the very same novel as he discovers Proust, Reacher turns his reading ability to greater effect – foiling the plot against the Vice-President – when he detects a hyphen in a letter, and an apostrophe (as a result of which I am still not sure if I should be putting the hyphen in Vice[-]President or not). Close reading is a form of forensic science.

Every investigation, conversely, is a form of reading, one of the branches of the 'cynegetic paradigm' (as Carlo Ginzburg nicely called it, from the Greek for dog, *kunē*). Sniffing out clues, following a scent, a trail, retracing the path taken by prey or predator: isn't that like reading a book? No wonder, then, that we readers demand a resolution, or at least a solution, some temporary satisfaction, at the end of our passage through the forest of symbols.

26

BREAKFAST, SUNDAY, 27
SEPTEMBER 2015

Sharon (theatre producer) and Ivan (pinball wizard) limped
into the diner on the Upper West Side. They were both walking
wounded on account of both, in a companionable way, having
had bike accidents just a few days apart. We ordered pancakes,
the multi-grain ones, so we could kid ourselves they were almost
healthy. With fruit.

Ivan had had more time for reading while semi-immobilized.
He couldn't do much else. He still refused to believe that Lee
hadn't done a ton of research for *Make Me*. I said I could remember him googling the word 'hale', which isn't even in the book,
but apart from that, nothing. He'd already done all the research
he needed to do, notably on the subject of suicide. Had checked
percentages and stats. The rest was all intuition and psychic
powers.

I had a pile of newspapers in front of me, taller even than the
pancake stack. In fact it was just one newspaper, but it seemed
like a hundred. Sunday edition of *The New York Times*. 'Hey,'
said Sharon, 'where's the theatre?' It was in there somewhere, you
just had to keep pulling out different sections.

'Here, check this out, though.' I fished out the Book Review. I
know I'd heard this already, from the horse's mouth, but it's different when you actually see it written down. Evidence. Exhibit A.
The bestseller lists. For 27 September (but drawing on data from
the period 6–12 September).

> **MAKE ME,** by Lee Child (Delacorte). In his 20th appearance, Jack
> Reacher pries open a missing-persons case that takes him across
> the country and into the shadowy reaches of the Internet.

Top of the world.

THE GIRL IN THE SPIDER'S WEB, by David Lagercrantz.

Lager pants ... 'nowhere'. At No. 2.

The other Lee (Harper) still at No. 3. *Girl on the Train*, No. 4. A rash of 'Girl' novels? The good news, looking at all this from a Lee Child point of view, was that Jonathan Franzen's *Purity* was now down at No. 6, behind *Star Wars: Aftermath*. Second week of publication and he was already on the slide.

Game over.

27

A BINARY PRAXIS OF ANTAGONISTIC RECIPROCITY

I don't know if anyone else has noticed, but there is a curious correspondence, almost an alignment, between *Make Me* and *Purity*, published in the same month. Both have at their core a murder story. I think there is one murder in *Purity*, whereas there are approximately 200 more in *Make Me*. Industrial-scale. Reacher has to solve that puzzle. Whereas in Franzen the murderer himself has to go and blab. He can't shut up about it. So the two writers must have been in touch recently – I like to imagine – just to compare notes and pass on tips.

JONATHAN FRANZEN REWRITTEN BY LEE CHILD
Begin with a backhoe. Obviously. Look at pages 134–5 [of *Purity*]: Andreas spends far too much time digging. With a shovel. Get some decent machinery in there. Why struggle? Dig the hole deeper, shove the guy in, cover it over. Job done. Don't sweat it. And look, you postpone the murder till after page 100. Which is too long. Postponement is one thing, but you are going to lose a helluva lot of readers that way. (And then you take pages and pages just to do it! What is your problem?) You either need to kick off with the murder and then Andreas is the bad guy who must be hunted down (by the way, your solution for what happens to him ... why the hell would he do that?) or ... and this is more promising: what if he has a far better reason for knocking off this guy than ... oh yeah, his girlfriend *asks him to*. 'Hey, Andreas, would you mind if ... ?' *Come on!*

    *Step*father? What about *God*father? What if you have Andreas, with all his skills, and his team of hackers, crack the mystery of this guy who must be channelling funds to Al-Qaeda while running drugs and girls and degraded nuclear material (probably polluting the environment too) and finally, and here we come to a climax, nailing this woman Pip, who is an ex-FBI agent (maybe abducting her, locking her up, *and* sadistically abusing …). And so Andreas is fully and righteously justified in offing him. No anxieties, no remorse. Maybe Pip could help bury him. A woman driving the backhoe. Which would be a breakthrough. Good revenge motive.

Question – what the hell happens to Annagret, the great girlfriend, anyway? It's like you've forgotten all about her!

Then again, maybe you should just have Reacher come along and straighten it all out. He gets off a train in Berlin and there is a mysterious woman waiting for him … Now I come to think of it, this is what your book (good read, by the way!) is fundamentally missing: a decent hero. A big guy.

Just a couple of minor details. Does everyone have to have quite so many relatives? They all have mothers/fathers/aunts/uncles … it's like a forest of family trees. I recommend a quick glance at Camus' *The Outsider*. The mother is dead in the first sentence. Good move, Albert. My advice: *Kill all your relatives!* You'll find it speeds the whole thing up no end.

And leave Shakespeare out of it. If you're killing someone, kill him. Don't have the hero dick around like this: 'If he let the native hue of his resolution be sicklied over with it [anxiety], he was liable to put down the shovel and go back to the city and laugh at the idea of himself as a killer' (page 136).

One final point: *the* final point. There isn't one. Your last fifty pages (maybe a hundred, I lost track) are a pointless add-on. Nothing happens! The parents are having another argument. The kids are sick of them. That is an ending? Your readers have had enough of that in their own lives – and you think they want to read about it too?

Here's a thought: I noticed that your characters are all quite small. Kind of weedy. What about a bit more size? And muscle mass?

LEE CHILD REWRITTEN BY JONATHAN FRANZEN
I loved *Make Me*. Really, I did. My first Reacher! I'm sure it won't be the last either.

We have so much in common, you and I, do we not? After all I have a hero (OK, protagonist then, or just *agonist*, whatever) who essentially wants to kill ... himself. And you have all these people (hundreds of them, thousands, I forget) who seek a quietus with a bare bodkin. If only the almighty had not fixed his canon 'gainst self-slaughter ... Oh, sorry, there I go again, fuckin' Bard always bubbling up. I'll try to get a grip.

And, look, you even have the Dark Web theme: all those sneaky addresses and passwords and whatnot – and nerdy guys who can hack into it. I've got all that too. We're on the same page here, surely? The idea that there is some schism between us, a cultural abyss, what I believe Kuhn used to call an *incommensurability* ... it's a joke, isn't it? A figment of the over-active media imagination. Genre? It's just retail! Consider this conversation to be an official rapprochement.

If you think about it, why does Reacher finally stiff all those guys? Answer: *because his girlfriend (Chang) asked him to!* He never would have exerted himself otherwise. And she has been begging for that bone from around page 2.

But, now you mention it, when it comes to the stuff that is missing, the lack, the Lacanian lack, one might say, *le manque*, yes, that very deficit out of which creativity springs forth like a ... OK, sorry, yes, Franzen, get to the point, my point anyway (not that there is one) is that if you compare *Make Me* with some of the classic novels, shall we say, *Madame Bovary* or possibly, I don't know, *À la recherche du temps perdu*, or *ja!* let *uns* get Germanic, what about Thomas Mann's *Magic Mountain*, or Hesse, the archetypal *Bildungsroman*, the thing that is missing is ... consciousness. It's like everyone is unconscious. They are already dead. Yes, it's a zombie novel, isn't it, at heart? Or rather, if it had a heart. So that is what we need to do, yes, put the heart back in, give it a heart transplant. Or a brain transplant maybe. Just a few touches, nuances really, to upgrade and enhance the old *Weltanschauung*.

Here's how I see the final scene, for example. So Reacher has killed all these guys, right? But he's already pretty depressed, isn't he? I like that. Vulnerable. A little screwed-up. Verging on neurotic. The concussion is just an outward (or is it inward?) symbol of his core angst or existential nausea. So that bit where he just ups and hops into the car and drives away with Chang ... what about if ...

CHANG: Hop in.

REACHER: I don't know. I'm feeling a bit broken up about, you know, the way the hogs got hold of that guy and just started chomping and scoffing ...

CHANG: Oh God, I know, it was awful, wasn't it? Nobody deserves that. We're sick, you know that?

REACHER: Sicklied or ... To be or not to be, that is the question. And you know what, I had a dream about my mother last night ...

CHANG: But you're supposed to be like my sublime father, you know, a stand-in or surrogate, because I never knew my own.

REACHER: I'm not feeling well. Is there a doctor in the house?

CHANG: Sorry, I have to go and vomit.

Something like that. What do you say? See what I mean? There's more of a swerve to the narrative, more depth, I guess. It's not quite so linear. Don't hit me, I mean, yes hit me, you bastard, I deserve it! Chomp me up and shit me right out again, like the hogs, but ... sorry, I guess I lost it there for a moment. What was I saying? Oh yeah, erm, it's like, you have this great narrative, OK cool, score one for you. But what about de-constructing it all over again, the way I do it, chop-chop karate, Joycean celebrity chef style. Turn it inside out, upside down, every which way.

And the backhoe – OK, but what about if, yes this is good, you know, the shovel just flops and drops right off? Like a bad dream. And the guy is left hanging there, drooping, impotent, totally limp and flaccid. *Moving* [first word] ... *needle* [last word]? How about: *Detumescing ... organ? Qu'en penses-tu, mein Kamerad?*

28

BACK TO SCHOOL

from: andymartinink
to: LeeChild
date: 29 September 2015
subject: Night School

Have you worked out what the medal is yet?

from: Lee Child
to: andymartinink
subject: Night School

Legion of Merit.

from: andymartinink
to: LeeChild
subject: Night School

So you're storming on with the third sentence?

from: LeeChild
to: andymartinink
subject: Night School

2 words long

from: andymartinink
to: LeeChild
subject: Night School

```
Is that the lot or what?

from: LeeChild
to: andymartinink
subject: Night School

I'm already onto the second page. Garber is back.

from: andymartinink
to: LeeChild
subject: Night School

You're on fire. Send a chunk my way?
```

He sent me chapter 1 and I caught up with him at his apartment a couple of days later. He was sitting at his desk, but somehow lounging in his chair, leaning back, hands behind his head, looking reasonably pleased with himself. 'Do you know what my favourite bit is?' he asked.

'Is it the bit about the Balkans? Why he got the medal. Had me laughing out loud.'

'Look at it,' he said, re-focusing on his screen. '"The Balkans, some police work, two local bad guys identified, and located, and visited, and shot in the head. All part of the peace process." Classic Reacher!'

'You're going to have to be careful with the passive, though. You don't want too much passive. Otherwise it's all "The bed was gotten out of, the breakfast was eaten, etc." It's OK as summary.'

'Yeah, Reacher has to be active. This is like a report to HQ.'

'No "whom", of course: "*who* Reacher knew from years before." Do you think you'll ever use "whom"?'

'Reacher would know about the difference between *who* and *whom*, but I guess I decided he just couldn't be arsed to do anything about it. He's just being lazy.'

'Or economical?'

'Economical.'

'I like how you go to Fort Z and then, lo! Reacher is to be found at Fort Belvoir. Coincidence or what?'

'Economy of invention. Waste nothing.'

The shrewd reader will have noticed that approximately half the time Lee Child thinks he is Jack Reacher. Or vice versa. One of these days, the distinction will be lost completely and he really will think he is Reacher and he will walk into a bar and try to head-butt half a dozen bad guys and that will be the end of him. Or possibly not. Maybe they will mistake him for Reacher too.

'"Reacher said nothing." I see you get that in. Thanks.'

'Now you think everything I say is just quoting *you*.'

'Yeah, well that's OK because I'm just quoting *you*. So it evens out.'

29

CAN I HELP YOU?

I would like to be able to write, *I was having lunch with Lee Child in the Tavern on the Green when ...* For starters, it's quite a classy establishment. Actually *in* Central Park. I mean, I usually end up in Starbucks. To be honest, I could have done with a decent lunch for a change. You know, salad, but with good ingredients, maybe some fresh-baked bread on the side, and so on. Sparkling water. Rather suave waiters and waitresses, a view out, table linen, actual glasses, the works.

In fact, however, Lee Child was having lunch with Karin Slaughter. Karin Slaughter was the author of some dozen previous novels and her book *Pretty Girls* was just coming out. Lee was interviewing her for *Playboy*, or she was interviewing him, either way. So I stood around, leaning against a pillar for a time, while they were yacking. Yacking and chomping. Finally Lee waves me over. I sit down. I say hi. 'Very much enjoying your book, Karin,' says I. 'Bold use of second person, I like that.'

'You see,' says Lee, 'this is what he is like, you can't stop him.'

And then this *maître d'*-type woman comes storming over and says, directing her words rather pointedly at me, you know, giving me the look and the whole thing, 'CAN I HELP YOU?' She spoke like that, in upper case. I was cool with that. She probably had a lot of hard-of-hearing customers, getting on a bit. So I sat there trying to think of ways in which she could help me. Menu would be good for one thing, I was thinking. I was pretty much ravenous by this point.

'It's OK,' says Lee, waving a protective hand like a shield. 'He's with me. He only looks like some poor starving wastrel.'

Starving wastrel more or less summed me up: like some Dickensian ragamuffin looking through the windows of the

Savoy. But the great thing, I realized, is that I had at last accidentally achieved the kind of status I had long hungered after, that of deranged celebrity fan. Her 'Can I help you?', correctly translated, meant, 'Get the fuck out of my restaurant, you weirdo!' Or, 'I'm dialling 911 right now, so you'd better get your ass out of here before the cops turn up.' With hindsight, wearing the Dr Martens (even if vegetarian) had perhaps been a mistake: the *maître d'* woman feared I was going to start something. I think I also managed to scare Karin Slaughter, herself author of many a scary tale – guys with knives and a propensity for sado-masochism – by ranting on about the *nouveau roman* and the *tabula rasa*. She scuttled off to catch a cab. Had to go on a publicity tour.

'Great name,' I said, 'for a hardcore writer. Makes your "Child" look just a little soft-centred.'

'Yeah,' he said wistfully. 'Come on, I've got to go and have a smoke. You don't want to have lunch or anything, do you?'

'Nah,' I said. 'Not bothered.' This may well be the biggest lie I had come out with for some time.

The *maître d'* came over. 'MR CHILD,' says she, 'PLEASE HAVE THIS LUNCH ON THE HOUSE. IT HAS BEEN THE TAVERN ON THE GREEN'S PLEASURE HAVING YOU HERE.'

Lee nodded gracefully, humbly, like a member of the Swedish royal family. 'Cor,' says he when she'd gone, 'if only I'd known I would have ordered more. D'you think it's too late to get a dessert?'

He agreed that the *maître d*'s swooping on me, virtually whipping out her gun (at least verbally), probably had something to do with the on-the-house gesture. Act of contrition. But he reckoned he was always getting this kind of treatment. The one guy in the world who least needed it, while all the waifs and wastrels were starving. And who would least appreciate it, moreover. 'The guy who first said *There is no such thing as a free lunch* was obviously never a writer. I've had so many free lunches. What's the problem with that?'

We wound up in a dark corner of a Starbucks on Columbus. Black coffee. And a cherry yoghurt for me. With granola. Free lunch (courtesy of Lee). It was almost like being a writer. If only I'd known, I would have ordered more. We were mainly talking about killing people, as a matter of fact. I can't remember if he said 'Kill all your relatives' first, or I did. But we were thinking along similar lines. Lee was talking about his own in-laws, to some extent. 'The whole point of my brand of mythic realism is to escape from your own family. This is why I had to have Joe the brother killed off in the first novel. The Dad is already dead.'

'The mother not far behind of course. Sturdy old Resistance fighter though she is.'

'You can't have a lonely drifter tough-guy hero and he has to call home every couple of weeks to talk to his Mum,' Lee reckoned.

It was probably the essential difference between what he was doing and what, for example, Franzen was doing: was there a big family drama going on or not? Franzen was all about the family drama and not much else; Lee more or less scorned the family drama, maybe one or two light touches of nostalgia for the good old days when Reacher had relatives. 'Everyone else is doing soap,' he said succinctly.

We were wondering whether we might feel bad about killing somebody (the way Andreas does in Franzen). 'I think this guilt and remorse thing is totally overdone!' Lee said with a degree of disgust. 'It's made up, pure fiction. Something they've worked up to justify droning on about their personal turmoil. It's a complete con.' He had heard a soldier once, on the radio, talking about killing. He was something of a sniper. Big rifle. Had taken out a guy half a block away, who really needed taking out. Had seen his head blow up. Good shot. 'And what did you *feel* at that moment?' inquired the interviewer, BBC-style. The soldier had had to think about it for a second. Then he replied: 'Recoil against my shoulder.' It wasn't a joke, he wasn't being stylishly witty. That's all he'd felt. Recoil not revulsion. Nothing else.

'It's easy to get used to killing,' Lee said. 'We used to do it all the time, had to. We've forgotten. But we soon remember.'

'But the amateur? The solo operator killing somebody, man or woman, that's different, surely?' I was trying to see the Franzen point of view.

'All this obligatory hand-wringing!' Lee said. It was one of those times where the word 'exclaimed' could be justified. Maybe he sensed I was taking Franzen's side. 'It's just ridiculous. How do you feel when you put down roach powder? It's got to be done. Sometimes. *How do you feel?*'

Lee pretty much hated the stupid 'How do you feel?' question (which is why I didn't ask it all that often). 'You might as well ask a cook in the kitchen frying an egg, "How do you *feel* about frying the egg?" *Come on!*' He was furious with the absurdity of it all. 'Eggs are going to get broken. It's no big deal. You can take anything, and it becomes normal.'

30

CUP OF TEA, WITH A
SIDE ORDER OF NAPKIN

'Sorry, everyone!' Karen said, unbuttoning her coat. 'I had to ditch Spielberg.'

Good line. We were having dinner at the Trattoria Dell'Arte on 7th. To celebrate total world domination: *Make Me* was officially No. 1 for the second week running. Lee, Joel, and I were working our way through a bowl of olives when she came sweeping in, looking fabulous. She really had ditched Steven Spielberg. Her movie, *Maggie's Plan*, was a roaring success at the New York Film Festival. Thousands at the Lincoln Center. They were all loving it. Massive global deals in the offing. South Korea, Cambodia, Brazil, they all wanted it. Spielberg was pissed because he had originally passed on it. But, to do the guy credit, he had turned up for the screening. Karen felt good about passing on him. 'Did you know he's really small?'

'They're all small,' said Lee, the lofty one. 'All of them.' He had been thinking about Henning Mankell dying that day. The (London) *Times* had called him up, asked him if he wanted to comment. He said he didn't. Boring old Wallander. Did he have to make his stories that flat? But, still, he was dead aged sixty-seven. Of lung cancer. Heavy smoker.

I piled in. 'Better than Larsson. He only made fifty. Diet of fags and coffee and burgers.'

Lee said, 'I'm running out of gas.'

Joel and Karen made noises of incredulity.

'Come on, I'm getting old. The next contract is the last one.'

'For how many books, though?' I asked.

'You know I've got books piling up. I want to just sit and read them.'

'I knew I shouldn't have given you the bloody Franzen,' I said.

'Yeah, I want to retire and read Franzen,' he said.

His other big idea was writing songs instead. At least the lyrics. There was even a group out there, Naked Blue, waiting for him to send them the song. He reckoned he could do a good job of that. 'Maybe I need to find someone to take over from me. To write the Reachers. While I write some short, lyrical heartbreakers and tearjerkers. To a thumping beat.'

Joel reckoned *he* could do it. Sweating the revisions to his latest novel, he had been going around saying he wanted to *be* Lee Child. One draft and only one. 'Come on, how hard can it be. *Reacher gets off the train. All hell breaks loose. The end.*'

'Don't forget the waterbed, though,' I said, between yet more olives. 'Can you do the waterbed?' It was something Lee and I had been discussing. The crazy stuff. The second sentence. 'It's such a stupid metaphor. And it's the second sentence!'

'Stupid?' said Lee. 'And it's a simile.' Lee Child, the pedantic, nit-picking academic. Shocking, I know.

'Trope then, Jay-sus. The point being that it's hard to reproduce, because it's dumb. It happened.'

'No problem,' says Joel. 'I can do the waterbed. Lee, I promise to slip a waterbed *simile* into the next one. *Reacher gets off the train. Gets on a waterbed. All hell breaks loose ...*'

Lee said, 'If Reacher got on a waterbed, all hell *would* break loose!'

Joel was kind of serious, though. He really would like to take over the franchise, I think. Someone ought to. Readers are going to be sobbing in the streets otherwise. Maybe we should all do a bit of a Patterson and get in a crew and start churning them out, three or four a year. They'd sell.

Lee was giving him hope. 'Look at Robert Ludlum. He's written more since dying than he ever did when he was alive. They're probably better too.'

He was eating a salad, but he managed not to eat the leaves, just scoffing up the Gorgonzola. He got nostalgic about great or not-so-great meals of his youth. He was about eighteen. On his own, and flat broke. He used to go into a cheap café called the Kardomah. On a dark back street in Birmingham. You could get a cup of tea in there for threepence. Not 3p but 3d. There was even a threepenny bit then, the golden age of LSD – pounds, shillings, and pence. He would knock back the cuppa. Even had milk in it in the old days. Not coffee but tea. Couldn't afford coffee. He would empty out the contents of the ketchup bottle (tomato, generally) onto his saucer. Then he would pick up a paper napkin from the dispenser and soak it in the saucer. Then he would suck the ketchup out of the napkin. Solid tomatoey flavour. Of course he would suck up some of the napkin too. Decided it wasn't too bad, all in all. More or less went for it. Soaked up some more sauce and then shoved in the napkin. All the way in. Bit by bit. 'It was that or steal. Filled me up. Kept me going. It's a good old stand-by.'

None of us could top that story. We'd never been that level of broke. Lee really had done it all. You could say it explained a lot about him. It definitely explained how come he remained so thin. The thinness got locked in early on. It also explained the truly gigantic wedge of cheesecake that sat in front of him right now. Monumental. He'd never get through it, but that wasn't the point. It was better than a napkin. A whole lot better. He held up the creamy table linen and waved it around. 'Where's the ketchup?'

As we were going out, Lee already reaching for the Camels, a guy with smoothed-back white hair jumped up from one of the tables and shook Lee by the hand, smiling broadly. Fan. 'I'm just reading your new one,' he said.

'I wish he would hurry up,' said his rather lovely wife, sitting on the other side of the table.

31

'YOU'RE NOT GOING TO BELIEVE THIS, BUT ...'

I didn't have to choose the waffle. Could have been pancakes. Or tacos, with extra potatoes on the side. It could have been banana waffle, but I went and chose the strawberry. It just felt like a strawberry waffle kind of day. Lydia was having the tacos. The waitress delivered our order. The waffle was punctuated by swirls of whipped cream. And, as per the menu, laden with slices of strawberry. I had to sit back and admire. It was a thing of beauty. Somehow I felt I had to take my phone out to take a picture. 'I have a dog called Waffle,' I said.

'Really?' said Lydia. 'That's a nice name for a dog.' We were sitting outside at the Guenther Mill on the river in San Antonio.

'My kids came up with the name. They were having waffles at the time.'

At that precise moment a text signalled its arrival with a brief throb. I still had the phone in my hand. I was thinking of putting it away, but I hadn't started eating, so I thought it was just about acceptable to check my phone. It was a message from CambVetGrp (a veterinary service back in Cambridge, England, several thousand miles away and several hours ahead, according to the clock). The first word was 'Waffle'.

```
Waffle is due his FLEA TREATMENT. Our records
show that you might need some more. Please call
01223 249331 to order.
```

I went ahead and ate the waffle. Having first smothered it in maple syrup. But I still have the photograph (with the time noted) and I kept the text, just in case anyone should doubt. Absurd, laughable, bizarre, definitely, perhaps even trivial. What are the chances? I think I can guarantee that this precise set of circumstances will never occur again in the history of the universe. But I believe it comes under the heading of what Jung would call 'meaningful coincidences' or 'synchronicity'. I eat a waffle in San Antonio, Texas, I speak of Waffle, and a text concerning Waffle from far, far away simultaneously materializes on my phone. Virtually from Waffle himself.

It was the kind of phenomenon that tended to happen around Lydia Lair. She was a magnet for weirdness, a regular lightning rod for the uncanny. She came to pick me up at the airport in her white Jaguar. About the first thing she said was, 'I'm not Emma Bovary or Anna Karenina. I don't have time for love affairs. I'm a business woman.' Lydia Lair was immaculate. She was always immaculate. She was slim with squarish glasses.

I said, 'I'm glad you're not Emma Bovary or Anna Karenina. They both came to a fairly sticky end, didn't they.'

She had been to see the ballet of Anna Karenina in Montréal not too long ago. 'What did they do about the train?' I said, never having seen it.

'Oh they had a train all right,' she said. 'The train steamed across the stage right at the beginning. And then again at the end.'

The invention of the train had expanded the ways available to unhappy people to commit suicide. I knew at least one guy who had chosen to go out that way (he was an economist – saving on rope or gun). The train was an effective tool, no question. Tough on train drivers, though, who were being used as involuntary executioners.

I loved San Antonio. It was summer again, in October. The Lairs lived in Alamo Heights. Lydia took me to the Alamo itself, which turned out to be a fairly small but rather beautiful fortress, all in white, in the Spanish hacienda style, downtown, just across the river. A lot of men had died there, heroically, back in the nineteenth century, besieged by greater numbers, in a way recorded in song and film. Davy Crockett/John Wayne had perished there. I saw them again in a glorious technicolour *son-et-lumière* show, together with the Lone Star, projected on the façade of the San Fernando Cathedral. Lydia took me on walks along the river and to an archetypal Tex Mex restaurant with amazing murals and real mariachis. I was forced to drink margaritas, champagne, and finally Armagnac. But I just about managed to hold it all together and concentrate on what I was there for, namely to talk about *Make Me* and her role in it. And the meaningful coincidences (which came to seem still more meaningful and ever less coincidental) that linked the character of Lydia Lair and the real Lydia Lair herself.

It was a phrase Lee had used himself when he inscribed a copy of the book to her. 'To the real Lydia Lair, with thanks for your kindness.' Which didn't surprise me. But it did surprise her. 'We were *flabbergasted*,' she said. A word you don't hear that often. A bit more than surprised. Astonished but (briefly) reduced to confusion and perplexity. The reason being: she didn't even know that she was supposed to be lending her name to a character in the book.

'But wasn't that the whole point?' I said. 'Wasn't that what you were paying for?'

She thought she was getting LUNCH WITH LEE CHILD. It said so on the list of auction items. Started at a thousand dollars and kept on going up in multiples of 500 or 250. A lot more than they had ever intended to pay. They never even intended to bid at all. But somehow they got caught up in it. And then their final bid had won the charity auction at the Hilton Head 'Heart' Ball. Plane tickets to New York. Three nights in the Roosevelt hotel on 45th Street. And lunch with Lee Child. No mention of a character's name. There had been a breakdown in communication. I knew all about it back in February. Lee had been pondering the name in Bermuda. We discussed it. He decided against renaming Stashower/Chang as Lydia Lair. 'Don't worry,' he said. He would find her something to do. 'Something poignant. Then she dies. Short and sweet.'

So Lydia never even knew what she was getting in return for her immensely generous contribution to the Heart Foundation. And then she found out. Over lunch with this 'prince among writers' (Lydia's words) in New York. *I* am in *your* book!? She opened *Make Me* with mingled excitement and trepidation. What would her character be like? Would she be young or old, ugly or beautiful? Would she get to make love to Jack Reacher or perhaps be killed by him? (Reacher had no qualms about killing women, if they needed killing.) 'Oh God,' she blurted out when a particularly unpleasant woman made an appearance, nameless at first. 'I hope I'm not her!' She wasn't.

She was glad too that she wasn't Chang. Obviously Chang was Chang (even though she had once been Stashower). Lee had saved Lydia Lair up for the part of ... Lydia Lair. In the home invasion scene. Lydia, her husband Evan, the daughter, her pre-wedding party – all thoroughly smothered, like a waffle in maple syrup, with assorted bad guys and guns and Reacher and Chang.

'That really was me,' she said. 'If it had been Chang, it would have just been a name, it wouldn't have been me.' Lydia was Lydia. She was completely caught up in it. Her heart skipped every time the name Evan came up. 'Dr and Mrs Evan Lair'. Pictured at a charity ball, moreover. She had been reading that bit on the plane home. She had to put the book down, she was too emotional. 'You're not going to believe this,' she said, heart in mouth, to her husband. It was like Lee was allowing her to live the life she might have led. Evan Lair, in the story, was a doctor (of the medical kind). Dr Evan Lair. 'Evan', Lydia's Evan, had been studying medicine when he was killed in the car crash. Straight-A student. She was studying French at Euphoria State and they had met through singing in the choir. They were both great believers, brought up in the Methodist church, and Evan had thought about becoming a missionary. They were engaged to be married. The date was set for June. Then he went and died in April. Aged twenty-one.

The eve of his death, Lydia had had a terrible premonition. A feeling of agony took possession of her. She was sobbing. Nothing like it had ever happened to her before. 'I'm afraid if you leave me tomorrow then I may never see you again,' she said. 'How could that be?' (Evan). 'Because you would be dead' (Lydia). 'And then I would live forever,' he replied, evenly, quite unperturbed. 'I would be with God, so there is nothing to fear, is there?' He had calmed her down with quotations from the Bible, reassuring her of their eternal life together, whether on earth or in heaven. And she had believed him. Didn't give it another thought. Then there had come the knock at her door at 2 a.m. A minister

116

of the church, knocking at 2 a.m. Evan was dead. His car had collided with a bridge as he drove home in the darkness. It was all her fault, she felt.

And now Evan, in *Make Me*, thanks to the divine intervention of Lee Child, was alive once more. He had attained eternal life after all, at least for a few glorious pages. ('How did he choose the name Evan?' she asked me. 'He needed two syllables,' I said, uselessly. 'But,' Lydia again, 'why *those two*?') And then she was preparing for the wedding of her son, just a week or two later, just as her character was preparing for the wedding of her daughter. And she had been brought up in Kansas, in an isolated township, just like Mother's Rest, on a wheat farm where she drove a tractor and milked the cows before school. It was entirely uncanny and utterly entrancing for her.

But it was the story of the brother that just about killed her. Lydia Lair's brother had gone missing – such was the premise of *Make Me* – and Reacher and Chang and Westwood were trying to figure out what had become of him.

It was after lunch. Her husband and his test-pilot friend Art had gone out somewhere. We were alone together, seated comfortably in her living room, next to the grand piano, deep in upholstery and cushions. A quiet, spacious house, a tree-lined garden, walls decorated with paintings, many of them by her husband. She wanted me to explain to her how Lee had come up with all his ideas, about the 'assisted dying', and all the poor devils who went to Mother's Rest to die. I recounted some of our conversations about different ways of committing suicide and the friend of his who had suggested climbing up a mountain in Austria and then chucking yourself off, a bit like that scene in *Crouching Tiger, Hidden Dragon*, now I come to think of it: half-falling, half-flying. She agreed that was never going to work: either you were too ill to get up there in the first place or you would be revived by the mountain air and would come down again, the slow way, only with a more positive attitude and the lungs thoroughly purified.

She wanted to tell me about her brother. The tragic brother. But first of all she revisited the suicide of her ex-husband. He was a lawyer, specializing in the oil and gas industry. They had kept on moving around, from Albuquerque to Dallas to San Antonio. And then he had to go back to Dallas. 'I'm staying here,' she said. She liked it in San Antonio, their kids were happy at school. He could go to Dallas on his own. Six months later they had divorced. Her ex-husband had remarried, but in a year or so he was dead. His second wife killed herself first. In a garage, the car engine running, the door locked. (An old Chevy – no catalytic converter.) Exactly three weeks and one day later, he died in exactly the same way. Garage, engine, door. He was an ex-ex-husband. Found lying by the door, not sitting serenely in the driver's seat, perhaps having had second thoughts, trying to get out and failing. He had told his and Lydia's children that there was no way he would ever commit suicide, so they were not to worry. *Liar!* Lydia had read his journal, after he was gone. Like a good lawyer, he had done his research. If the spouse committed suicide *within* three weeks of his partner, then any life insurance was null and void. He had left it precisely one day more than the three-week waiting period. Looked as though he was impatient to be gone. Only really waited so his kids would collect. It was just a question of timing.

It had taken Lydia – unlike her first husband – years before she was ready to remarry. So when Jean-Pierre came along, Lydia told him to go away and leave her alone and never to call her. He duly went back to Paris. *Adieu!* Then nine months later she called him. She was in the south of France.

But, as I say, it was all about the brother for her. Whenever the question of the mysteriously missing brother came up in *Make Me*, she was torn apart. Again and again. Her reading was bliss and it was torture. In the Kansas that was not in Lee Child's head, her brother, Duke, had died only three months before. 'In a tragic accident on his farm,' she had written to me. Maybe she even believed it then. For a while. She wanted to believe it. But Lee Child wouldn't let her. *Make Me* told her everything about her brother. On the one hand, Lee was giving her Evan back again; on the other, he was taking away her brother, once and for all. It was fair. She needed to know what had happened. And now she did.

She had told me about the 'accident' on our walk along the river. Duke had been repairing one of his vehicles in a shed by the wheat field. A big heavy vehicle, a grain-feeder. About three in the afternoon. He was fixing the hydraulics, which had a habit of failing. The front part of the vehicle had to be craned up so Duke could slide underneath it and get access. But it was supposed to be supported on blocks so that it couldn't ever flop down and squash anyone who happened to be underneath. But Duke had done it a 'gazillion times' and he was confident. He didn't bother with the stupid blocks. Inevitably, the engine had collapsed right on top of him and crushed the life out of him. Like he had been stomped on by a giant hoof from above. Aged just fifty-eight. Lydia had been given the job of phoning around all her sisters (there were seven children, six girls, and just the one brother, the youngest). It was a 'freak occurrence' of just the kind that happened on farms all the time: people died in grain elevators, for example (just like the ones in *Make Me*, 'as big as an apartment building'), drowning in wheat. Chopped up into tiny little pieces in giant shredders. Turned to pulp in pulping machines. And so on.

But now we were sitting comfortably, as I say, next to the grand piano, sinking into velvet upholstery. And Lydia changed her story. I wasn't interrogating her, as such, not much anyway, no third degree, no thumbscrews. We were just talking. But I guess it was the talk of *Make Me* and mountains in Austria and all that. 'I didn't really put it together before,' she said. 'Not until I read Lee's book. And then I started thinking …'

It was the phone calls. 'I love you for ever and ever,' Duke had said to her. It was his last phone call. She was just leaving for South Carolina, but she would come and see him in Kansas soon (and she did but he was already dead). She knew he had been in a slump recently. Had started putting weight back on. Was due to go into hospital for surgery and he didn't want to go into goddam hospital for surgery. Hated doctors, didn't trust them. And the wheat crop had been pretty much destroyed in a storm. He was in trouble with the bank. But then he was always in trouble with the bank. He was a farmer. It was normal.

It was the other phone calls that really did it for her. He had phoned all the sisters (she discovered later). A night or two before. Had said he would love them all forever. 'He didn't call me for two years and then he called me and then he died,' said one of her sisters. Or more than one. It was the same thing, over and over again. That 'accident': he was too smart for an accident. And smart enough to stage one too. It wasn't a suicide, *prima facie*; but then again, it was. He was calling them all to say goodbye. Almost like a suicide note.

'The last straw was the election.' Duke was a popular guy in town. Perhaps even the most popular. He was always donating stuff to worthy causes. Everybody loved him. He was a happy-go-lucky kind of guy, with a nice wife and son and daughter. He ran for county commissioner. Came in runner-up by about three votes. Laughed about it. Was philosophical about it. Stoical. And then again, maybe he was in fact deeply depressed by it. Had never quite got over it. Felt as if he had been rejected by everyone in the entire community. Betrayed, in a way, after everything he had done for them.

Then he died, flattened like a pancake, under the greasy engine of a grain-feeder.

And she had understood his last text to her. In March 2015, when Lee was approaching the climax of *Make Me*, when Reacher was close to figuring out what had happened to that elusive brother. 'Lydia, what are your plans for next week?' Her plans didn't include her only brother's funeral. Lydia showed me some pictures of him. Grinning at the camera. Cheekily. Arms around his family. A little overweight, maybe, but he carried it well. He looked cheerful enough. Maybe a little *too* cheerful?

And now she realized: there were other farmers out there, killing themselves. The shotgun to the head. The horse tranquillizer. 'How can you live?' she said, with an air of desperation. 'There are no jobs.' It was pure *Make Me*. *Make Me* was the story of Lydia's life. With a few twists. But it was all there. 'When I read the book,' she said, 'I realized: *this was my brother!*'

'That Lee Child must have googled you!' said her sceptical aunt over the phone. 'It's the only way.'

I knew he hadn't. He only knew two things about her, technically speaking: 'Lydia' and 'Lair', in that order. No more. Didn't have a clue about her beyond that. Had no idea where she came from or who she was, least of all who her brother was. Or Evan. Or anyone else. And then he had just gone right ahead and written the story of her life (with a few minor alterations). He had done a Cuvier and reassembled the whole creature out of a mere heelbone of a name.

Lydia knew her aunt was wrong anyway. How many Lydia Lairs were there? And even if you zeroed in on the right one there was never going to be that amount of information about all the other people in her life.

The *unus mundus*, Jung liked to call it. *Mysterium coniunctionis*, recalling the mystic fusions of the old alchemists. All those unfathomable connections that went beyond time and space at the level of the collective unconscious. Like worm-holes in space, providing a short-cut from one distant galaxy to another. Weaving in and out of black holes. Synchronicity. That non-Cartesian realm in which waffle calls unto waffle across the miles like stranded whales, beached upon foreign shores. Or maybe like the mosaics that Lydia Lair herself liked to create, sticking together disparate fragments, broken shards, to form some kind of pattern. Lydia Lair had been a cheerleader, a bassoonist, a mother, and a business woman. She was a fan of Andy Williams, Tony Bennett, Neil Diamond (especially Neil Diamond), and Barry Manilow. And she had always been strong in the faith. 'Pure, honest, wholesome, unbleached, and free from chemicals.' I'd read it in the Guenther Mill, referring to 'Pioneer Flour'. But you could as easily apply it to Lydia Lair.

When she had that lunch with Lee Child, it was not in the least like going to meet her Maker. Or maybe it was. To a degree. He was *a* Maker, after all. The Maker of *Make Me*, at any rate. He who knew things about her. Things that nobody ought to know and that he had no right knowing. He was, as he said himself, just a 'little bit omniscient observer here'. He was a god who smoked, admittedly. 'He is going to die, you know,' said Lydia, with a touch of regret. 'Tell him that.'

I went out through the garage of their house. It was where they kept the great invention behind their business success. And it really was great, I'm not kidding. Their original folding ladder. I saw it in action and I definitely want one too. Basically everyone is going to want one. Or two. It used to be called the 'Auto-Lad'. Now it is known, more prosaically, as 'The One-Touch Electric Attic Ladder'. Retails for around $3,500 or so and it's worth every cent. Her idea, designed and built by Jean-Pierre (who, apart from being a gifted painter, is also an aeronautical engineer, specializing in the 'reverse-thruster' on Gulf Stream jets). You know all those terrible ladders that come down out of your attic? Kind of come down, but don't, not properly. They're all stiff and useless and awkward. You can't really work them. They don't slide. The good news is that they are a thing of the past – thanks to the One-Touch. Press a button and it's like grace descending. The ladder folds down out of the ceiling. All controlled by a computer, not sensors. It's like a dream.

And you climb up it with total confidence. Broad steps with excellent grip. You don't climb, you ascend. Like an electric stairway to heaven.

32

JOUÏSSANCE

It was typical Lee Child.

Not long before, he had been ranting on about how you had to kill off all your relatives (speaking aesthetically, but with a definite sense that art is murder) and how much he hated all those family trees in the classic novel. He was anti-genealogy. No begats. You can't have an XXL ex-military vigilante drifter roaming about and he has to call up his old mum every couple of weeks. That sort of thing.

Now he was saying, 'What if his mother comes back? Madame Reacher. You know, but young. In the Resistance. A kid. Before she became a Reacher. I love that period. The Nazis marching down the boulevard. Sartre and Camus writing in the Café de Flore. Most of the Resistance fighters achieved nothing, beyond getting themselves tortured. Useless, a lot of them. But the couriers – they were really something. They saved lives.'

We were crossing the street at Columbus Circle, weaving around cars and buses, riffing on the phrase 'San Fairy Ann' (the Anglicization of *Ça ne fait rien*), deriving from our Second World War-era *franglais*-speaking fathers. Neon-lit darkness. Only a hazy idea where we were supposed to be going. We'd just finished the *New York Times* job in the Starbucks across from Lincoln Center Plaza. Lee was looking particularly disreputable for some reason. Maybe it was the stubble or the jeans-and-t-shirt combo. Piratical. Like, if you were sheriff, you'd want to run him out of town before he started anything.

'I thought you had a rule about relatives?' I liked the old ma, but you had to get the aesthetics right.

'Maybe I could kill off all *her* relatives? That could work. It is the bloody war after all, much harder to keep 'em alive then.'

'You can't kill her off, that's for sure. No Mum, no Reacher. He's not born yet!'

'Yeah, that's a problem. Everyone will know she has to live to a ripe old age. What was it? Sixty, I think. My age …Then she conks out.'

It was all down to a reader, as usual. A Canadian reader. Lee had been up in Toronto at a bookstore, doing his usual author gig, and a woman had stood up and asked him if he would ever bring the mother back. She liked the mother. There was a definite ripple of enthusiasm for the idea – no doubt from all the mothers in the audience. He had said no one had ever asked him that question before and he was quite struck by it. Maybe he would, one day. Hence, thinking about it as we crossed the street.

To me it was like asking Albert Camus if he wanted to bring back Meursault's mother. That's what readers were like these days: controlling. It wasn't enough to read a book; they wanted to write it too. Or press the buttons on the remote anyway. In this case the rewind. Can we have the one with the mother back, please? Lee recalled a similar issue with Marilyn and Chester Stone, in *Tripwire* (Reacher 3). People wanted to know what had happened to them at the end. The author hadn't said. Just left them swinging in the breeze. After everything they had been through (at the hands of Hook Hobie). 'What do *you* think happened?' he replied, sophisticate that he was. Cue outraged reader. *He* was supposed to know, not them. But it was like the reader was getting him to rewrite everything. 'Makes you wonder, though, doesn't it? I could just *extend* every novel. Stretch it out a bit more. Go forwards, go backwards. Easier than writing a new one.' Which is what he was in fact trying to do, when not distracted by about a hundred other things. And readers pulling his strings.

'Starts to sound like my distant relative George,' I said. 'George R. R. "Game of Thrones" Martin.' There has to be a connection.

'Our colleague at Random House. I think he slipped in the R. R. Just to sound more like Tolkien.'

We were only a block out from the Random House building. 'You could bring back everyone we thought was dead,' I suggested, helpfully. 'Like Gandalf.'

'Isn't that the kind of thing you do?' This was prefaced by an explosion something like a 'Ha!' He was not a great *Lord of the Rings* fan, mainly on account of Tolkien having been at his old school: King Edward's Grammar, Birmingham. Reacher vs the little hairy hobbit. It was no contest. Ring or no ring. Maybe he had even come up with Reacher as a kind of protest *against* hobbits. 'I bury 'em and you keep digging 'em up again. So I guess I don't need to.'

This was his notion of hermeneutics. The writer goes about killing people, and the critic goes about excavating the bodies all over again. A would-be resurrectionist. Like in *Pet Sematary*. Or archaeologist. Maybe forensic pathologist.

Lee had a house in France. Was good at French. Spoke it fairly fluently. Here's proof (of the fluency): the other day a French couple had come up to him a couple of blocks from the Apple Store on 56th. They wanted to know where the Apple Store was. They spoke only French, no English. And, this was the problem, they had just walked straight past the Apple Store, didn't even realize it was there. Lee had to explain to them, in French, that the Apple Store was in fact concealed beneath a glass cube in a square and they had just looked right through it, what with it being transparent and all. Not unlike the Pyramid outside the Louvre. I was wondering how well I would do. I would have struggled in English.

Thus Lee Child knew all about the difference between *le plaisir* and *la jouïssance*. The classic Roland Barthes distinction, in *The Pleasure of the Text*. Flaubert (*jouïssance*), Dumas (*plaisir*). Translated into our current – recurrent – terms it was Franzen vs Child. The standard English translation of *jouïssance* was 'bliss', which was OK so long as you didn't forget the sexual connotation, or possibly denotation (orgasm). Lee was definite. Explicit. 'The reader has to have an orgasmic experience reading Reacher, it can't be anything less.'

'Of course, it's ambivalent, the *jouïssance*. There has to be a degree of pain alongside the pleasure. That's the difference.'

'I can do pain,' he said. 'No shortage of pain.'

He was right of course. Look at Lydia Lair. It was all bliss (Evan) and torment (brother) for her. Maybe that is the way the

Reacher books work: they are an equation, a pendulum, bisecting pleasure and pain, ultimately with a slight tilt in the direction of pleasure.

'I'm held to a higher standard,' Lee was saying. We were wandering about looking for the Trattoria Dell'Arte. We were in no hurry. 'Great city, isn't it?' It was a warm night and the streets around 57th and 7th had a certain *joie de vivre* going on, verging on *jouïssance*. A Lee Child book had to be like the New York of literature. With all the lights on. Electric darkness.

'Think about it,' he was saying. 'I can't afford to let the reader off the hook. It has to be intense *all the way through*. If the reader ever says, "Yawn, I'm bored," I've failed. Whereas, consider Franzen. The Franzen reader expects to be bored, some of the time. The point is buying the book in the first place. The actual reading is almost secondary. You got more out of the buying than the reading. There can be long stretches, *longueurs*, where nothing is happening. A hundred pages maybe. Of ennui. Where the reader doesn't even care. You can put it down for months.'

'Years in my case,' I said.

'You finished *Purity*, didn't you?'

'*Freedom*. Still about fifty pages to go. I'd better pick it up again and finish it. If I can find it.'

'You see, that's exactly it. There's no compulsion. You can take it or leave it. Pick it up or put it down.'

'You often use the analogy of being in a car going somewhere. Usually a nice car. A BMW or something. Maybe Franzen is more like just wandering about, on foot. What we're doing now in fact.'

Lee thought about that one. We still hadn't found the Trattoria Dell'Arte. We were relying on the city to find it for us (neither of us was tempted to use a phone). 'Reacher does a lot of wandering, of course, doesn't he? It's his whole *raison d'être*.' He chuckled, only because he'd managed to get the phrase *raison d'être* in there. But it was true: he gets off the train only because he likes the name, Mother's Rest. He's not going anywhere as such. 'But look: he has to find the diner. He has to get the cup of coffee, eventually. Otherwise, he curls up and dies. Then it's pure Beckett.'

'The endless waiting. Nothing happens.'

That was the cynegetic paradigm: directed wandering; aleatory, but teleological. Lee Child wasn't the opposite of Franzen (or Beckett). It wasn't linear. Maybe it was just more *transparent*. If you wait long enough for Godot, then Godot really will manifest himself. All 6'5" and 250 lbs of him. Maybe this, finally, was the point of Reacher: to level the playing field and abolish the hidden hierarchies (aka 'bad guys'). Reacher wasn't God, but he was Godot.

Which is when we finally came across the Trattoria Dell'Arte. Right opposite Carnegie Hall. I could have looked it up properly and we could have gone straight there and we would already be putting away the hors-d'oeuvres but, then again, we'd have missed out on the wandering. We got somewhere, but without knowing exactly where we were going. I think it was the Lee Child method at work. Seek and ye shall find. He also fancied the look of the 'Grill' place next door and said he'd rather go there next time.

33

ON THE FIRST CHAPTER OF LEE CHILD'S *MAKE ME*

I should have taken a photograph, just for the record. A world first: Lee Child spotted writing in a Starbucks. It'll be airport lounges next.

To be fair, I guess I pretty much made him sit down and write. It was just a conversation in a café, but we had to write it down. It was something we were doing for *The New York Times*, an analysis of a page or two, to go online. We half-talked, half-typed, sitting on stools, looking out over Broadway, sliding the laptop to and fro along the counter like a couple of cowboys in a saloon sliding a bottle of whisky from one to the other. Lee was trying to move forwards with *Night School*, but he didn't mind going back to *Make Me*: it reassured him – if he could finish the last one he could finish the next one too.

Moving
MARTIN: You start with a participle. I like that. Verb of action. Transitive. We have an action taking place, and an object (corpse, one, large). But we don't know who is doing the moving. So, covertly, you're posing a question, right at the beginning, that won't be answered till somewhere near the end. Who are these guys? Who is the subject of the verb? The 'hermeneutic code' (as Roland Barthes neatly called it) is like a long, serpentine fuse leading to a big barrel of gunpowder somewhere down the road. You just lit it. Expect fireworks.

CHILD: The first sentence arrived fully formed. And it had to put us right alongside the bad guys, struggling with their midnight task. I didn't want, for instance: 'Keever was a big guy and it was hard to move him.' That's too flat, too start-from-cold, too declarative. I felt 'Moving a guy as big as Keever' was somehow real-time descriptive, a little breathless, as if grunted by a guy occupied with the problem. The sentence had to do two things: launch the action *in medias res*, as they say, and hint at a kind of inarticulate, rural vernacular.

Keever
MARTIN: First proper name. Like an inscription on a tombstone. Keever, phonologically a close approximation to 'Reacher'. A para-rhyme. What you're saying is: this could happen to Reacher as well, if he's not careful. Keever is a big guy too. And look where that got him! (In with the hogs.) Maybe there's also a faint echo of (John) Cheever, the writer, in there too? But more likely it's Kiefer (Sutherland). You have to bump off the star of *24* in the very first sentence. *Before* the first sentence. You don't want any competition.

CHILD: That's an academic thinking. The writer says he doesn't know where it came from. Cheever? Possible, but so far removed from a hog pen at midnight that it's unlikely. Kiefer? I'm more a fan of his Dad. (Who once wrote to me saying he wished he was younger so he could play Reacher in the movies.) 'Keever' probably just bubbled up from somewhere in my subconscious. Maybe I just liked the sound ...

like trying to wrestle a king-size mattress off a waterbed
MARTIN: The leitmotif of sheer size gets bigged up all over again (and it comes up once more with the silos at the end). But you want to know the thing that kills me about this sentence? Try getting 'Deep Blue' to write that line! There will come a time when machines will write novels. Maybe it's already here and cyber-authors are simply masquerading as human beings. But I guarantee IBM or Google are not going to come up with this crazy waterbed image in a million years. Where did that even come from?

CHILD: I try to respect the physical reality of death and corpses, to some extent. And they're floppy and hard to move, especially the big ones. I was once in a hotel in California, trying to nudge a waterbed mattress straight, and it felt like the right image. But I agree, machines will never have that kind of crazy free association.

buried
MARTIN: Begin with a burial. How can that miss? It also picks up where the last one, *Personal*, ended: with another burial. So there is a sense of a continuum. But I know you were rereading Stephen King's *Pet Sematary* at the same time you were writing this book. All those zombies on the rampage. And isn't there a sense in which Keever just won't stay buried? Like the ghost of Hamlet's father, crying out for revenge, he keeps on popping up, despite the best efforts of the bad guys.

CHILD: Keever was dead before the book began, but in a parallel way he wasn't … his fate drove the whole story, we learned some poignant details about him. For a dead guy he ended up a rounded, well-developed character. So in that sense, yes, he refused to stay buried.

Which
MARTIN: It's like you've got two voices going here at the same time. Like a harmony. On the one hand, you've adopted the point of view of the farmers, the hog owners, the guys who are doing the killing and the burying. It all 'made sense' to them to do exactly what they were doing. Coldly logical (the word 'therefore' comes up twice here). Ruthless, of course. It's the Flaubertian *style indirect libre*, what James Wood calls the 'semi-close' third-person voice. But the way you're starting a sentence with the beginning of a subordinate clause: that is pure you. That is your voice. One of your syntactical quirks (egalitarian perhaps? – no subordinates!). So it's like you're letting the reader know that you're still there. Buried, but irrepressible.

CHILD: And 'Which' at the head of a sentence is an accelerative word – it launches the new thought with pace and momentum. Very valuable. But I have to be careful not to overdo it. It becomes a habit. Two or three in sequence is fine, but those sequences need to be separated.

harvest
MARTIN: They are farmers, after all. If only they would stick to the farming! They shouldn't be using people as fertilizer or hog snacks. Harvest would typically have fairly positive connotations. Not in the works of Lee Child! Admit it – you hate the pastoral. The nomadic warrior is the opposite of the farmer. It's an opposition that goes back to the shift from hunter-gatherer to agricultural home-makers. Is this still the fundamental theme of your work, first aired in the Book of Genesis – *Cursed is the ground for thy sake, in sorrow shalt thou eat of it ...*? And 'harvest': it has a weird sort of Stephen King echo to it – what the hell is going to leap up out of the earth? That old Greek myth of the 'autochthonous' guys ... these are people connected to the earth in some way. Chthonian, subterranean. Which hooks into the very end of the book ... The descent into the labyrinth.

CHILD: I guess one writes what one knows, or at least has sympathy with. And the opposite. It's not that I particularly dislike farmers (OK, a bit) but more that I scorn the unexamined assumptions that litter our discourse. Farmers are good and wise? Well, not really. Not always. Farmers have screwed up repeatedly (Dust Bowl, BSE, etc.) – they're as dumb as anyone else. I think that should be pointed out occasionally. The myth of agricultural wisdom.

nothingness
MARTIN: There is plenty of 'nothing' in your work. 'Reacher said nothing,' for example – one of your most recurrent phrases. But *nothingness*: it's a rarity. This is only the third time in twenty novels that this word has been used (I know, I checked). The first page of *Make Me* and you pull out the nothingness card. And only once in the course of this novel, likewise. What is this word even doing here? A faint allusion to Sartre's *Being and Nothingness*, perhaps? The pastoral is all about nothingness; the nomadic warrior, on the other hand, is the incarnation of pure being. A higher level of existence. And, without giving it all away, the whole plot is right there, at the very beginning. Like a hologram. The temptation or the dread of nothingness.

CHILD: It was somewhat declarative – here we have a tiny cast on a gigantic empty stage. I wanted a strong sense of absolutely nothing, with a bright pool of light in the centre of it. In the context of the first page (especially considering the way I write, which is not to know the second page yet) it would be bogus to claim much meaning in it, beyond an obligation to tell the reader, OK, the setting is miles from anywhere in farming country. Information, rather than metaphor. I find it more organic to come back and decide what was metaphor later (and then develop it) rather than decide ahead of time.

backhoe
MARTIN: You really like this word, don't you? And the size of it. Maybe Reacher is modelled on a backhoe. But I like the way you really give the machine character and dignity and power. Look at it go! All those beautiful lights. And all the different kinds of work it can do, 'straining', 'roaring', 'scraping', and all that. It's lyrical. Your hymn to *tekhnē*, the love affair between man and machine. The cab 'falling and rising' – inanimate and yet so alive. We instinctively feel that we are not done with this backhoe, just yet. It did a similar job in *The Hard Way*, I recall. With Reacher in the driver's seat.

CHILD: I like machinery, sure. I grew up in a city that made that stuff. [*Birmingham, England.*] But again, at this point all I wanted was to create a picture of vast, dark emptiness, with a tiny hot-spot of light, noise, and nefarious activity at its centre. You're the analyst, I'm just a working hack. This is housekeeping – setting the scene for the reader, but through action, so it's not boring. But yes, it's a good American word; they don't have it in England (where it's 'JCB').

fluent, articulated
MARTIN: Verbal words applied to the machine. The machine speaks more than the anonymous farmers. And look at the description of the train too. With its 'mournful whistle' and the rails that 'sang'. It's like they have real feeling and poetry, which the humans lack. The machine sings the blues. But we

are reminded too of the thing that is missing on this first page, something you might reasonably expect: dialogue. There is none. Surprising?

CHILD: I wanted the sound of the railroad to emphasize the silence and loneliness. No dialogue? Absolutely, and that's a choice. Lots of writers use dialogue from the top, to make the page look accessible to a bookstore browser. White space is less intimidating than a dense wedge of text. But Reacher is not a talker. I don't want to give a false impression. But if I do the opening right, I think I'm saying to the reader, don't worry, you're in for a fun ride, and there will be plenty of talking later. On the other hand, in the third person, it often feels like dialogue even when there isn't any. It's all down to the voice – or *voices*.

Jack Reacher stepped down to a concrete ramp
MARTIN: I remember you originally had something to do with 'dirt' here and you changed it to 'concrete'. Is concrete more Reacher? You didn't want him getting his shoes dirty right off the bat. He's a warrior not a farmer, after all. What's that phrase in *Shane*? 'Sod-buster'? Reacher is more of a head-buster. Here he is getting down off his steel horse: like a knight in disposable chinos and t-shirt.

CHILD: I wanted to separate Reacher's initial environment from what we had seen around the bad guys. I needed it to be a clear two-world situation – here are the bad guys, and here is Reacher, different in every way. Yes, he's a descendant of the ancient knight errant tradition.

And they would use the air, for a guy like Keever.
MARTIN: I almost forgot. You went back and put in the comma in this sentence, didn't you? The humble comma. You'd think a big bone-cruncher like Reacher wouldn't have time for a mere comma, but he notices the little things, doesn't he? Solves a case by reference to an anomalous hyphen. Spelling. And the comma – it's all about the music, isn't it?

CHILD: There was no comma on the first pass, but I wanted it to sound slower, more considered, more ruminative, slightly inarticulate, slightly low-IQ. Even though no one talks in the first section, I wanted to mirror a halting, slow-witted style of speech. Flaubert!

dream
MARTIN: 'like a vision in a dream'. It wasn't *like* that – it really *was* a 'vision in a dream', wasn't it? Isn't that how it came to you?

CHILD: It's a funny old job, mine. I get paid to sit around and daydream. Everything else is just typing.

elevator
MARTIN: Very Don Quixote, with silos in place of windmills. Or rather this used to be 'silo' – you've changed it to 'elevator'. Don't you like silos any more? But more importantly I recall that you originally had 'bigger than an apartment house'. Now you have 'as big as'. Is that downsizing? So everything comes down to sheer *size*: the lifeless bulk of Keever, the massive presence of Reacher. Even the shed has to be 'enormous'. It's like you're saying, OK now it's Reacher vs silos (or elevators) – who will win?

CHILD: Cervantes was too satirical of the heroic tradition. I never liked sidekicks like Sancho Panza either. But you're right, I wanted to echo the opening. Make it more like a refrain. And *elevator* – it was the sense that there could be machinery at work rather than just a storage facility. Or maybe it was all those syllables. Size, yes, I always want Goliath to win, not David.

toothbrush
MARTIN: I know, it's not in the text (not till several chapters in). But it has to be in Reacher's pocket, right? The folding toothbrush. Or is it the kind you screw together?

CHILD: It clips together. I have hundreds. People send them to me all the time.

MARTIN: I'm hooked all over again. Another reader, desperate to know what happens next. How do you do that? Is it something to do with the *agon*? You've set it up so there has to be a clash, a show down, somewhere down the line. Or is it to do with that teasing, did he see something or nothing?

CHILD: It's all about asking questions and not answering them for ages. Who is Keever? Who are the folks who killed him? And why? Why was he important? Did Reacher see the lights? Is that why he gets off the train? For a first page I thought it did its job. I was happy with it.

ADDENDUM

Unusually, instead of butchering what we'd done, they asked for more. 'They' in this case was a nice guy called Scott, an editor at *The New York Times*, who was a fellow surfer. The conversation was going online anyway, so there was room. Hence, a few days later, we came back to the point that had worried me from the beginning and is still bugging me, even now.

midnight

MARTIN: Not only do these mysterious Keever-killers live in the state of nothing and nowhere, but they have no time in which to do a proper job either. There is a manifest contradiction to do with trains which Agatha Christie for one would never have tolerated. Look at your impossible timetable. Your bad guys only get started at midnight. And you have them being disturbed by the train in the middle of their fairly thorough grave-digging. Yet the train is supposed to leave Somewhere at seven. It's five hours late, so it arrives in Nowhere (i.e. Mother's Rest) at midnight. *Therefore* (to use your word) the time it takes them to do the job is exactly ... zero. The train takes ages to go by ('forever') and yet: it is *still* 'midnight' when it's gone. It's like the whole oneiric plot exists in non-time and non-space. Is this Lee Child subtly deconstructing the whole genre and saying to the shrewd reader, it really is all airy nothing?

CHILD: Sometimes you just have to get it wrong to get it right. I liked the emphasis on 'midnight darkness' for one thing. It just felt right that way. For a clandestine burial. I didn't want to be a slave to train timetables. And then once it was done, I was reluctant to go back – like Agatha Christie – and finesse it. I like it a little rough and ready. And rely on the readers to get it right for me.

34

HIS DYING WISH

Jeff had a successful career as an industrial chemist. He had made some good chemical cocktails over the years. But, well ahead of the financial curve, he had retired young to (really) spend more time with his family and his kids, before he was too old or worn-out to enjoy it. So it was that one fine afternoon, instead of cooking up some new potion, we find him playing football in the park with his son Keith (aged twelve). It is a lovely sunny afternoon and Jeff is wearing shorts. He is feeling as fit as ever he did as he weaves around his boy, feinting left and going right, and putting the ball high into the back of the net while the crowd (in his imagination) goes wild.

Jeff goes off in pursuit of the ball and trots back with it, a triumphant grin on his face. Hey, come on, he can still outwit and outrun his own kid, maybe not for much longer. He can make the most of it while it lasts.

'What's that on the back of your leg, Dad?' says Keith. 'Is that some kind of mole?'

'What? Where?' says Jeff, feeling down the back of his leg.

CUT TO: Hospital. Senior surgeon. 'I'm sorry, I have some bad news for you.'

The bad news was really bad. In fact terminal. They gave him six weeks to live. It was nothing to do with the chemicals. It wasn't work, it was the holiday that was to blame. Too much sunlight. That trip they had made to Florida last year. Yes, it was true, he had got a nasty burn, but he hadn't given it too much thought at the time, just lathered it with lots of cream. And made sure to put the old sunblock on next time around. But sometimes one major sunburn is enough. It was like some people only smoke one cigarette and get instant lung cancer. This was similar. He had melanoma, advanced, malignant. And metastasizing like mad. One mole, but loosely connected to a whole subway system of murderous cells. 'Funny,' said Jeff, 'I didn't feel too bad when I walked in here.'

CUT TO: Jeff, a few weeks later. Gone from fit footballer to cadaverous shadow of his former self. But he wasn't dead yet. He called up his old mate Tel. 'Tel,' he said, 'I'm dying.'

'Oh fuck,' said Tel, never one for speeches.

'Can you do me a favour?'

'Anything. You name it, it's yours.'

'You're an old friend of Lee Child's, aren't you?'

'From schooldays.'

'I'm a big fan,' Jeff said. 'I've read 'em all. Twice. I hate having to wait a year. When's the next one due out?'

'September.'

'Tel, I'm going to be dead in September.'

'Fuck,' said Tel.

So it was that Lee received an email from his old friend Tel around the beginning of August 2015. He phoned up his editor in London. She phoned up the warehouse.

The following day, Jeff's wife walked into the bedroom, where he lay, surrounded by cards, grapes, and flowers. He was a popular lad among his fellow industrial chemists. 'Look what arrived for you in the post,' she said.

Jeff looked up and cracked a smile.

That September, Lee was in Manchester, doing a signing at Waterstones. He drove out to see Tel. Maybe he could drop in on Jeff too. 'Did your mate Jeff get his copy of *Make Me* OK?' he asked, solicitously, over a beer in one of the old pubs.

'He loved it,' said Tel. 'He really did. Said he could die happy now. And then he actually died. Happy. You know, sort of.'

Lee smiled. He wouldn't be driving over to Jeff's place after all. He hadn't really known Jeff. Let us be plain: he really did not know Jeff. But he had no difficulty putting himself in Jeff's position and imagining what it was like to have killer melanoma. And imagining, further, what it must be like to read *Make Me* in those circumstances. It was a form of assisted dying. *Make Me* was like morphine to a man in pain.

'You know what he said about it?' said Tel. 'He said that all those stories of everyone dying in pain, he was really sobbing over them. But he reckoned he felt better afterwards. You know, as if it didn't hurt so much and he could take it. At least no one was locking him up and beating his arse with a baseball bat and filming it.'

As he drove away from the pub, Lee thought that maybe that was the great consolation of the book, any book, not just his own. It was the one thing that all books shared in common. They all had an 'End'. There was a last word. And a final, terminal, full stop.

WINTER

35

CARL (1)

'I think I may have just broken the record for the disproportion between the amount of selling and any actual sales.' Thus spake Carl.

He had had the kind of coverage most writers would die for. A front cover of T2 in the (London) *Times* and a big page in the *Guardian*. He had done his share of TV shows. And he had just returned from giving a talk about *The Wellness Syndrome* at the Stockholm Public Library. Big audience, around 200 or so. Which was encouraging, surely?

Except when one of that audience, in the Q & A, stood up and said, 'Really interesting. You ought to write a book about it.' The only book of Carl's they had on display was a copy of his PhD thesis on Lacan. For which there were few, if any, takers.

I was there for Lee vs Lagercrantz. But behind the scenes gang war was breaking out. *Intra* not inter. The worst kind. With a dash of Nordic noir.

I guess it was all Carl's idea. He was a new Reacher reader. But a convert with boundless enthusiasm. He had gone to New York to launch *The Wellness Syndrome* in the US. I took Lee along and he instantly recruited him to the Child gang. For one thing he liked the umlauts in his name. He was tall, even taller than Lee. But above all he approved of his book, even bought a copy, because it appeared to give intellectual and political ballast to his semi-religious conviction that any hint of physical exercise or healthy eating was automatically bad for you. Trying to be well made you unwell, trying to be happy made you unhappy, in fact generally trying too hard at anything was uncool. Such was the diagnosis of Dr Cederström. He was spelling out the fundamental Reacher philosophy. He was *in*. Without trying, of course. It was the only way. If you tried, you failed; only if you failed to try did you stand a chance. It just had to happen that way.

Anyway, he vowed to bring us both to Stockholm. Without really trying of course. Which went pretty well, it has to be said. For a while.

First of all, *Babel*, Sweden's No. 1 literary television show, wanted to talk to us about the great scientific project that was *Reacher Said Nothing*. One week it was Franzen, the next it was Child/Martin. They were into Lee Child, they were fans, but they were sold on the idea of having a crusty old academic shadowing his every move. It was weird enough to be different. Carl had scored. And he was going to write an article about the meta-book. It was going to be the first meta-meta-article. Probably the last.

Then he got crushed by the Lee Child publicity juggernaut. Her name was Lina. Pronounced Lean-er. And she leaned on people for a living. Carl was an innocent by comparison. Collateral damage. For one thing she was trying. Really really hard. Which was almost like cheating from his point of view. That was the thing about the cool, deeply stoical, not-trying method: it ran up against all these uncool, trying types. Like Lina.

'Fuck you, Lee Child!' That was the essence of Carl's reaction. It was a line I had heard a few times over the ages. It was a line Lee Child himself loved to hear. Music to his ears. Carl was revolting against the gang leader. Threatening to hand in his card. Maybe he would join the Franzen gang instead.

'It's like fighting against giants. These people. Now it's all Lee, Lee, Lee. *Reacher said nothing!* that's a joke. You can't stop him! He's everywhere.' His head was in his hands. 'It's like standing under fuckin' Niagara. An endless torrent ...'

'Carl, I get that metaphor.' Carl, though Swedish, has brilliant English.

'You know what I mean then.'

'Totally.'

'He is some kind of monster.'

'Of course.'

'You don't mind that?'

'*The Wellness Syndrome* teaches us: don't fight, don't struggle, let it be.' I was trying to tell Carl what his book said. He wasn't convinced by my interpretation.

We trooped around Stockholm together, crunching over the ice in big boots. Went to the modern art museum, bathed in a roomful of yellow light. But it was when we were on the Larsson trail that Carl took a call on his cell. He clicked off. 'My life just changed,' he said. He was a tall white guy. But he had just gone a whiter shade of pale.

36

ELSA (THE OPPOSITE OF THE TOOTHBRUSH)

It was *Make Me* that started it. Carl had been carrying a copy around with him and she thought it looked interesting. But she still hadn't read *Make Me*. Obviously she couldn't read that one before she had read all the other works in the Lee Child oeuvre, in order, chronologically. So she rushed off and bought *Killing Floor*. She just hadn't realized how many there were, not at first. But now, like all Lee's readers, she was starting to worry there weren't enough and she was having to slow down, postponing *Make Me* still further.

But, to be fair, Elsa had got off to a cracking start. She had read twelve in five weeks and was now well into the thirteenth, *Gone Tomorrow*. Some of them she had read in one sleepless night and then slept the whole of the next day. It was a full-blown addiction that was throwing the rest of her life into disarray. She wanted to *be* Jack Reacher. Which was difficult, given that she was also the mother of a ten-year-old daughter. And she looked way more like Lisbeth Salander. In fact, a lot like Lisbeth Salander.

We were having dinner in a little restaurant around the corner from the Opera House in Stockholm. I was sitting next to her on a velvet-upholstered bench. I felt a bit sorry for the daughter. Aside from the fact that Elsa was giving priority to Jack Reacher in her life, she had also refused to watch the Eurovision Song Contest with her. She knew she ought to, as a good mother. But she had had to refuse on aesthetic grounds. She just couldn't bring herself to watch such unmitigated trash. Four million out of a total population of nine million in Sweden would be watching it. 'I don't want to waste my time,' she said. 'There's just too much bullshit.' But it gave a certain authority to her judgement when it came to Reacher. 'Lee Child is an artist,' she said. 'He has such deep knowledge of his character. Of everything really.'

She had mentioned Lee Child to a friend. The friend made some condescending remarks. 'What!? You're reading that!?' The friend was unfriended then and there. She would never be seeing her again. 'I'm very discriminating,' she said. 'I scare people, I'm so picky.' Normally she was to be found reading Jonathan Franzen or Martin Amis or the Swedish equivalent. She summarized her attitude succinctly. 'I give a shit about the things I give a shit about.' It was the kind of line Reacher would have understood, I felt.

There were no visible body piercings, but I was guessing tattoos, yes, a few. Slim, black shirt and trousers, fine bone structure, page boy haircut. An intense gaze. But she was scared. 'I'm scared I'm going to run out.' It was the classic addict's anxiety. Where was the next fix coming from? Lee was like her dealer. Or maybe more like Heisenberg in *Breaking Bad*, cooking up another batch of super-high-quality crystal meth, the kind that people will kill for.

'I try to have something in my life,' Elsa was saying. 'To escape.' Once it had been books about lightning. They had to be about lightning, specifically. She had exhausted that vein. Then it had been Candy Crush for a while. Now it was Reacher, who was like a man-size reefer of lightning and Candy Crush all rolled into one. She had had to go back to the beginning and *Killing Floor*. 'I started when there were no cell phones and computers.'

We both ordered avocado and tomato salad. And extra olives. She said she couldn't live without olives: it was a bond.

She dreamed about Reacher too, apparently. In her dreams she spoke with the voice of Reacher. Elsa said she definitely wanted to go and head-butt somebody. (She mentioned a name but I had a feeling it could have been almost anyone.) Back in her youth she had been into *Modesty Blaise*. She had read them all, aged fourteen, and thought of herself as Modesty. Willie Garvin, the Cockney sidekick and comrade, who called her 'Princess', was a kind of precursor to Reacher, big and muscular and cool. And come to think of it Modesty was a precursor to Salander, with similar combat skills, only (if I remember the comic strips correctly) more voluptuous and less of a techie. She had a special technique of whipping her top off, to distract the bad guys, from time to time, while Willie punched their lights out. The topless move not only worked but it looked good on the page too. And Modesty and Willie remained gloriously Platonic to the end.

'I love Neagley,' Elsa said. Neagley being that inexhaustibly ruthless comrade of Reacher's who does not like to be touched. Ever. Elsa and I instantly found ourselves revisiting the erotic scene in which Reacher finally touches her for the first time. She has a hand on the wall (for some odd reason). Reacher's hand goes over the top of hers. Their fingers meet. It's the kind of thing that is not supposed to happen, like a particle and an anti-particle getting up-close and personal. There is an immense discharge of voltage: nothing happens beyond that, but it is enough. She shoves off, he shoves off, they kill a few people who badly need killing and they part, as before. But the blue touch-paper has been lit. It's almost Platonic, but not quite.

Elsa was not a huge fan of Tom Cruise. 'If you get a man below 1.70, it's not the same. You have to over-compensate. You have to talk too much. Like a chihuahua.' Not that a chihuahua talks much, but you get the idea. 'Whereas Reacher is calm. That calmness comes from his size. It's the essence of Reacher. I tried to explain it to my boyfriend. He's into theory. He listens to podcasts all day long. If I like a room, he'll say it's neo-classical or something. I like to think with my gut. Like Reacher.' She had clashed with her boyfriend over Reacher. He thought she should be reading more Tolstoy. 'I don't give a shit,' she said. 'He gets scared if I raise my voice and get passionate.' It was clear that it was something she did from time to time.

Another thing she liked about Reacher: he doesn't mind being wrong. Or other guys being good at stuff. 'It's rare in a man. He would never want to push someone over a cliff because they're better than him.' Similarly, she didn't mind not being what she wasn't. 'I will never wake up blonde and tanned. Reacher is like that. It's a confidence thing.'

There was a tinge of sadness to her voice when she admitted that, unlike Reacher, she couldn't drink coffee. One drop and she feels nauseous. She was using the books, which are mainly about drinking coffee, after all, as her caffeine substitute. I mentioned the article I had read that said that if you drink enough black coffee you turn into a psychopath. 'I'm not a psychopath,' she said. 'But I am ADHD.' She was definitely obsessive. But attention deficient? OK, she couldn't handle gas bills or taxes, but I wasn't convinced that someone with ADHD would be able to concentrate on Reacher stories all night long. It was more OCD to my way of thinking. The compulsion to keep on reading Reacher over and over again. I had that too. We agreed that our condition had something in common with the dyslexics and illiterates who found that they could actually get a grip on Reacher. And then having got a grip they were a bit reluctant to let it go again.

In the great Lee Child vs David Lagercrantz debate she was, naturally, anti-Lagercrantz and refused to read *The Girl in the Spider's Web* on ethical grounds. She thought Eva Gabrielsson had been ripped off. But anyway she was just too busy reading Reacher. She also thought it was obvious that someone like Lee could simply intuit the entire life of Lydia Lair. 'David can't do that,' she said. 'He's a mechanic, not an artist.'

We finished dinner, and eventually we went our separate ways, Elsa to the south island, I to the north. Stockholm is all about islands. (I heard that there were fourteen of them.) But I had a feeling there must be something more to explain her Reacher compulsion. 'There has to be more!' as Reacher says in *Make Me*. So when she called me up a couple of days later, my last day in Stockholm, and invited me over to her 'studio', in Gamla Stan (or Old Town), I had to go. I was curious.

My default metaphor is Aladdin's Cave. But it was up several flights of stairs. And it wasn't jewels, it was clothes. Her studio was stacked from floor to ceiling (I am not kidding here – the crates really reached up to the ceiling, and it was a high one at that) with clothes of all kinds: dresses, but lots of guys' stuff too – DJs, or gorgeous Sergeant Pepper-style jackets, in profusion. A whole apartment, several rooms, virtually a penthouse at the top of an old building, and it was crammed. I asked for the craziest thing I could think of at the time – a straw boater. She found one for me in about five seconds, and it fitted. Hats galore. Shoes, boots, ties. Regalia of all kinds. Even about fifty different kinds of glasses. It looked like utter chaos but there was some secret order to it all, a code that would decipher the apparent gibberish. 'I need all this shit,' she said. 'This is what I do.'

I realized I had forgotten to ask her about her job. All we had talked about, in our obsessive way, was Reacher. Maybe we were both ADHD. She was a costume designer for theatre and movies. Didn't fully approve of the way they had dressed Salander ('It's like they googled "punk look"'). She had just got back from Rhodes and (she explained) dumped a load of stuff on top of all the other stuff. 'So it's more zen underneath?' I asked. 'No, it's a nightmare,' she said. I took a picture of her in the middle of all her kit. She looked like a little girl – maybe Little Red Riding Hood (except in black) – disappearing into a dark forest of clobber. She was being *clobbered*. She was drowning in clothes. She was being buried in an avalanche of clothes.

'You don't own things, they own you.' She didn't really have to say this. She only had to show me. I understood why she was such a confirmed Reacher freak (not that you need a reason). This was like the exact opposite to the folding toothbrush. When she landed at Stockholm Airport she was carrying – single-handedly – thirteen separate pieces of luggage, each one weighing 40 lbs or more. She had to pay a fortune in supplementary baggage charges. Something that never happened to Reacher.

She was rooting through some stuff. 'God, I hate mixed bags.'

She gave me a couple of ties. Again something Reacher would never do. 'Are you sure?' I said.

'Please!' she said. 'I have thousands of ties. Save me from two of them at least.'

It was my Reacher gesture for the day. They tried to grab me round the throat, but I deftly took control and dealt with the two bad ties.

37

THE MAN WHO REFUSED TO READ
MAKE ME

Peering at the screen over his shoulder, if I screwed up my eyes, I could just make out the word 'cappuccino'. It was like a bad dream: *What!? You're putting milk in your coffee now. What is wrong with black?* I scanned along the lines. There was no more Reacher. It was all 'Mikael' and 'journalisticht' and 'interessanta'. Maybe I could have made some helpful remarks on the grammar and lexical choices, but it was all written in Swedish. Or *Svenska*.

I tried out a joke on the natives. 'I have total command of *Svenska*,' I would say. 'Really?' they would say in perfectly fine English, maybe with a hint of disbelief. 'Yes,' I replied, 'the word *Svenska*. I'm a bit hazy about all the other words in the Swedish language, though.' I had in fact once studied Swedish, strangely enough (the Swedes certainly thought it was strange), and if not for that Swedish girl who dumped me, I could even now be speaking it quite fluently. David Lagercrantz agreed, however, that I had an excellent pronunciation of 'Malmö'. We were sitting in his office in his apartment on the south island. I was watching him write the sequel to *The Girl in the Spider's Web* (which would become known as *The Girl Who Takes An Eye for an Eye*). Another gang member was betraying Lee Child, going over to the opposition. He lured me in because he told me how much he loved my book, but also partly because he said that he was *not* reading Lee's book: he hadn't read it and he wouldn't be reading it. Why? I wondered. 'His review in *The New York Times* was so ... *ungenerous*.' Whereas the *Guardian* and *Le Monde* and other Americans had been much more Lagercrantz-friendly. Apparently, his publisher in England, when he read it, had phoned him and said, 'How could they let him do this?'

'That's what Lee said!' I said. '"How could they let me do this?"' I tried explaining to David the deep background: that Lee was fundamentally concerned about someone else taking over his own character and alter ego. But David was already thinking dark thoughts and plotting revenge. When I told him the story about Lydia Lair, he thought that maybe Lee could pay himself some money and put himself in his next novel – 'and then Reacher could bump into him and kick his arse'. Reacher vs Child. It was a good twist. But Reacher would clearly be stunt double for Lagercrantz himself.

The meeting, on the previous day, between Lee Child and David Lagercrantz had gone supremely well, on the face of it. Harmoniously, one might say. They were perfectly amicable and polite towards one another over a period of several hours. In fact, when David walked through the door of the common room in the Stockholm Business School, he not only smiled broadly but bowed down, deeply, theatrically, reverentially, and said, 'Ah! the master!' Maybe overdoing it just a touch, I thought. But OK, better than locking antlers or whatever. He had a cameraman and a sound man following him around, tracking his every move, for some documentary. I suppose this was similar to me following Lee about, but they didn't say quite as much. The conference was just fine too, with a wonderfully responsive audience (and they even got me to sign a few books, for which I became 'Åndy Märten'). But there was a definite *frisson* when we were all up on the stage, holding forth about this and that.

It was all my fault, I suppose. I was the guy in the middle, nominally the 'moderator'. I sketched out a hypothetical scenario. Lee Child had just run up ten flights of stairs, à la Larsson (I didn't need to say 'à la Larsson', not in Stockholm). In New York. Lot of stairs in New York. Say, his elevator has broken down. It's almost plausible. So he goes running up the stairs, but – uh-oh – having got to the top of his apartment building in Manhattan, he drops dead. It's all too much for his old ticker, what with the smoking and Sugar Puffs. Everyone is sobbing their eyes out, not so much because Lee Child is dead (well, just a little maybe, a few close friends), but mainly on account of Reacher. *What will happen to Jack Reacher?!* the cry goes up. If Lee is dead, does that mean

Reacher is dead too? There would be a gnashing of teeth. *But,* I suggested, all would not be lost, because (and here I swivelled around in my chair in the other direction) David Lagercrantz would come to the rescue, and do for Reacher what he had already done for Lisbeth Salander. Lagercrantz would resurrect Reacher (even if Lee himself was definitely a goner).

Lee's answer fell into several parts. Part 1, 'I would never run up the stairs. I haven't run anywhere for about forty years. I consider running to be strictly for emergencies.' Part 2, 'Well, I would be dead, so I wouldn't care.' This was always his feel-good fall-back position: cosmic indifference. Part 3 was a bit more problematic. When he tried to answer the question. Unusually for him, he was stumbling and stuttering. A bit. Could someone else take over Reacher? He wanted to say, *No, no way José!* At the same time, he didn't want to be rude to David Lagercrantz. It came back to the question he had raised in his review in *The New York Times*, which he had answered in the negative. Sensing a weakness, David stuck the boot in. 'Well, Lee, what do you think? Could I do it or not?' Obviously, he thought he could.

And it was a theme he picked up when we were all having dinner together, in that little place by the Opera House, with Carl and Elsa and David's very shrewd agent, Magdalena, who had set up the big deal with the Larsson estate in the first place. David thought he could do a Bond book, easy; Lee reckoned no one could do a decent Bond book these days.

LEE: Bond was a consolation for the loss of Empire. Now the landscape has changed. Partly because of Bond.

DAVID: But you could change him. He can adapt.

LEE: He is not Scottish, he is English.

DAVID: He can be whatever you want him to be. It's only literature on top of literature.

Lee had turned down an offer from the Ian Fleming estate. Twice. David, in contrast, was open to offers.

David struck a knife against his glass, commanding silence, and made a charming speech. I remember him saying, 'My publisher told me, "You won't be No. 1 for very long – Lee Child is coming!"' He also said he would be delighted for me to go and watch him writing the next one. But the thing that sticks in my mind is, during coffee, when David's agent turned to Lee and solicited his opinion on how they ought to spend all the money they had earned from taking over the Larsson franchise. They really wanted to know, David agreed. 'What do you do with all your money?' he asked, flat out. They didn't have the experience of rolling in it, which they were fairly sure Lee did have.

'I spend it all on drink, fast cars, and women. And the rest I squander,' Lee said, adopting the classic George Best line. I had to point out (Tonto assisting the Lone Ranger) that his squandering included setting up scholarships for young wannabees and random gestures of benevolence, like buying a house for one of his former teachers who had become destitute, and a wheelchair for an old lady. David thought they might donate some of the money to illiterate kids in Malmö. He wanted to tell them they couldn't all be Zlatan Ibrahimović (David had ghosted *I Am Zlatan*, the autobiography) and the next best way out of the suburbs was being able to read.

LEE: You can be the Zlatan of reading.

ME: Give them some Lee Child books to read. Illiterates and dyslexics love his stuff.

LEE: They think it's like not really reading. Which is how it should be.

David said he also wanted to know more about Camus, which he was relying on me for. But he could quote more Camus than I could, probably. For example, he managed to reconstruct most of that perfect opening sentence of the would-be writer Grand in *The Plague*. 'Hey!' he said, from the other side of the table, 'are you working right now?'

'I'm eating,' I said, 'not working.'

'But am I going to be in your next book?'

'Nah,' I said. 'I'm working on readers not writers this time. Different sort of thing.'

So it was that I ended up, the following day, at David's apartment on the south island. When he started writing *The Girl in the Spider's Web*, he had to go out and buy himself another computer. It was part of the deal with the publishers and the Larsson estate. They didn't trust anyone. The point about the new computer – which he was writing on now – was that it had to be isolated from the outside world. If he wanted to send any emails or look up something on the web, he had to use his old computer. The new one was an island, like one of Stockholm's fourteen, but built deliberately without any bridges, completely cut off and insulated. Even though (or because) he was writing about Lisbeth Salander, the person they feared most in the world was ... Lisbeth Salander. Or someone like her. In other words, hackers intent on ripping off his latest novel. If the computer he was writing on was hooked up, then they could just reach right in and steal it and publish it and make a fortune, without writing a word. It was industrial espionage, applied to literature.

David had to write the opposite way to Lee. He had been required to write a synopsis first, to map it all out in advance, to convince the estate and the publishers. 'I remembered this story from when I was a young reporter: a savant eight-year old kid who produced a detailed drawing of a traffic light. And I wondered what it would be like if he witnesses a crime.' And then he also wondered if the ruthlessly mathematical Lisbeth Salander, who would have to be hacking the NSA, could ever have anything like mothering instincts. Impossible, and yet ...

I guess Elsa had a point: David didn't have the 'calm' of the big guy. He described himself as a 'snobbish neurotic' (and another time as a 'neurotic snob'), and it's true he couldn't seem to settle down to the job for long periods. He was always jumping up and showing me stuff. He tended to agonize over things like whether to call back his agent or his mother first. He said he had been 'driven mad' by hour upon hour of interviews and signings and talk shows, trying to keep a smile on his face since around May, together with taking a high degree of flak. He had been 'plundering the grave', 'stealing ancient artefacts'. Cross-examined on *Babel*, when he described himself as *manic-depressive*. Henning Mankell, for one, had gone public saying, *'Don't let Lagercrantz do it!'* and then that he had 'betrayed literature'. Even his ex-wife called and left a message saying, 'You have gone over the edge.'

'I was being treated like a politician. Or a monster.' He was depicted as the evil bourgeoisie preying on the proletariat (Larsson). And he'd done a midnight opening at a bookstore, signing till 2 a.m. Some bugger had even published a review by

7 a.m. the next morning (not favourable either, in fact 'terrible'). I could see how that sort of thing could drive you a little crazy. Or 'schizo', as he neatly put it. He had been filmed cracking up finally, kicking a door in because a news anchor had 'gone too far'.

He twisted around, looked up at me with sad eyes, and ran a hand through his luxuriant hair. 'It's kind of tragic. You don't enjoy it as much as you thought you would.' David Lagercrantz was a bit of a Hamlet figure in my eyes, with the madness and all, a prince of sorts, even though Swede rather than Dane, and the ghost of his literary critic father was dripping poison in his ear too. The deceased Dad (name of Olof, big deal according to Carl, huge symbolic capital, Amis and Franzen all rolled into one, fan of Dante, Strindberg, and Joyce) kept telling him *literature* had to be 'serious' and anything 'commercial' was just trash. And yet here he was, the son, writing about illiterate footballers and tattooed female hackers. And cracking deals with Hollywood on top (news of which was just breaking while I was there). Wasn't he tarnishing the old escutcheon? Wasn't he a traitor to the family crest? (I have no idea if he really has a family crest, but he has one tattooed inside his head.) He wanted to write the perfect book, like a poem, and David kept saying to himself that a book could be serious *and* commercial ('there is no contradiction'), but he didn't believe it in his heart of hearts, so he felt guilty, even though enormously successful, and half-agreed with the people who denounced him, and was trying to give away all the money he earned. No wonder that he was a bit sicklied o'er with the pale cast of thought. 'I once wrote a fine literary novel,' he said. 'It's still on my computer somewhere.'

While we were sitting there he had one passing guy punching his doorbell and asking if he could come up and discuss literature, if he had a spare five minutes. David told him, over the intercom, to send him an email. I said I thought that Stockholm was like an immense academy, made up of professors and students, and the students could come and make an appointment at any time to discuss some knotty aspect of their essays. Or maybe more like the Business School: they want to work out how to be more successful in their writing.

'Yeah,' David said, still a bit jittery. 'But there is also the possibility that he wanted to break in and steal the next novel. That's the only way they could do it. Physically remove the computer. Old school.' At night he locked it in a safe. Just in case.

38

MAMMA MIA! (× 5)

I started it by boasting about my command of Swedish. To Lina. Lee said his fondness for Sweden had a lot to do with Abba. Not so much Björn Borg, or Strindberg or Larsson or Lagercrantz. Or Bergman (Ingrid or Ingmar). We were all sitting in the back of the car going from the Grand Hotel to the talk at the Stockholm Business School.

Lee Child: an Abba fan?! I was shocked. Imagine Jack Reacher listening to 'Dancing Queen'. No, the idea is absurd. He listens to blind blues singers, not Swedish bubblegum bands. But there was more. Lee reckoned he had been to see *Mamma Mia!* no fewer than five times. 'It's a great show,' he said. 'You don't know what you're missing.' His top Abba tune was 'Super Trouper': it was some kind of role model, he claimed, his whole game plan, right there.

'I went to Cambridge to get away from Abba,' I said. I had a weakness for Beethoven's late quartets at the time. 'And here I am back in Abba land. Where did I go wrong?'

As Carl had discovered, Lee was rather popular in Sweden. He had spent the day before being interviewed and photographed, from dawn till dusk. But it hadn't always been this way. When Lee presented *Killing Floor* for translation into Swedish, he was slapped with a morally superior response from the Swedes. 'Have you any idea how many people die in this book?' they asked. Lee said, 'No, I have no idea.' He thought it was quite a lot. They said, 'There – you don't even care!'

'I guess they had a point,' Lee conceded. 'Reacher, as someone once said, is the only detective who commits more murders than he solves.'

Lee was in full on wolf mode, in publishing terms. He and his agent had recently closeted themselves away for a few days and hammered out their Napoleonic campaign for the next book, or rather books. They were going for another three-book contract. And the numbers had to be even more telephonic this time. *Or else.* 'We're upping the stakes.'

'What about Karen's idea,' I said, 'that (a) you don't need the money, so (b) why don't you relax where the advance is concerned and take the pressure off yourself?'

'(A),' says he, mockingly, 'ridiculous! We have to *shake the tree.* And (b) it's not an *advance* anyway. We're going for *licensing* this time. This is the future. Advances are history.' It was all down to the way books were being sold, and the percentages; the way they were being *bought* in the first place was going to have to keep up.

I had the impression that if he had been driving, in place of the extremely well-behaved and placid Swedish chauffeur, he would have been putting his foot down and screaming through red lights and forcing innocents and police pursuit cars alike off the edge of the road and down into the abyss, where they would burst into flames. And he would have no idea about how many bodies would be left behind.

Not being a great Abba aficionado, I had to look it up on YouTube. 'Super Trouper', that is. I'm still not that much of a fan. Nice white suits and all. Incredible English. You could understand what they were saying. But I couldn't help noticing the 'Feeling like a number one' line. And the blonde woman actually thrusts one finger up at the sky. In some obscure way, Abba gave birth to Reacher.

39

JACK REACHER VS LISBETH SALANDER

In the final showdown, who would win? That was my question. Inevitably. In that conversation at the Stockholm Business School. Lee snorted at the idea that it could be anything but a walkover for Reacher. David thought Salander and Reacher would go off and have a coffee together, realizing that, in essence, they were on the same side. But there was another question a guy in the audience asked: 'What is your favourite English word of the moment?'

Forest
Child's word. Not a big deal, he said, unless you are very into trees. Which he was, while writing 'Not a Drill' (the short story that came after *Personal*), most of which takes place in a forest. But the interesting thing about it was that, etymologically, a 'forest' didn't have to contain trees. In its origin it meant simply a place that was good for hunting – it could be anywhere, a grassy savanna, for example. But it gradually came to be associated with trees, where most of the predators and predated tended to hang out. He also had recently been taken with the word 'saturnine'. And among Swedish words he liked *skum* (even though he mispronounced it); meaning: foam (he had seen it on fire extinguishers).

Pekoral
Not English. But maybe it should be, thought Lagercrantz. You're a kid living under the stairs – but you're secretly a wizard and the fate of the world depends on you; or like in Disney movies, the young girl gets the prince. It's awful, but you have to be close to that. Lisbeth Salander was *pekoral*, in part, and Jack Reacher, when he walks into a bar and beats up six guys, had, if he may

say, a touch of the *pekoral* about him too. Lagercrantz looked it up on 'Google Translate' and it came out as 'drivel', which was wrong. He thought maybe it was somewhere between 'gimmicky' and 'kitsch'. But, this was the thing, all good books had to be a little bit *pekoral*. All fine literature since Hamlet is about losers, but you have to be able to love the hero.

Aleatory
Still my favourite word. Guided (or misguided) by chance. Throwing the dice and seeing which way up they land (*alea* = die).

40

CARL (2)

There were a couple of things going on with Carl that Lee was impressed by. The first was that there was a heavy dude who was threatening to beat him up. On TV. He was a big gym animal and he didn't like Carl's book.

'Are you saying going to the gym makes you stupid?' says the guy.

'No.' (Carl.)

'Are you saying we should exercise less?'

'Not exactly.'

'That's good, because I would have crushed you.'

A woman was also threatening to beat him up because she felt her right to bake was being infringed. For some reason Carl had made some anti-baking remarks.

Lee approved of all this: he thought that too much exercise and cooking would damage the brain. (It's the recurrent theme of *Persuader* [Reacher 7], the exercise part anyway.) The second thing that Lee was taken with was that Carl taught at the Stockholm Business School. 'So he teaches business?' he said with a new note of respect.

The answer was yes, but then again, no. It was more like the opposite of business. Carl told me about one of his courses. There seemed to be three key elements:

1   reject professionalism;
2   embrace the amateur;
3   unlearn how to write.

Recommended reading consisted of back numbers of the *New Yorker* magazine. Also his main business theorist was Jacques Lacan, the cryptic French psychoanalyst.

This all came up while we were following the Larsson trail. On our left we have the café where Blomkvist would come and drink coffee. On our right we have the Blomkvist pub. And over here we have the building where Larsson ran up the stairs and then dropped dead. And so on. There was a lot of Lacan on the way. Most people are confused by Lacan. Carl is the only person I've ever come across who says, 'Whenever I'm confused I go back to Lacan: I find that soon clarifies my thinking.'

Carl would give his students a questionnaire after his first lecture, asking, for example, 'WHY ARE YOU HERE?' Possible answers included:

1   I find these classes interesting.
2   I have no idea what to do with my life.
3   I thought this would give me a well-paid job.
4   My parents forced me to come here.

He thought the students who ticked number 2 tended to be the best students. They were more 'open'. He rejected the 'incremental' approach, and quoted Yeats: 'Education is not the filling of a pail, but the lighting of a fire.'

In case education didn't work out for them, they could always commit suicide. That was another of his courses. He liked to give lectures on the variety of ways business people had offed themselves over the ages. He called it 'human resource management'. Apparently jumping out of high windows is still popular. One guy had taken the phrase 'falling on your sword' rather literally, in the middle of a meeting, moreover. Another rare case involved the 'lighting of a fire' (not the Yeatsian kind), and a car, while sitting in it. Carl's most popular course was 'NEGATIVE THINKING'. It was a business school, but not as it would be understood in the US. Carl mentioned there was another course he had been required to teach which had some complicated and ugly acronym, 'PCUTL'. 'I still don't know what it means,' he said.

Carl was a lot fitter than Larsson, but he had some things in common with the character of Blomkvist. He was a very forgiving sort of guy, for example.

'You know how you basically hate everyone?' he said.

'Yes.'

'In airports, specifically.'

'Especially airports.'

'Well, I try not to.'

It was when we left the Blomkvist café, the one with the KAFFE sign outside on Sankt Paulsgatan, that he took the call that would change his life. 'I've just got three years' funding,' he said. From the Swedish Academy. 'What's the surfing like in Hawaii?' But this was more under the heading of expensive hobbies he might take up. His actual project involved performance-enhancing drug-taking in New York. He was planning to write a whole book in one month (high on a cocktail of drugs) and then come over and dangle Ritalin or Modafinil in front of Lee's nose at the point in his writing arc when he was starting to get a bit panicky.

'He'll go for that,' I said. Obviously I have no idea, but a guy who smokes a pipeful of marijuana as part of the 'creative process' is surely not going to draw the line at a little Ritalin. Anyway, it was all part of a vast scientific and anthropological experiment.

'In March?' said Carl.

'March is the best time,' I said. 'He'll be trying to hit the dead-line. Running out of time and possibly ideas. He'll be begging for more.'

Carl came to see me off on the train for the airport. He had been thinking about everything and was starting to see the world through Child-tinted glasses. 'You know what I need?' he said.

'Ritalin?'

'An agent like Lina. This is the kind of person you need. I'm sick of well-meaning idiots. I would love to have Lina. At least she is selling his books.'

Carl was officially back in the gang.

As a parting gift, standing around at the train station, he offered me a Lacanian reading of Lee Child. He thought Child was more 'addictive' than Lagercrantz and he was trying to work out why. I guess he was 'clarifying' his thought, by reference to Lacan. 'This is how it works,' he said. 'There is a split in the other. Thus the reader is fundamentally broken, fractured, fissured, suffering from a lack that the book, i.e. Reacher, is supposed to fill.

164

This is why they read; to try to heal the fracture. Of course. But the really interesting thing about these books is that the writer is just as fissured and fractured and screwed up as they are. Which is why they love him. They lack, he lacks ... *Lack* Reacher.'

41

MISERY

I just want to make one thing clear. Never, at any point, did I threaten Lee Child with sledgehammer, axe, or shotgun. Nor did I handcuff him. Or drug him into a stupor. Or run anyone over with a lawnmower. It was all totally consensual and voluntary. My year of being a literary voyeur, I mean. I didn't *make* him write *Make Me*. He would have done a decent enough job of it even without me looking over his shoulder in his office across the street from Central Park, keeping a close eye on his grammar and punctuation and font size. And what he put on his toast. After all, he'd already written nineteen previous Reachers, so he probably didn't need a whole lot of back-up to write the twentieth.

On the other hand, this scene definitely looked familiar. A desk, a typewriter, a writer – and behind him the devoted reader, observing intently. 'So what happens next?' asks Annie Wilkes, annoyingly. 'No! Don't tell me.' I guess I must have said that a few times.

We had gone to the Broadhurst Theater on Broadway, Lee and I, to see a production of Stephen King's *Misery*, directed by Will Frears, with Bruce Willis in the part of the immobilized writer, held prisoner in the wintry wilds of Colorado, and Laurie Metcalfe as his nurse and tormentor and deranged, obsessional reader.

Unlike Annie Wilkes, I never went about crooning, 'I'm your number one fan!' (Contrary to a *Prospect* magazine article that came out in England around this time, which has me saying just that.) I guess I could be more like number two or three. In fact, now I come to think of it, there are plenty of people who know the collected works better than I do and are more fanatical – and more than a few who are acting them out, as we speak.

And, unlike Paul Sheldon, Lee never moaned, 'How do you expect me to work with you in the room watching me all the time!?'

Still, there was a kind of madness to the whole business of trying to catch the creative process on the wing. It is true that when I saw Annie Wilkes rolling around on the bed in a state of ecstasy as she leafs through Paul Sheldon's latest chapter while the snow falls outside, I was bound to think: Annie Wilkes, *c'est moi!* 'You know that bit where Paul Sheldon picks up the typewriter and clobbers her over the head with it,' I said to Lee, nervously, at the end. 'Did you ever feel like that?'

'It was like watching you and me all the way through,' he said.

He deserved a medal for putting up with having a spy in his office nearly every day. Maybe that's why he awarded one to Reacher at the beginning of *Night School*. To be fair, though, I reckon I had to put up with a more-than-doctors-would-advise share of involuntary inhalation. Writing is a dangerous business. But so is reading. Books are all about an intimate, intense relationship that can blow up in your face at any time. Which is what Stephen King was going on about, I think.

Apart from the appeal of gazing at a horror movie mirror-image of the two of us, writer and reader inhabiting the same space while a whole novel is being written, there was another compelling reason for going to the theatre. Bruce Willis, in his early *Die Hard* persona, was one of the precursors of Reacher. But Reacher is a more muscular avatar of Lee Child himself. Very approximately, Child = Reacher = Willis. So it was tough on Lee to see hard man hero John McClane strapped to a bed with smashed-up legs, turned into yet another writer held hostage by an unhinged reader.

King imagines his alter ego Paul Sheldon turning out a series with the recurring protagonist Misery Chastain. But her creator is desperate to get away from Misery and write some different books for a change, so he kills her off, fictionally speaking. Annie Wilkes, the reader, is so attached to Misery that she forces him to bring her back to life, and stands over him, equipped with assorted carrots and sticks, till the job is done. Something similar was true of Conan Doyle – he shoves Sherlock Holmes over the Reichenbach Falls, but his readers insist on summoning the detective back from the dead.

Talking of Conan Doyle, I like to think I'm more like Dr Watson to Lee's Holmes than Wilkes to his Sheldon. 'Of course!' I am apt to say, rather annoyingly, Watson-style, when he explains the reasoning behind his latest brilliant move. 'It's obvious.' That sort of thing.

As we came out of the theatre into the driving rain of a November night on 44th Street, Lee said, 'Stephen King really has this writer-paranoia thing to the max, doesn't he?' It comes up again in *Finders Keepers* where King has a devoted reader blowing out the brains of the elusive and mystically talented John Rothstein in order to run off with his notebooks.

I have a feeling that if I had suggested this whole risky, virtually impossible, semi-insane project to Stephen King towards the end of August last year ('Hey Stephen, how would it be if I come and watch while you write your next novel?'), he would have run a mile. His worst nightmare. 'Yeah, sure, you effin' freak! – what's it going to be, axe or shotgun or what?'

Rather like Reacher, Lee never loses any sleep over bad guys. Even when this sinister dude in a baseball cap came running up to him just down the street from the building where John Lennon was shot dead by a nutter fan, he took it all calmly in his stride. He likes readers. He doesn't plot, he doesn't plan, he just lets it all happen, in some sublimely confident, laissez-faire, stoical, fatalistic way. Like a reader, in fact, more than a writer. Roland Barthes argued that the reader should be more like a writer (or 'scriptor'); Lee thinks that the writer needs to be more like a reader, with no clear idea what is going to happen next, nothing but hazy hypotheses. So his answer was more, OK, whatever, sounds good. 'I'm starting Monday,' he said, 'so if you want to do this you'd better get over here.' I didn't have to drag him out of a car wreck and lock him up in a room till he'd finished.

Pascal said that all human misfortune springs from one thing: our inability to remain at rest in a room. The philosopher, obviously, was capable of sitting for long periods, and writing down his *Pensées*. I sort of wonder if he would have been so good at it if there had been someone else in the room with him, watching what he was doing.

42

BOOK ENDS

PART 1

You could say he resembled Lee, up to a point. He was tall and thin. And he had hair. I wasn't crazy about him otherwise, though. I mean, I started out neutral enough. I was just asking him about a book, after all. Not my book. I just need to get that clear. I was asking about *Beatlebone*, by Kevin Barry. Because I couldn't find it and I couldn't remember the name of the author (sorry, Kevin, I've got it now). The thing I remembered was a joke in it (as per in a review): Dodgy Irish hotelier: 'Do you have a reservation?' Lennon: 'I have many. But right now I need a room.'

I was in Book Ends, the Upper West Side indie bookstore, scene of Carl's New York launch of *The Wellness Syndrome*. I had bought books there in the past and I was on their email list. I wasn't a total nobody. The tall, thin guy went to check his computer. He couldn't find the book. 'That would be *B-e-a-tlebone*,' I said.

'B-e-e-t, surely,' he said.

'Well, it's sort of about John Lennon. In Ireland. So I'm guessing it's like the Beatles.' He looked nonplussed, like some old judge peering over the top of his spectacles. That sort of look. 'I guess they were a bit before your time,' I said, forgivingly. He wasn't that young. Nobody was that young.

'Ah, here we are ... B-e-A-t.' He said it as if I hadn't already said just that. 'It's over here.' He led me over to the fiction shelf and pulled out a copy and I took it in my hand.

I thought I'd better get it out there. No point beating about the bush. I try never to be discreet unless I really have to be. 'Look,' says I, 'I've got to ask because I can't quite see it at the moment, and I scoured the non-fiction table, but do you have my book in stock? It's about Lee Child. *Reacher Said Nothing*. I have to ask because he's coming into your bookstore tomorrow and I'm supposed to be coming with him and I just thought, you know, it's going to be a bit embarrassing if you don't have this book, which is by me and about him.'

The dude went back to his computer. He clicked for a while. 'Ah. *Reacher* Said *Nothing*. I thought you said *Says*.'

'Ha ha.' Yes, that was nervous laughter.

'No, we don't have it.'

'Ah.'

'We could order it.'

'Well, here's the thing, I know he's coming in tomorrow, isn't he, to be a "bookseller for a day" and all that.' There was some kind of charitable thing going on.

'Mmm,' says he. Consulting computer still. 'You see Mr Child lives near here.'

'Yes, I know that. He is a "local author".'

'And he sells millions of books.'

'Around 100 million I believe, by the last count.'

'But you know he doesn't sell that many with us.'

'Well, I notice that his book is buried at the back of the "Mystery" shelf.' I was thinking it would help if it was a bit more visible, but I didn't like to state the obvious. 'And why don't you have my book? Because maybe I need to have a word with Random House if they haven't got the book out properly or something.' At that point I genuinely thought it was a glitch. Naïve

'The buyer must have assumed that your book, being about Lee Child, wouldn't sell here either.'

Cue outrage. 'Oh really!' says I, snapping. Looking desperately around for some kind of comeback. So naturally I slapped *Beatlebone* down right in front of his computer (again, sorry, Kevin, nothing personal). And I meant that gesture to sting. It was like, *I'm never buying a book in this bookstore again!* I was flinging down the gauntlet.

Faint note of apology. 'Of course, that doesn't mean that we won't *ever* get your book in.'

Too little, too late, mate. Exit irate author. Anyway, that *ever* got on my wick, like he was dangling some distant carrot in front of my nose. I calmed down by the time I got all the way down-town (and the subway was in a mess, so I'd had to go uptown to go downtown, and the whole thing took ages). So it was that I sent off a measured sort of email to Lee.

```
from: andymartinink
to: LeeChild
subject: BOOK ENDS MUST DIE
```

It wasn't so much the not having my book that got to me (well, it was partly that, obviously). It was more – and I haven't really brought this out yet – the tone of total snootiness. The Book Ends guy was tall and thin – 'reedy' would be about right – but he didn't have to be snooty too. And this was the thing, snooty to me *and* Lee. The local author who was putting himself out to come and support the bookstore for 'The Small Business Weekend'. Actually sell some books, not just his own. He was doing his good deed. And they were slapping him down, like he was James Patterson or something. And me too of course. *Bastards!*

I would never enter that bookstore again in my life, I vowed. *I'm going over to Amazon and Kindle*, I said to myself. To hell with indie-book-stores-that-are-so-fucking-snooty-they-can't-even-sell-Lee-Child-for-chrissake. Let them die. It's the Upper West Side, not the far side of the moon.

I got the usual lapidary response.

'See you there at three. Coffee afterwards.'

PART 2

I was standing outside Book Ends, reading a book. *Men*, by Laura Kipnis. The bit where Andrea Dworkin is saying how all sex is rape.

'She doesn't like your masculinity,' I felt obliged to point out to Lee, when he appeared out of the mists. Laura Kipnis had men-tioned it to me a day or two before.

'What's wrong with it?'

'It's too *transparent*.'

'Would she rather it was *opaque*? Or *disguised*? What kind of masculinity would be acceptable, other than none at all?'

'I can't go in,' I said. 'I've taken the vow.'

So we go in. 'Get used to it,' Lee was saying. 'I get it all the time. Now you're going to get it too.'

'Great,' I said.

'This place is a war zone. No actual bodies. People walk out. But it's vicious. You're opening yourself up to snootiness and disdain.'

The tall, thin dude was floating around somewhere, but he kept his distance. Still looking down on the whole wide world. A nice young guy called Cody came up to us. He was from the downtown store. He had squarish glasses and a beard and long hair.

'Mr Child!' says he. 'So good to have you with us today.' He was beaming.

'I want to introduce you to my good friend Andy Martin,' says Lee. Nice. 'He's written this book mainly about me called *Reacher Said Nothing*.'

'Ah, Professor Martin,' says he. 'Of course, I recognize you from the *New York Times* article.' He was talking about the cartoon.

'Yeah,' says I, gritting my teeth. 'I know you don't have the book or anything. I was a bit put out by that but I'll get over it.'

'We don't have it!?' said Cody. 'I'm sorry, that's a terrible mistake, I'm going to rectify that right now.'

'I may have written something hasty to the effect that BOOK ENDS MUST DIE. Or KILL BOOK ENDS perhaps. Either way, delete all that.'

Cody rushed off somewhere. Lee introduced me to some of his other writer friends. 'You're that guy!' said a man named Chris. 'I'm going to buy that book right now,' said his wife.

'You can't,' I said. 'They haven't got it.'

She wouldn't be put off. 'I'm going to pre-order it.'

'I think you'll like it,' said Lee. 'It's full of stuff.'

'Like what, for example?' This was Chris again, not his wife, she had gone off to pre-order.

ME: Well, if you want to know what size font he uses, this is the book for you.

CHRIS: I like to use Times Roman, 12 point.

ME: He uses Arial.

'10 point,' said Lee.

'Yeah,' I pointed out, showing off my knowledge in these arcane matters, 'but he cranks up the magnification.'

'Double space, though?' said Chris.

'Single!' said Lee. 'I like to be able to see the whole page.'

Chris's wife came back. 'It's ordered,' she said. I was kind of moved by all this. Someone ordering my book while I'm standing right there.

'He's working on the sequel right now,' said Lee. 'You'd better watch out. It's all about readers.'

'Turns out he has quite a few of them,' I said.

I also met Gordon Burns while I was there. He was quite short, though, and I had to bend down to say hello. He had a rather edgy bandana and his flowing hair was brown and white. He was a dog. I was giving him a pat while his owner, a woman wearing a turban of some kind, explained to me about how I really needed to use dog toothpaste. Beef or chicken flavour. I mean, on my dog. It was so much better for their oral hygiene. Gordon Burns had lovely teeth, I had to admit. I was a bit of a convert. I'd probably been using the wrong toothpaste before. Even a dog needed the old folding toothbrush from time to time.

Cody came back to us. 'There,' he said. 'Your book will be in on Tuesday. I do hope you'll come back and sign a few copies.'

'I don't want to seem like I'm hyping it up, but I honestly think it ought to be here. It works as a kind of complement to *Make Me*. Being about the making of *Make Me* and all.' I felt a bit pushy. 'I'm sorry, the only selling I'm doing here is trying to sell my own book, which isn't even here.'

'Don't worry about it,' said Lee, popping up. He'd done his bit of bookselling for the day. 'Grisham sold his first novel like that. Yard sale. Worked for him.'

There was no way around it. Kevin Barry, you'll be glad to hear this. I had to go and buy *Beatlebone* finally. I knew exactly where it was on the shelf too. I mean, *noblesse oblige*. It may even have been the same copy I had slapped down on the counter twenty-four hours earlier. To tell the truth I'd been wanting to use that 20% off discount card for a while, before it expired or something.

Cody took a picture of us ('Booksellers for a Day!' was his caption) and Lee and I sloped off to the Starbucks a couple of doors away. It was small and packed but we finally got seats. He told me he was a few thousand words ahead of where he was last year, but at the moment he was stuck. He was always stuck. Then he mentioned what had been really worrying him. 'We are definitely going down,' Lee said.

'Hey, it isn't even Christmas yet,' I said, trying to be upbeat.

'They're doomed,' he said, gloomily. He was talking about Aston Villa of course. Bottom of the table. Rock bottom. Only seven points on the board. 'Derby went down with only eleven. We're aiming to beat that.' He meant beat them in the wrong direction. Excessively minimalist approach to points accumulation. 'There just aren't enough games left. It's already too late. We'd have to get a point and a half out of every game till the end of the season. We haven't come anywhere near that for years.'

He also thought I stood a chance of making a decent career out of football management. It wasn't too late for me. I ought to give it a go if I had nothing else on. 'José Mourinho started out as a translator. Worked his way up. Produced a fanatical scouting dossier, ridiculously detailed, like a book. You've got a bit of the Mourinho about you.'

We walked up Columbus in the rain. Lee was having a laugh at the headline in the *New Statesman* describing him as the 'Camus of Crime'. It was a review of my book. 'There's two things I like about your book,' he said. 'You get the *inaction*. It's not a boys' adventure story. Reacher isn't always getting into fights. And then the onomatopoeia. It has to *sound* right. No one ever really noticed that before.'

'I think the reviewer thought I was being a bit superficial.'

'I've never been overly keen on profundity,' said Lee. 'Everything is surfaces, glittering surfaces. I'm going to have to start introducing you as my superficial friend.'

'Nietzsche reckoned it was all the fault of Christianity, or Judaism, you know, searching for the invisible soul.'

'"I'm going out to get kitchen towel and toothpaste."' He was quoting a line from *Reacher Said Nothing*. 'That's exactly what it's like. Everyone thinks you're going to be cracking open a bottle of champagne, like the guy in *Misery*. But it doesn't work like that.'

He ducked into a deli and I kept on going up the hill in the rain, heading for the subway. I had to go and walk Vince, Joel's dog. I was thinking he could do with some of that beef toothpaste.

43

SAM

I have to bring in Sam. I can't leave him out. Unless, that is, I come across some other guy capable of representing that proud constituency of Reacher readers who regularly douse themselves in elk urine. A small but hardy crew. Maybe, like Sam, they all prefer to read their Reachers up a tree. (Always providing it's not snowing: Sam notes that he has not yet worked out a way of protecting the book and reading it simultaneously in adverse weather conditions.)

Sam has lived several lives already. The way he is going he is liable to run out of lives one of these days. He started out as a skinny, ascetic poet, with a life-size photo of Jacqueline Bisset blu-tacked to the wall of his study-bedroom. He was a Yank-at-Oxford, an English undergraduate at Christ Church College. His father was an English professor, the author of books that I had read and admired, and his mother was also a writer. He lived the ultimate scholar's dream when he had sexual congress with one of his own tutors (a woman, to be specific) in the hushed precincts of the Bodleian Library; but he was duly discovered by a passing librarian, denounced, and removed. When he dropped out and landed in New York, he was a novice grad student and would-be writer. He had done enough studying of Chaucer, Milton, and Wordsworth, and wanted to give it a shot himself. As it happened, he produced a timeless work in circumstances that neither Chaucer, nor Milton, nor Wordsworth could have dreamed of. Not unless they were on steroids, that is.

It has to be understood that this was the eighties in New York. It was the era of *Death Wish*. The struggle for survival was at its most nakedly Darwinian. The subway was like Dante's Inferno. Just walking along the street was asking for trouble. Muggers, murderers, rapists, rampaged freely around the land. Joggers in Central Park were just moving targets, easy meat. But enough nostalgia. Sam had an important insight at this point. He needed to big himself up. It was something I had been taught by friends concerned for my well-being as I took my life in my hands and opened the front door on the Lower East Side: you had to look mean enough and ugly enough that all the bad dudes out there would pick on some other poor devil. It was a good basic principle and it saw me through, almost unscathed. Sam went a step further: several highly enhanced steps further.

He was tall, yes, but he was thin, like Lee. In England they called him 'Beanpole' or 'Lofty'. In New York he looked like a stick insect among buffaloes. Having borne witness to the customary random street violence, among the denizens of Hell's Kitchen, his first thought was to wear armour as he ventured out. His second thought was to armour-plate himself from the ground up, to re-engineer his body to make himself overwhelmingly powerful and, effectively, invulnerable to attack. He wanted, in short, in the terms that concern us now, to *be* Jack Reacher, even though Jack Reacher did not yet exist. He was a proto-Reacher type. He had the height. But in order to be Reacher he would have to bulk up and put on at least another 50 or 60 lbs of solid muscle.

He hit the gym and he attained his immediate goal readily enough. No one in his right mind was going to mess with this guy. But Sam had unleashed a monster. Big was not enough, it had to be huge. Huge was not enough, it had to be colossal. His quest for bodily metamorphosis soon assumed the form of an obsession. It was art for art's sake, at the level of glutes and abs. Hours every day in the gym, a ridiculous consumption of steaks and raw eggs, and still he hungered for more muscle. He had (to his now absurdly distorted way of thinking) 'plateau'd out'. Thus he took off to the mecca of pharmaceutical supplements, otherwise known as the West Coast. Here he gorged on steroids and took to performing adequately in body-building contests, before the bubble finally burst and he wrote his unforgettable account of his own experiences, his romance with himself and his own body, but with a satirical swerve. A love affair, but with the full arc from ecstasy to post-coital angst.

One scene that for some reason springs to mind: he and a comely female body-builder go back to his apartment and attempt some kind of union. But each of them is so muscularly inflated that the other simply bounces off. There are castle walls and turrets and crenellations, but no drawbridge. It was probably just as well. The steroids were known to have the unfortunate side-effect of impotence.

His book attracted innumerable admirers (I was one), but Sam also found that he was threatened and hunted by gangs of steroidally over-grown maniacs (another of the numerous side-effects – stupidity) all determined to deny, destroy, and annihilate any hint or whisper that any of them were on drugs. Sam's book was brilliant because it was seduced by myth, it was pervaded by corporeal fantasy, but analysed all the hype and the poetry, coolly, almost scientifically, like a Christ Church English graduate carefully weighing the versification of a sonnet. The Hard Men wanted the legend, not the truth. They didn't want anyone deconstructing their 'protein' shakes. So Sam went on the run. Actually, he was not running, he was riding. He bought himself a big old BMW motorbike and toured the nation, easy-rider style, from east to west, north to south. He went up to Alaska and way down to Louisiana, picking up odd jobs here and there, and keeping out of harm's way, by and large.

Then he went truly primitive, building himself a log cabin somewhere in the backwoods of Montana, a troubadour among survivalists, fully resolved to live off the land, hunting lunch with a bow and arrow. (He also had an array of guns – pistols, shotguns, rifles – that he would teach me to shoot.) And, for a living, he dived down into deep frozen lakes to fish up dead bodies for the local police department. Which introduced him to Reacher. And he found in Reacher a mirror-image of himself, in many ways. All his experiences gave him a privileged and exceptional perspective on the text of *Make Me*, about which he made several profound observations. But first of all I need to mention his original encounter with the works of Lee Child.

It came, a few years back, through one of his comrades in the Flathead County Sheriff Dive Team. Sam had passed on to him a Redmond O'Hanlon book (with its singularly British locutions), and he in return gave Sam the gift of a Reacher: *61 Hours* – which remains his favourite, even now, perhaps because of all the snow, although he cites the requiem-like intonation of how many hours are left at the end of every chapter. He went on to read nineteen of the twenty, still missing out on *Running Blind* (aka *The Visitor*, Reacher 4). His source for all things Reacher was the Salvation Army 'buck-a-book' stacks, where people dump their discards. It was a treasure trove of old, beaten-up, coffee-stained paperbacks of just the kind that Reacher himself would approve of.

He had reservations about *Make Me*. Maybe it was the lack of a ticking clock. He was similarly sceptical regarding a chapter in *Reacher Said Nothing*. The mysterious Quiller in a pub near the British Museum once mooted that he had only encountered four distinctive voices in all his years studying English and American literature: they were Ernest Hemingway, Raymond Chandler, J. G. Ballard, and, finally, Lee Child. The odd thing was that Quiller was another Christ Church graduate, but they diverged considerably on this matter. Sam thought that four was a ridiculous underestimate. In fact he was furious about it. He cited a whole list of other options: e.g. Henry James, Herman Melville, Dashiell Hammett; and what about William fuckin' Faulkner for chrissake!? How is that not an original voice???!!! Maybe he had a point; I wasn't sure. But Sam was sure and he wanted to track down the other Christ Church guy and shove those names straight back down his damn throat. He wanted to overwhelm and crush this puny fool and his pathetic crew of four.

And one final reservation: that idea of relying on the local hardware store to pick up some fresh clothes along the way? Laughable! In the kind of true wilderness that was Sam's natural habitat, the chance of running across a handy hardware store every few miles was practically zero. Only in Sam's ultra-rugged *Weltanschauung* could Reacher appear as an effete sophisticate, a stylish urbanite. A 'lightweight' (as he put it). He hungered after a showdown, confident that he could kick this prissy little pseudo-hard man's arse.

He did explain to me about the elk urine, finally. He said that the key to all hunting was the tampon (fragrance-free). You soaked a few of them in said liquid and hung them on the branches of trees, like Christmas decorations. There was a method in his madness. But the reality was that he ended up soaked, tampons or not. In fact he was known to sprinkle it on the heels of his boots as he walked into the forest. Anyone who is going to jab a syringe into a dead coyote's bladder or redistribute wolf excrement is never going to smell like a host of golden daffodils (as he once had so, so long ago). He recalled one incident in which he had gone into the local store for supplies and a PETA woman came up to him and started haranguing him, but then paused to sniff, and said, 'Is that elk urine?' And he said, 'Does it turn you on?' She fled, of course. That was the idea. But I floated the theory that just as so many drunks get drunk in order to cover up the fact that they would be idiots anyway, even without the drinking, so too it was possible that Sam was dousing himself in elk urine to give himself a solid alibi for his inadequacy where women were concerned.

That got his goat all right. He snapped back a reply (over email, but still it was pretty snappy – I wouldn't have even started this particular conversation face-to-face). Any notion of seduction was now 'incompatible with his values'. In other words, he wanted to be a wild man of the woods, he wanted to be all alone in his log cabin. Just him and the bears and the elks. And a dozen or so assorted handguns, rifles, and shotguns. No more sex, just killing; *la mort* not *la petite mort*. He loved the hunting because it 'intensified' his life. He could see better, hear better, think more clearly, he was living right on the edge; it wasn't all 'shoot, shoot, shoot'. And it kept him leaping out of bed at 4 a.m. Sam said, 'You must have your own rules, in advance, just in case. Reacherlike, in a way.' To my way of thinking he was well beyond Reacher. Even Reacher has occasional flings before hitching a ride out of town. Intimate photographs showed Sam getting cosy with dead deer and bears.

He had once wondered if Lee would like to go hunting black bear with him. With a bow and arrow. Preferably in the middle of winter, in a blizzard. But Lee turned him down on account of having nothing against bears as such. There was one other email message he sent me that seemed to undercut some of those resolutely loner values. Spending most of his days up a tree or down in a 'blind', huddling against the bitter cold, he had plenty of time, even while trying to focus on the next deer to wander by, to reminisce, to think about things that had happened, and other things that had not happened. And he thought especially of the women in his past, women he, in his monastic way, had now foresworn. Women he had loved and some of whom had loved him. But there was one woman in particular he often thought of. She had once told him, even while walking out on him, 'In twenty or thirty years, I'm going to come knocking at your door and, because you love me and you will always love me, you will let me and my bags in.'

'But what if I'm married?' he had asked, reasonably enough.

She was not to be deterred. 'It won't matter. If you're married, you'll put me in your guest room and I'll seduce your wife and that way I'll get to you and sleep with you again.'

She had said all this back in 1985. And Sam wrote, 'I'm still waiting by my door.'

Maybe she will come. I just hope she's not too fussy about elk urine.

44

CLUELESS

'Some fucker's only gone and written this article saying you're "Clueless".'

'You?'

'Well, it was that or *Aleatory*.'

'"Clueless" is cool. I like that. The allusion to the 'tec narrative. Let's have a look at it then.'

He had a look (on his phone). We were sitting in some Starbucks somewhere, on stools, at the window. He was stuffing his face with lemon cake. It's weird getting instant feedback from someone you're writing about. It's probably a mistake too. But it wasn't as if there was some rulebook I could consult. It just happened that way.

Nobody really believes him when he says this. And in the end I guess that it is unprovable. But I can put my hand on heart and say, having been there, and watched him at work, that Lee Child is fundamentally clueless when he starts writing. He really is. He has no idea what he is doing or where he is going. And the odd thing is he likes it that way. The question is: Why? I mean, most of us like to have some kind of idea where we are heading, roughly, a hypothesis at least to guide us, even if we are not sticking maps on the wall and suchlike. Whereas he, in contrast, embraces the feeling of just falling off a cliff into the void and relying on some kind of miraculous soft landing.

Of course he is not totally tabula rasa. *Because he, and I, had a fair idea that the name Jack Reacher was going to come up somewhere …*

He looked up. '*Tabula rasa*. It's one of your phrases, isn't it?'

'Yeah.'

'Becoming a habit.'

'Like your "Which" at the beginning of a sentence.'

'Yeah, but … try putting "tabula rasa" at the beginning of a sentence and see where that gets you.'

It's probably a defensive reflex gesture, but I sometimes like to joke that, when I had this crazy idea of watching a writer write a book from beginning to end, I first contacted Amis/Tartt/Franzen/ Houellebecq and when they were unavailable I only asked Lee Child as a desperate last resort.

'You would have to bring *them* in. Franzen. Amis.'

'In order to eliminate them from our inquiries.'

'Bastard.'

'Read the next sentence.'

The reality is he was the first writer I thought of. He has always struck me as a blessed (and I don't mean by that successful) and exemplary incarnation of what Borges called 'the spirit of litera-ture'. He is, more than anyone I can think of, a pure writer, with a degree zero style. Maybe sub-zero. He doesn't plan. He doesn't premeditate. He loves to be spontaneous. Which explains two things: (1) That he said yes to my proposal. (2) That he also said, 'I have no plot and no title. Nothing.'

'*Blessed!* Makes me sound like a saint. A secular saint. I like Borges. Anything but Franzen.'

'Have you read *Purity* yet?'

He went back to the article.

When I got there, on September 1 of last year, to his apartment on the Upper West Side of Manhattan, overlooking Central Park, just up the street from where John Lennon once lived (and where he was shot dead by a deranged fan), all he had was sublime con-fidence. And a title, which he had come up with the night before: Make Me. He just liked the sound of it.

It had to be September 1…

'Blah, blah, yeah all that stuff about the beginning. The back-hoe, the hogs, the guys, the Flaubertian point of view.'

He skipped a couple of paragraphs.

For the next few months I looked on with a degree of anxiety. Maybe he would never finish this one. The whole project looked doomed. Reacher was wandering around this small town, trying to work out mainly why it was even called Mother's Rest. He didn't even know that Keever was a dead man at this point. He was a fairly useless detective, because he couldn't even figure out what the crime was, let alone solve it.

So too Lee Child. He wandered around New York, then drifted off to the West Coast, then Madrid, then Sussex, and still had no idea what the hell was going on in his book. If it was a book. Around Christmas time I spoke to him on the phone and he said, 'Maybe it'll make a good short story.' And added, 'Maybe I should go back and work in television. I hear it's improved a lot since my day.' And tossed in stray remarks like, 'I guess I'm all out of gas.' He was partly winding me up of course – if he didn't finish then neither would I. But after phase 1 in his writing (what he calls 'the gorgeous feeling' of the beginning) there is a phase 2, which puts him in mind of Sisyphus and his travails. He struggles and meanders. Smokes more and drinks more black coffee, if it is possible to drink more black coffee. Puffs on the occasional joint in hope of inspiration finally ...

'I wasn't winding you up. That was real. It still is.'
'I'll get you another coffee.'

Some time in January, it started to crystallise in his mind and he gave me the Big Reveal. Looking back at my notes, I see that I said to him, in a tone of mixed awe and horror, 'You evil mastermind bastard.' I realised that there was a simple mistake I had been making all along. I had been mixing him up with his hero Jack Reacher. Whereas I now realised what I should have realised long before that he was also every single bad guy he had ever dreamed up. All those fiendish plots were actually his. The role of Reacher was to stop him plotting and for all I know taking over the world. Reacher keeps the author in check.

'"Evil mastermind bastard"?'

'What do you think?'

'I like it … it's fair comment. I guess it's lucky for the world at large I'm a writer rather than a full-on criminal.'

'Sometimes it's hard to tell the difference.'

Then, in his phrase, it was the 'marathon sprint' to the end. He got to the final page on April 10, 2015, surviving on a diet of Sugar Puffs and Alpen and toast, garnished with mucho caffeine and nicotine.

Having feared he would never get to the end, I was not sure I really wanted him to finish. Or whether I should be there to watch. It really seemed as if I was transgressing and crossing the line into some sacred place. I was bearing witness to the creative process dying. But without which the book itself could never be born. Last word: 'needle'. 'Moving … needle'. The whole book was there.

He stopped, so I stopped. That was the rule. I started when he started, so I had to finish when he did, or the day after anyway. No additions, no time for further reflection. It all had to be done according to the same principle he had adopted. He didn't want to change anything, so neither could I. Hence it took me several months to work out why it was that he worked in this fundamentally terrifying, angst-inducing way. Actually several explanations have occurred to me: sloth for one. He just can't be 'arsed'. And then there is what he says, which is that he would be 'bored' if he knew what was coming next. But contained in that statement is a hint of what I think is the case and in fact is the secret of his whole writing.

Lee Child writes his books as if he were the reader not the writer. When he is sitting at his desk in that back room in Manhattan he is only typing. The real work takes place when he is 'dreaming', when he is being just another reader, wondering what is coming next, waiting to find out. It probably explains too why he allowed me to look over his shoulder and watch his sentences taking shape even before he knew how they would end. He feels a natural sympathy with readers because he is one.

'Do you remember when I was just lying on the sofa, smoking?' he asked.

'And you said, "I'm working!"'
He laughed. 'And you bought it!'

I sometimes like to claim – with absurd grandiloquence – that my book is some kind of first in the history of mankind, sitting around watching another guy write a whole book: but in fact that would be a lie, because I had to run off from time to time so as not to curl up and die of involuntary inhalation. But the 'first' that I really would like to lay claim to is this: I am the first reader of a Lee Child novel to read it slowly. I had to keep stopping because he kept stopping. Because he really had no idea what was coming next. 'Why did you stop there?' I asked him one day, feeling he hadn't really written enough for that day. 'I had to stop there,' he said. 'I have no idea who that guy in the Cadillac is.'

'That is my method. You nailed it. *Clueless*. I tell you what, though,' he said, crushing the empty Starbucks cup in his hand. 'I could really do with a clue right now. An honest-to-goodness clue. I don't have one. I'm stuck. Again.'

'So you're sending Reacher back to "Night School" ... Is that you, basically? You feel you ought to be going to school, finally? To learn how to write ...'

'I did too much fighting the first time around,' he said. 'If only I'd been a proper student ... Maybe he can find a note or something. That would help.'

45

KARINA

She said she would never finish the novel she had been reading at the exact time her husband died. It was 'brilliant'. But he died so it died, necessarily. She couldn't go back to it. But she would have to read *something*.

Karina, born in Poland, was a writer in Cape Town. She was also the widow of a much older writer. She read his books first, chaired seminars about him, wrote essays about him, then married him, when he was already getting on a bit (but still in good nick), and then he went and died on a plane, in February 2015, flying back from Belgium, high over Africa, aged around eighty. She wasn't even forty. They had spent a decade together, talking or being silent, hardly ever apart.

Now he wasn't around any more. He didn't exist.

Which is when she espoused Reacher. He didn't exist either of course. Which probably explained why he was so enormously hard to kill off. This is what she wrote on her blog.

I reached out to *Killing Floor* at a time in my life when everything had become difficult, including breathing. And to stay alive, I need reading as much as I need breathing. It is a matter of survival, of being who I am. In the early stages of widowhood, I had to learn everything anew. How to breathe, to sleep, to eat. To smile. I picked up books in the hope of reclaiming a little bit of myself, a sense of stability, some solace, and an escape from my unbearable new reality, but every page was a struggle. Books which would have taken me two or three days to read, lasted for long agonising weeks. I was desperate. Until I picked up Jack Reacher on a roadside, typically hitchhiking out of town.

It turned out they had a coffee habit in common, and a certain passion for numbers and chronology. Karina quickly started consuming Reachers the way she drank coffee. With an addictive fervour.

> I was hooked after only a few pages. The exhilaration of devouring a book again at breakneck speed came with such a relief that I immediately bought the next one, and the next, and the next (once I even ventured out into a freezing and rainy Sunday night at quarter to nine and sped like a maniac through town to Exclusive Books before they closed because I'd just finished a Reacher novel and couldn't bear to face a night without the following one in my hands).

Her diary entry for 22 April records that she spent the entire morning in bed with Reacher and that 'I have fallen for this guy, big time.' On 28 April she 'took Jack to dinner at Karouk' (where she ate steak and chocolate mousse). A few days later she is having 'a lovely long candle and chamomile and Jack bath'. She was no particular fan of thrillers (the exception being the Larsson trilogy, which she and her late husband had both 'devoured' – I forgot to ask her about the Lagercrantz sequel). But where Lee Child was concerned she was a total convert and she went about converting others around her until there was a thriving South African branch of the Jack Reacher fan club. She would send out tweets like this:

```
Come to the Reacher Side, @pamelapower! We've
got bloody good books! Twenty of them.
```

And:

```
Becoming a Reacher Creature has been one of the
most rewarding experiences as a reader for me!
@pamelapower
```

Karina organized Reacher parties/seminars at the 'Book Lounge' in Cape Town ('We Love Jack Reacher' was their tagline). Karin

Brynard was there (the writer whose novel she would never finish).

I hardly need to say this, because Karina says it all herself, but I'm going to say it anyway: the works of Lee Child came to fill the void her husband had left behind. Reacher was, in effect, a surrogate partner. A stand-in. One who would never die, on a plane, over Africa.

> With the Reacher books, my hunger for all kinds of reading returned to me. Back in full force, it is the only thing from my past which has pulled me through the greatest loss of my life unscathed.

She tweeted about it too:

```
@andymartinink @Heckitty As you know from my
blog, I owe a lot to the Jack Reacher series.
The books made many unbearable moments bearable.
```

She wrote to me the following: 'The books are almost like talismans of good luck for me. I take them with me for moral support whenever I feel vulnerable because I can disappear into their world.' In Sweden, Reacher had helped Elsa through the long hours of darkness; in Cape Town he guided Karina through the valley of the shadow of death. He became her 'perfect companion'. Like Elsa, Karina went back to the very beginning and read them all in order. Or nearly all. She had had to read *Worth Dying For* 'when I couldn't find a copy of *61 Hours* in time'. And then her friend Elleke Boehmer, a literature professor at Oxford, had brought her *Make Me*, on the very day it was published in England, 9 September. She was the first reader of the hardback in South Africa, perhaps the whole of the continent. Even the guys at Random House in Cape Town hadn't seen it yet. It was her first Reacher in hardback.

Karina was anything but a naïve reader. She loved not just Reacher, but the women characters too, and she loved the 'poetry', which she quoted:

> 'It was raining and grey on the western peaks, and in the east the sun was slanting down through the edge of the clouds and gleaming off the tiny threads of snow in the high gullies.' (*The Visitor*)

She admired the way he could nail a character in a couple of lines:

> 'She looked like a solid, capable woman. She was about sixty years old, maybe more, white, blunt and square, with blond hair fading slowly to yellow and grey. Plenty of old German genes in there, or Scandinavian.' (*Worth Dying For*)

And she thought the opening lines were great too:

> 'I was arrested in Eno's diner.' (*Killing Floor*)

> 'The cop climbed out of his car exactly four minutes before he got shot.' (*Persuader*)

> 'Moving a guy as big as Keever wasn't easy.' (*Make Me*)

She added one more thing:

> And! The sex is good.

She even liked the movies. Thought Tom Cruise was just fine.

I first heard from her in November, shortly after *Reacher Said Nothing* came out. Somehow word had reached her, in Cape Town. Her radar was attuned to any mention of Reacher, or maybe it was her Twitter feed. Having read *Make Me*, she would now have to wait till the following September for the next one. Except that *Reacher Said Nothing* was like the next best thing, because it at least *mentioned* Reacher and sent news from Leelandia.

This tweet appeared on my timeline:

```
Nov 29: 'What could possibly make you happy for
Christmas?'
Karina said nothing. #ReacherSaidNothing by
@andymartinink pic.twitter.com/cWbsr5Xkl2
```

I had to tweet her back.

```
I'll send you one for Xmas.
```

I don't care how ruthless, cynical, and Scrooge-like you are, you would have said the same. She was so damn nice about it.

```
I am not only a Reacher Creature, but in my head,
I live in Leelandia (wonderful word I got from
@andymartinink). It's a really great place!
```

Then Karina's friend contacted me. She was flying to South Africa soon. Maybe she could take her a copy.

```
@Heckitty Nov 29
@KarinaMSzczurek @andymartinink Oh, we have to
make this happen! I'm in rural Maine. BUT: this
country has reliable mail!
```

The end of it all was that I took a copy to Lee and he signed it and I sent it off to the address in rural Maine. He was happy to sign it. Partly because she was a fellow writer. But mainly because she was a fellow reader. And a loyal reader at that. (@heckitty's tweet: 'Holy wow! @andymartinink we OWE you. Going out in search of vast mug of coffee, and will raise it to you & Lee.' She said it was a Christmas miracle.)

'Reacher would make such a poor husband,' Lee was saying. 'In reality. Forever running off and coming back home a mess. And he would never mow the lawn either.'

'But as a symbolic husband ... ?'

'Yeah, the unreal kind, he is just fine.'

In the diegetic realm of the novel, Reacher was always drifting off, like Shane, hopping on another bus. But if you consider it from the point of view of a reader, then Reacher, on the contrary, is always coming back. Every time you pick up one of the books. In fact he never really goes away, just pauses, if you pause. He is easily summoned, like a genie in the lamp. All you have to do is ... open the book. Reacher helped Jeff out of the world; he helped Karina remain in it.

I had some notion that Reacher had saved Karina. There was

a line in her novel *Invisible Others* where a character picks up a book 'like a lifeboat after a shipwreck'. Maybe, I thought, it was like that. But if there was one more tweet from Karina, not addressed to me at all, that stuck in my mind, it was this:

```
Juan Salvado makes me think that sometimes you
believe you are saving someone's life, but it is
actually the other way around.
```

I think Lee would say the same: it wasn't so much that Reacher was saving any of his readers, it was all those readers who were saving Reacher. Without them he would be dead as a dodo.

46

ZENO AND THE ART OF THE HEAD-BUTT

Vaughan, the cop with the brain-dead soldier husband, calls Reacher 'Zeno' the first time she meets him (in the pages of Reacher 12, *Nothing to Lose*). They have a couple of exchanges about Zeno of Cittium (or Cyprus), the founder of Stoicism, on the city line between Hope and Despair. She tells him to 'stop being so long-suffering' (page 49). Don't be a stoic. But is Reacher seriously stoical? It was something Lee had floated once on a rooftop in Madrid. 'Philosophically, Reacher is a stoic. Stoicism is about all he has by way of philosophy.'

At one level, he meant that Reacher could take anything anybody could throw at him. He could put up with unbelievable amounts of pain or basic discomfort without moaning about it. More than anyone could reasonably stand. As regards pain, Reacher is adept at giving; but he can take it too, when he has to. He can reset his own broken nose, for example, as in *A Wanted Man*. And tape it up afterwards with silver duct tape. He bears the scars of numerous wounds – something that always elicits a ripple from his audience when he whips off his shirt. But his stoicism is dramatized in the head-butt.

It's for when you want it to be all over, in a hurry. But the head-butt is a complex operation, both giving and taking away. With pain on both sides, albeit unequally distributed. If you do it right, argues Reacher, it doesn't hurt that much. Thus, stoical. But the head-butt also demonstrated why it was that Reacher couldn't possibly be a stoic. The true stoic wouldn't be head-butting a soul.

Zeno, other than fragments, is lost. So I went back to the *Enchiridion* to check. Epictetus, one of the theorists of stoicism, may well have had a lot to be stoical about. Some said that he was crippled at birth, others that he had been injured, or that he

193

had been deliberately hobbled by his owner. The former slave Epictetus formulated a philosophy in which everything ought to be exactly the way it is. There is no distinction between an 'is' and an 'ought'. Anything that occurred was fine just the way it occurred. What was the worst that could happen? You die or everybody you know dies. So it goes. Plane crashes, car wrecks, ship wrecks, plagues, volcanoes erupting, tsunamis, disasters of all kinds. It was no kind of big deal, according to Epictetus. We just had to get used to it. Thereby attaining *ataraxia*. It only required superhuman reserves of indifference. Ataraxia was probably what Elsa had in mind when she rhapsodized about the 'calm' or tranquillity of Reacher.

Epictetus gives a simple example of something going wrong. Your servant, he imagines, drops your favourite vase and shatters into a thousand pieces. Do you crack up and punish the servant? No, he argues. The correct attitude is this: that vase (or jug or plate) has not been broken, it has been 'restored'. So, similarly, when the whole world is falling apart (or you are), do you need to complain or get hysterical? No. You simply say to yourself, 'It is being *restored*.' This is what Reacher, in his conversation with Vaughan, calls 'the unquestioning acceptance of destinies'.

Is Reacher a stoic? Only up to a point. He can take it, true. But fundamentally he gets fed up with the way things are, after a while. He can't stand it any more and it has to be put right. In *Make Me*, for example, he tries to remain 'stoical', in the Epictetan sense, for as long as possible. Doesn't give anyone a beating for some considerable time. Tries to concentrate on the meaning of the name 'Mother's Rest', tries to ignore missing detectives. It's none of his business. He is indifferent, *au-dessus de la mêlée*. But then he gets drawn in. The woman waiting at the station. The mention of 200 deaths. The weird townspeople. That creepy rubber store. Something is rotten in the state of Kansas. By extension, the world, as Reacher sees it, stands in need of correction. A rectification. 'Is' is not 'ought'. *Is*, in fact, is generally a long, long way from *ought*. Response, on an ascending scale: a sense of injustice, indignation, righteous fury. The broken jug is crying out for fixing and it takes Reacher to fix it.

Hence the head-butt. When Reacher head-butts one of his adversaries, it is his way of trying to restore things. He is an interventionist. He has to be because of all the other people who are also intervening, in the other direction.

He is anything but a stoic.

But he has to be a stoic, to deliver the head-butt.

He is and is not a stoic. Maybe a Reacher book is all about symmetry and balance.

At one level Reacher is pure myth. At another – specifically at the level of someone on the receiving end of the head-butt – Reacher is the real. The principle of pain.

We were having a pizza somewhere when Lee put down his fork and said, 'Stoicism used to mean something like, *go with the flow*. Doesn't sound much like Reacher, does it? He hates the flow.'

I guessed he was thinking about *Night School*. It was time for Reacher to stop being quite so damn philosophical. To stop being so long-suffering.

47

REACHER VS WEST GERMANY

Night School, 1 December.

Lee was saying that it was Reacher let loose inside a classic espionage novel. Not exactly John Le Carré, but verging on. Sober, disciplined, repressed, almost scholarly, and then Reacher, a Dionysian principle trampling all over the Apollonian. It is 1991. Reacher is in Hamburg. Other than that, little changes. He is hunting for coffee, as always. The quest for the bean never stops. It brings him up against a lot of guys – skinheads, neo-Nazis, and the like – who seek to prevent him getting coffee. Big mistake, as they quickly discover. But a few deftly delivered knockout punches are as nothing next to his killer one-liner.

Lee had lured me over to his place with talk of his 'best ever alpha male' sentence. I should have guessed it would have something to do with the Second World War. Lee is too young to know about the war at first hand. He was born between the wars. If I had had to guess, I would have said that he derived his feeling for the war from the 1966 World Cup (soccer), in which England defeated West Germany 4–2 in the final. (And as all Germans will tell you, with regard to the third goal, 'the ball never crossed the line!') It was possibly our greatest ever moment as a nation, on the sports field. But it wasn't that.

Oddly enough it was at a tennis match. Lee was around ten at the time and some uncle had taken him along. It was a Davis Cup game, England vs West Germany, in Edgbaston, Birmingham, and England were getting massacred. It was like having Panzer tanks roll all over your nice lawn. Really, we had no option other than to mention the war. It was our default rhetoric when it came to the Germans. So this was fifty years ago, approximately. But the line had stuck in Lee's mind, it was always there, stashed away, but clamouring to get out again. And now Reacher was in Hamburg it was the perfect opportunity for payback.

'Hold on a second,' I said. 'What happened to school? Don't tell me he's dropped out already?'

'Turns out that was all a cover story.'

'It's called *Night School*.'

'Misdirection.'

'I was looking forward to seeing Reacher back at school. Hogwarts and all that.'

'Nah, he's got better things to do than play Quidditch all afternoon.'

'It's you, isn't it?'

'Yeah, I always hated school.'

The guy behind the bar doesn't want to serve Reacher, who has already beaten the living daylights out of four poor devils outside. Now he is inside. So the barman doesn't have a lot of option. But he's not really into it, making coffee for this *Schweinhund* of an American. It feels like still having an army of occupation. But Reacher is determined to get his coffee come what may, so he's not going to slug the barman. He has to be in shape to make the coffee, after all. On the other hand, Reacher needs to wind him up and crush him verbally. So he comes out with the worst thing he can think of, for a German. It's the line Lee first heard fifty years before, chanted by the English crowd, riled by German supremacy, at Edgbaston:

'How does it feel to lose a war?'

Maybe the barman should have snapped back, 'I don't know, I wasn't in Vietnam.' But maybe he doesn't feel like verbal jousting with Reacher. Anyway he slinks off to make the coffee. One way or another, Reacher gets his point across. And he always gets served his coffee.

Simple message: guys, do not take Reacher on, because you will lose.

But what about women? This is what Lee was, to some extent, worrying about. The Laura Kipnis effect. He wasn't alpha male to women. He was egalitarian. He'd had to kill a few (see *Gone Tomorrow*, for example); had made love to many more (e.g. *The Affair*, *Killing Floor*, *Die Trying*, etc.). But he was anything but

God's gift. And he was no Don Juan, not a hint of Lothario. Sex was not like coffee to Reacher. He didn't really need it: he could, semi-monastically, go whole novels without (*Personal*). Maybe his closest relationship is with Neagley, whom he is not even allowed to touch, apart from her hand, once. On the other hand, if it comes along, then fine. 'Obviously,' says Lee, 'he is competent. It's not like his driving or something. I had to give him his inability to drive to make up for all the other stuff. To balance up the physical prowess.' Bond would easily outmanoeuvre Reacher in bed or in a car – a bar-room brawl would be another matter.

Now Lee was looking ahead to the next novel, beyond *Night School*. No. 22. I was still carrying around *Men*, the Kipnis book. I plonked it down on the window sill as I perched on the couch. It wasn't provocative, it just happened that way. But it provoked him anyway.

'Look,' says I, 'I don't want this to screw you up or whatever.'

'It won't.' But Reacher would have to become more 'self-aware'. The same way he had adapted to the internet. He would have to tune in to the zeitgeist. And Kipnis, just at that moment, had registered in Lee's mind, as a primo zeitgeist exemplar, an ambassador from feminism.

'He can't do it in this novel. He's back in 1991. He's too young. Unreconstructed, basically.'

I opened *Men* on page 21. A typical Kipnis line (this one re. Larry Flynt): 'I had remade him into something palatable and he had nicely gone along with it. If only more of the men in my life had been like that.' I listed some of the types that provided her chapter headings. 'The Con Man', 'The Groper', 'Cheaters', 'Self-Deceivers'. We agreed that the 'type' Reacher came closer to was 'The Manly Man'.

By the way, I should add that she had written in my copy, '*Quel homme!*' I like to think it was benevolent. Possibly ironic. Maybe I am just making her palatable and hoping she will go along with it.

'But not macho,' I said.

'He doesn't have to be,' Lee said.

It was something we had agreed on in Madrid, while contemplating bullfighters and the legacy of Hemingway. There is no machismo in Reacher. That overly 'transparent' masculinity meant that he didn't have to put anything on. Unlike almost everybody else, he doesn't have to try to be masculine, he just is. There is no scintilla of indeterminacy.

It wasn't explicit in the book, or maybe it was there on every page. Kipnis hated the 'over-compensators'. You're suffering some deficit, you try to make up for it, by overdoing everything, hyping it up, in search of dominion. She saw this as the root of all evil.

Lee was totally with her there. 'There is a real estate equivalent,' he said. 'People live where they live, good or bad. But if you live in a rough neighbourhood, you always hear this, people try to make up for it by saying, "But we have the *greatest* deli in New York just around the corner." They lay claim to local knowledge. No one ever says *"and the shops are crap"*.'

'Baudrillard said, "Masculinity is an exhausting and eccentric condition."'

'Only for Baudrillard,' Lee said.

And maybe that was true too for Hemingway's heroes, who, even when they aren't suffering from war-induced impotence, are always anxious. The fishing and the fighting is a way of trying to hold the anxiety at bay. Reacher doesn't have anxiety. 'He doesn't think too highly of himself,' Lee was saying. 'But in the next novel, I'm going to make him more self-aware. Maybe he can meet someone like Kipnis.'

'You're sure this isn't going to screw him up for all time?'

'Nah,' said Lee. 'He often thinks about things. Doesn't screw him up or paralyse him, though.'

I felt a sense of relief, as if a great surging torrent that I thought, for a moment, was about to be dammed up or put in a bottle had been allowed to roll on, mightily, flowing ceaselessly towards some distant ocean.

The *Übermensch*. It was odd that I had never noticed it before. Reacher/Nietzsche. A perfect rhyme. I had been misled all along by his speaking French. Phonologically, Reacher recalled the German philosopher of the will to power and eternal recurrence. Reacher was back in his intellectual homeland, even if he couldn't speak the language. He didn't need to speak it: he *was* the language.

I had to tweet Karina and let her know what had become of Reacher. She tweeted me back:

```
@andymartinink. It is so good to know Reacher is
in Hamburg in 1991. That is perfect. That is just
where I want him to be.
```

She was so easy-going. I still thought he ought to be writing essays or doing his sums. *Night School* on the cover and inside it's wall-to-wall brawling and coffee. *No School* would be more like it.

48

BUT WHO IS GOING TO PLAY LEE CHILD IN THE MOVIE?

If you look carefully around any bookstore, I guarantee you will find a reasonable number of books that carry recommendations from Lee Child. He probably won't get quoted on the back of the Lagercrantz paperback. But, for example, I picked up this one, Suzanne Chazin's *A Blossom of Bright Light*, and it says on the front cover, '"A tremendous talent" – Lee Child'. Funnily enough, Suzanne Chazin herself was standing right there and she had a confession. 'You know, he never said that.'

'Wow,' I said, impressed by the sheer brazenness of it. 'You just made it up?'

'Not me. The marketing people. When they heard Lee was going to come up with a blurb, they got so excited they just made some stuff up as a place holder. Then they forgot to change it to the real thing.'

'What did Lee say?'

'Said he didn't mind and he thought what they said was just fine. He was very forgiving. I guess he could have sued or something.'

On the back cover, there was another recommendation from Lee for another book of hers, *Land of Careful Shadows*: 'This is everything a great suspense novel should be – but it hits the heart, too, not just the pulse, with people you come to care about. First rate and highly recommended.' And that was authentic, so he really did like her stuff.

I came across another one he had lent his name to, something to do with pirates and treasure. He liked that one too. 'And it really happened!' he wrote. Lee said he gets about four or five requests *every day* for blurbs. He has to turn nearly all of them down otherwise he'd never get anything else done; he'd be writing nothing but blurbs for a living. But he hates to say no. 'It makes me die a little every time.'

His most understated blurb ever, for a book called *Potboiler*, was, 'Of all the books I read this year ... this was one of them.' The author, Jesse Kellerman, loved that because he was sending up the whole genre. The hero is an academic who gets to take over his famous friend's thriller when he is lost at sea – sounded reasonable to me. If Lee ever does a *Titanic*, I'm ready to step in; I'm probably not going to push him in front of a subway train or anything, though.

We were all – Lee Child, Suzanne Chazin, and I – in the newly opened Scattered Books bookstore in Chappaqua, an hour out of Manhattan. Mingling with the customers, doing a bit of book signing (Lee was doing most of it). There were a lot of writers there as well as readers. Chappaqua is a highly literate town.

Suzanne wanted to know what the 'relationship' was between us. Basically, I had no idea. Did we even have a 'relationship'? I was still trying to be scientific about it: guy in a white coat keeping him under observation like he was some kind of super-powered lab rat. An anthropologist trying to blend in with a tribe of one.

'I hate him,' Lee said, looking up from signing about ten books. 'I'm worried his bloody book is going to start outselling mine.' Suzanne and I were just standing there at the time, watching his queue. 'It keeps me awake at night.'

It only took me about half an hour to come back with a riposte. When we were wrapping up and having a last coffee for the road and putting our coats on, he was telling Suzanne how having Tom as Reacher had enabled him to sell about another ten million books worldwide, in places he wouldn't otherwise have hit: China and Korea and Brazil. 'So who should play *you* in the movie of my book then?' says I. 'I reckon Tom Cruise would be perfect.' Lee was going down to New Orleans again in a few days to shoot his scene with Tom. As usual he would have to be sitting down while the main man towered over him.

'He can play you,' he says. 'I want Jeremy Irons to play me.'

Maybe whom you would choose to play you in the movie of your life is the key to your personality. It is how you see yourself, maybe slightly buffed up and sanitized. Lee's alter ego had little to do with Irons' more recent big-screen career, but more his earlier incarnation as Charles Ryder in *Brideshead Revisited*, the brilliant Granada TV series that Lee had worked on many moons before. 'Come to think of it,' he continued, 'you're not unlike Anthony Andrews – maybe he'll make a comeback for this one. A Jeremy Irons and Anthony Andrews reunion – how would that be?'

Andrews played the part of the decadent gay Catholic aristocrat at Oxford with a teddy bear under his arm all the time. Close.

'I was thinking Liam Neeson, maybe,' I said as we climbed into his Land Rover to drive back to the city. 'With glasses.'

He lit a cigarette and blew smoke out of the open window. 'You are so ... Fuck me!' He was looking down at his phone. 'Bournemouth 1, Chelsea 0. Mourinho's out on his arse this time. Anything can happen this season.'

49

TWO NEW YORK SCENES, ON THE SAME DAY, CONTAINING ANTITHETICAL REACTIONS TO LEE CHILD

(a) The New York Times

They were queuing up to meet him and shake him by the hand. The day before, it had been Bernie Sanders, candidate for the presidency. Today, Lee Child. We were in the *New York Times* building (built by the same guy who did the Shard in London). We were on the thirteenth floor. The land of the op-ed people, the opinion-formers, or those who try to be. They weren't having a lot of luck with that just at present. They had just published a front-page opinion column (a fabulous rarity) protesting against gun violence and outlining perfectly reasonable and even Constitution-compatible measures that could be taken to effect some kind of reduction. Meanwhile, the 355th mass shooting of the year had just taken place. And previously law-abiding Islamist terrorists were killing health officials in San Bernardino. On top of which, some firearms fundamentalists had taken the *New York Times* front page and shot a load of holes in it. Sometimes it's tough being on the thirteenth floor. It was like being President or something.

That 'queuing' is a slight exaggeration. We were the guests of one guy, the Sunday Review editor, and there was one other *Times* man who wanted to meet Lee, the op-ed editor, and a woman who was a debut novelist. A small queue, but still, it was the hallowed thirteenth floor. And there was a lot of respect for Lee. 'You won't believe the fans you have in this building.' We ended up in the *Times* café on some other floor, drinking black coffee. Lee had a couple of cookies. I think it's fair to say no one at *The Times* identified Reacher with unrestrained gun violence.

We talked about Bernie Sanders (lovely guy – doomed); Vladimir Putin (resemblance to Daniel Craig; rendition of 'Blueberry Hill'); Sean Connery (Russian accent in *Red October*); *Day of the Jackal* (the Jackal demands a paltry half million for assassinating de Gaulle); a million used to seem like a lot (mainly Lee); the whole of the universe adds up to zero (mainly me): in Lee's case a lot of zeroes (that got a laugh); Second World War (Sunday Review's Dad was a general: still had a Luger he had taken off some dead Nazi); Travis McGee, hero of John D. MacDonald's books; surfing; Whitney Dangerfield; the 'Out of Eden' walk, by Paul Salopek, replicating the migration out of Africa by early humans; the Exoneration project; Tom Cruise (Lee due to go and shoot his scene with Tom down in New Orleans the following day).

We were on our way out of the building when Lee said, with a degree of respect, 'You're outselling Stephen King!' He had noticed that I was now No. 1 on Amazon ... under the specific heading of 'Advice about writing from people like Lee Child'. The King book he had in mind was *On Writing*, not *The Green Mile* or *Carrie*.

Lee headed uptown towards a barbershop. He wanted to smarten himself up for his stint on the silver screen. I went and had a doughnut in Starbucks on 34th and 7th. That was what I tweeted about: the doughnut, nothing else. With a photo. 'Awesome #totally.' Dumb, I know, but it was easier to summarize a pastry with a hole in the middle than all the other stuff.

(b) Anonymous High

Joel has two sons. He had recently returned from spending ten days in Costa Rica *en famille*. The younger of his two boys had taken Will Durant's *The Age of Faith* with him to read on the beach. A massive 900-plus pages long. And it weighed a ton. I had been impressed by his studiousness. The other was trying to concentrate on his college applications. As Yoda would say: good intentions the way to hell paved with is. The older kid reads Larsson's *Millennium Trilogy* and watches the films when he gets back too. The younger kid somehow gets his hands on Lee Child. Joel's fault, most likely. He races through four in ten days. *The Age of Faith* returns, pristine, intact.

So the kids go into school and the English teacher says, 'Well now, class, tell us about some of the books you have been reading recently.' They like this teacher. He is bright, fun, friendly, open, easy-going, pluralistic, laissez-faire. *Except* where Child and Larsson are concerned. The boys get a tongue-lashing for slumming it so egregiously. 'Lee Child? Loathsome trash! Larsson, cheap and sensationalist.' Other words ending in '-ist'. Completely unsuitable for young minds. Tending to corrupt and deprave.

The teacher hands out a sanction: they have to go and read Thomas Pynchon's *Gravity's Rainbow*. It happens to be the teacher's favourite book. It is worse than corporal punishment to Joel's way of thinking. 'Pynchon is such a pile of horseshit!' he opines.

'Yeah,' I say, 'It's a baggy shopping bag of a novel. He chucks it all in. But, you know, in a line-to-line way, he's great, don't you think? I mean ...'

'He is crap,' said Joel. I had been telling him about Lee at *The New York Times*. 'Bet they don't roll out the red carpet at *The Times* for Pynchon!'

Tweet from @AnonymousHigh:

```
Any students found in possession of works
by @LeeChildReacher or so-called Scandi Noir
authors will be excluded from school until their
behaviour improves.
```

I made that up by the way, but I think it captures the doughnut mind, in which Lee Child is a hole in the middle.

50

ENNUI

I'm keeping this chapter as short as possible so nobody gets bored. I'm cutting all the references to Pascal and Borges and Baudelaire in case they were just a little boring.

Beyond pure terror and fear for his life, we had been wondering if Michael Scott Moore, held hostage by Somali pirates, had got bored, especially in the absence of something to read. Similarly, the globe-trotting Paul Salopek. Lee said he would never be bored. He never *is* bored. Could hardly understand anyone who was bored. And it was true, I had never seen him bored or complain of boredom or even clamour for greater excitement. Rather the opposite: the classic case that springs to mind is the time he turned down the offer of a potentially romantic candle-lit dinner with a Bond girl. 'I didn't fancy all the excitement,' he said.

Isn't there a hint of boredom on page 1 of *Make Me*? The anonymous parties who are burying Keever, courtesy of a back-hoe, are situated squarely within a panorama of 'nothingness'. Perhaps there is a hint that it is the very potential for boredom in this vastness that inspires the murderous enterprise that Reacher must discern and unravel. It was almost like a defence in court: 'We had to do something, your honour! We were bored out of our skulls. Nothing but wheat for miles around.' Comparable to an insanity defence: a *boredom* defence. But perhaps all criminals could plausibly have recourse to the same argument. We crave risk and excitement, which drives us to transgress. Without that, maybe we would even be good …

Reacher is never bored. He's always attending to *something*: when there's nothing to attend to he simply switches off his power of attention. He is always reading something – only rarely a text, but the world always presents itself to him as a puzzle to be solved or deciphered, interpreted, exegetically.

It was while I was chewing over this boredom problem that I wandered into Albertine, the French bookstore opposite Central Park. I was looking for Baudrillard's *Amérique*, but I couldn't help noticing a new translation of Georges Perec's *Attempt at an Exhaustive Description of a Place in Paris*. This is the book in which Perec sits around in the Place St Sulpice, drinking coffee, for three solid days, one October. Nothing really happens: there is no drama, nobody dies. And yet it is packed with happenings: buses go by, pigeons take off, there are interesting clouds. Traffic wardens pass by, and occasional old friends. For anyone who has ever listened to cricket commentary on BBC radio, it's like that, only without the actual cricket. Apparently trivial, banal, utterly forgettable, and yet every micro-event is freighted with significance. Perec called it the 'infra-ordinary'. All the stuff that most people don't notice.

Reacher is like Perec. He is into the infra-ordinary. He listens, he watches, he is on the alert for sense data. 'I notice things,' he says at the beginning of *The Hard Way*. He is a big guy who is perpetually struck by small things. Lee is a bit like that too, I think. Likes the little things, gets excited by the stuff that people often don't bother about, like commas and hyphens and short sentences.

51

THE WOMAN WHO HATED REACHER

Lee has never even met her. I just drop occasional comments from her into his ear (or vice versa). And yet she certainly feels she has had a full-on personal encounter with him. Possibly too personal. Her word for it is: *unpleasant.*

The full arc of the virtual relationship is there, in the margins, between the lines, under the covers. She never wanted to get involved with this guy. She didn't like the look of his sentence structure at all. His lexical choices were entirely unsuitable. His stylistic nuances and hers were clearly incompatible. She, a hip New York intellectual, and university professor, moreover, had a reputation. She liked wiry, witty, historically astute guys, as a rule. Guys, in short, who weren't that dissimilar to her (slim, fit, *soigné*, well dressed). No way was she going to hook up with a hulking 6′5″ ex military cop/drifter vigilante/muscle-bound galoot who bought his clothes in hardware stores. Imagine showing him off in the senior common room!

And yet, all the above notwithstanding, she was still irresistibly drawn towards the works of Lee Child. She held out for years. Then something tipped her over the edge. The *something* in this case was, as it happens, me, but it could have been anything, a friend, a word, a review, a dog-eared paperback in a bus station. Even a film. Oddly enough, she had seen the movie, with Tom Cruise. Thought it was just fine, as these things go, just hadn't made the connection. Tom had failed to sell a single copy of a Reacher book to her. And then I came along, not twisting her arm or anything, not being overly evangelical, just happening to mention *en passant* Elsa or Karina or Sam or that girl in Washington who said reading Reacher made her feel 'smart'.

She was having a cappuccino in a place in West Village and

telling me how she had succumbed to *The Hard Way*. She didn't actually *like* it, I should stress. Lucky for Lee Child that she wasn't reviewing it. Intellectually, she objected to the profusion of 'coincidences'. 'So Reacher just *happened* to be there!' she said, with her characteristically abrasive insight. It's true, the opening on 6th Avenue is exactly that: a coincidence, dramatically conceived, in which Reacher witnesses an exchange taking place, without even knowing that's what it is. 'And when he gets to London, that woman just *happens* to be there.' And so on. Fair comment. I guessed that Cervantes, Tolstoy, and Simone de Beauvoir might not be devoid of coincidence, but still she had a point. All those quantum collisions. She was a loyal Freudian and thought of everything in terms of splits and fractures and repressions. I was more Jungian, so welcomed the *coincidentia oppositorum* as an integral part of literary alchemy.

Which is what brings us to the 'unpleasant' part of the reading experience. I should have guessed that she would have a typically screwed-up, deconstructed, neurotic reading. That Reacher would constitute a trauma in her life. I guessed, in a way, it was another of those coincidences that she was so sceptical about. She is sitting all alone in Manhattan and then *kaboom!* this book just happens to fall in her lap. How ridiculous and unbelievable is that?

The thing is, she couldn't put it down, but she wanted to put it down. There was something about it that kept her reading, sheer momentum, a compulsion she struggled against in vain. She kicked and she screamed about coincidences and still she had to go on, all the way to England and East Anglia and the climax and the backhoe. She found that she couldn't stop. This was what she hated. A loss of control, something she was not used to. No laws had been violated, so far as I could work out. She would have to admit in court, she had signed up, she had bought in, she had said yes. But it was the kind of yes that contained a lot of no. A grudging, half-hearted consent, followed by an awful lot of regrets in the light of day. And the vow: Never again!

Maybe Reacher would approve of the attitude. It was a casual encounter. Strictly no-strings, no commitment on either side. She would move on, bruised perhaps, but not seriously wounded. She wouldn't be seeing Reacher again, ever, no way, not on your life, not if you paid me …

There was only one thing, which I had to point out. She hadn't read *Make Me*. Too bad. She would have loved the assisted dying theme. The obsession with death, voluntary or involuntary.

'Assisted dying?' she said.

She was into assisted dying.

FOOTNOTE. I was having lunch with Lee in Almond, on 22nd, an old downtown haunt of his. Or, to be exact, *outside* Almond, on the terrace. It was one of those crazy December days that were so warm. 'I agree with her, in a way,' he conceded. 'That's always the difficulty – getting going. Why does Reacher even get involved? So he is sitting there, but he notices things. Not everyone does. He files it all away. But it's right there on the first page of *The Hard Way*. *There are eight million stories in the naked city.* You're in the wrong place at the wrong time, it happens. I actually say how banal it is. "It was just an urban scene, repeated everywhere in the world a billion times a day: a guy unlocked a car and got in and drove away." But you are relying on the reader to give you a pass on one improbability – that Reacher should witness a significant event. One get-out-of-gaol card free, that's all you ask. Everything follows from that.'

'She says you're unpleasant.' I had to mention it.

He chortled. He loves it when people find him unpleasant. 'She is like the entire population of Sweden then. "It's so unpleasant!" they would say. But they kept on reading anyway.'

52

TOM

I want to try to explain why it was that he *had* to insist on the private jet. It was all set for flying *back* from New Orleans. *No problem, Mr Child.* He had an urgent appointment the next morning at Random House. That seemed fair. But then he demanded the private jet for the flight down there too, on that Thursday morning in December. Yes, both ways.

It was, let's admit it, just a little bit prima donna. But then, this was the movies after all. Didn't they all behave like this? Why should he be any different? You were virtually obliged to be a git so as not to stand out from the crowd. And he didn't fancy having to get up early in order to take the scheduled flight from La Guardia. He would arrive feeling wrecked and in no mood to shoot his scene. It was all in the interests of making the movie as good as it could be, in other words. *We understand, Mr Child. Consider it done.*

But there was, in truth, a more subtle rationale in play. It was all about *status*. Hollywood was status obsessed. It was a highly feudal regime, *Game of Thrones*-style. Were you going to be one of the high lords or one of the peasants? Lee didn't fancy being a swineherd; he was only a troubadour, singing for his supper, but still he wanted to be seated right up there at the top table. Otherwise you were capitulating. You had already lost the battle.

So it was that he went not to La Guardia, not to JFK, but to Teterboro, in New Jersey, just on the other side of the George Washington Bridge. They sent a car for him, of course. Come on, he's not going to hail a cab! The *grands seigneurs* do not hail cabs. A three-hour flight, but he has a six-seat charter plane to himself, no security, no hanging about, no queuing. Just flunkeys, bowing down. And at the other end, at the Louis Armstrong New

Orleans International Airport, for Mr Child's further convenience, he didn't even have to leave the building. They still sent a car for him, though, driven by some intern kid called Tyler. One of the lower echelons. Took him from one part of the airport to another. Paramount were using an entire terminal, abandoned by American Airlines, for their set. It didn't need a lot of Industrial Light and Magic to get an airport terminal looking pretty much like an airport terminal. But it had to be both an airport in Norfolk, Virginia (which Reacher is leaving), and the airport in New Orleans where he is landing. Cue lots of posters saying, 'Come to sunny Virginia!' or similar. Cheap but effective. How the hell else were you supposed to show it was Virginia?

Lee was playing the part of a TSA security officer (Homeland Security) checking Reacher's boarding pass and ID. They had to make the smart blue shirt for him specifically, they couldn't just go and buy one. Nobody else was as slim as he was with arms as long as his. Sarah was his 'make-up artist', a Brit who had come over specially for the movie. She spent more than an hour making him look good. First the haircut (he hadn't quite made it to the barbers the day before), then the shave, and finally the moisturizer. This was a first for Lee: he had never used any moisturizer himself, ever. Decided he wouldn't bother in the future either: got as much moisture as he needed from coffee.

They were shooting from six in the evening till three in the morning. It was all about the night shots. Easier to do at night sometimes. But they did Lee's scene first, given his high feudal status and all. The way it was set up: the camera over here, Lee over there, sitting at his podium. In between a queue of people snaking around, going through security. The camera would begin shooting raw film, then it was 'Background!', i.e. the queue, then it was 'Action!', i.e. Lee and Tom. Tom was second in line. There was a young black woman in front of him, going through the same routine, presenting her boarding pass and ID. She was only an extra, but she had the important part of Woman Who Goes in Front of Jack Reacher. It was her real ID, a driving licence. They had to shoot the scene about six times. She says to Lee, 'Now you'll be able to stalk me.' The driving licence had her real address, but because he wasn't wearing glasses it was all pretty hazy anyway. Tom comes up behind her and says, 'He wrote the book!' There was definite respect. Maybe a degree of amazement too. She was flabbergasted. For a short period in her life, she had the unusual privilege of being sandwiched between the father of Reacher in front of her and the guy behind her who was pretending to be Reacher.

They had lunch around 10 p.m. Hollywood hours. It was clear from the conversation that Tom had read the book. (Lee didn't like to ask, as such.) And all the other books in the series too, it turned out. He was really quite knowledgeable. Obviously he knew *One Shot* (Reacher 9) inside out. And now *Never Go Back* (Reacher 18) too. But then little pearls of wisdom would escape his lips. 'Reacher wouldn't say x,' or 'Reacher would do y' – that sort of thing. He'd come out with stray Reacherisms: 'You can walk out of here or they can carry you out in a bucket!' The director and the producer were both fans of the books. So was the woman playing Reacher's successor at the head of the 110th, Major Susan Turner. ('The book is better,' she said to Lee – I guess she had to say that.) Status of girl playing the putative Reacher 'daughter', unknown, except that she was good at stunts (with safety wire attached, of course – it would be digitally edited out later – she was only seventeen, and had to have her mother chaperoning her). But to have Tom Cruise reading the books too, that was something. Someone had once said of Tom that 'At least you don't have to worry about him breaking in and stealing your library.' But maybe that was no longer true. He had taken to reading Reacher with a passion (or maybe listening to the audio book, or having fellow Scientologists read to him of an evening, or whatever).

It was three years to the day since the UK premiere of the first Jack Reacher movie. A day that was hard for Lee to forget. On the positive side: the full red-carpet treatment. Shamelessly enjoyable. Who would not get a kick out of being flown around the country in a helicopter? Delivered to Leicester Square in a stretch limo. It was like he was a movie star. And when they got out there were as many fans yelling, 'Lee! Lee!' as 'Tom! Tom!' He signed as many autographs. He even wore a shirt and tie for the night, really made an effort. Put laces in his shoes. The works.

But, on the downside, he was working, although he didn't realize it at the time. He was being used to legitimize the movie for readers. It was an impossible task, doomed to failure from the very beginning. And the interesting thing was that, to Lee's mind, it had nothing to do with Tom Cruise. It was predictable that readers were going to hate the movie. You could take a 6'5", 250 lb guy who looked like Reacher and whose name was Reacher and who had once been a military cop and give him the part, and they would still hate it. Didn't make any difference. Reading was private and movies were public. You *owned* the book; you didn't own the movie. On the page, Reacher is my guy. On the screen, he becomes everyone's. It's like I have been robbed. Of course I am going to bellyache about it. I had this secret thing going on, and now it's been exposed, and devalued. Naturally, readers were always convinced that the book was better. So Lee, in linking himself to the film, was bound to be scapegoated. It was all his fault. The best of times and the worst of times.

I mentioned this theory to a few friends. 'Ha!' they would typically reply. 'What about Harry Potter?' or 'What about Bond?' and so on. 'It is all down to Tom!'

But perhaps, I thought, there was something specific to the figure of Reacher that made him harder to translate to the screen, that was maybe, secretly, covertly, bookish. This was why Lee was filled with fresh hope: because Tom was becoming a reader. So he had a chance of being Reacher.

53

PSYCHOSOCIAL ACCELERATION THEORY (*NEVER GO BACK*)

Lee did a rough calculation in his head. New York was around 1,200 miles north; the flight took slightly over three hours; therefore the plane was flying at roughly 400 m.p.h. All very approximate. He could get it more exact if he took the trouble. No point. It wouldn't speed the plane up. It was (he guessed without looking at his watch) ten minutes or so before midnight.

But the question that exercised his brain at this late hour, 20,000 feet over Virginia, in the darkness, was not what speed the plane was flying at, it was: what speed were his thoughts travelling at? How long did it take him to work out that the plane was flying at 400 m.p.h? He'd never wondered about that before. Whatever it was, Reacher would do it faster. But he, Lee, would still have to write it slow. It was one of his rules: *write the slow stuff fast and the fast stuff slow*. Perhaps it was his only rule.

Back on terra firma, going much more slowly, there was something adjacent I had been thinking about: what makes Reacher better? Of course, he was a man mountain. That helped. And he had all the street fighting moves, elevated to a level of surgical precision. But even that was not his real trump card. What set him apart and gave him his edge was a certain quality of thought. He 'noticed' things. He had read Nietzsche and a few pages of Proust, but he was not a major intellectual in any academic sense; and his database, though large and varied, could easily be surpassed by Wikipedia. But he had something else going on: his speed of thought. Which meant that everything in his perceptual field seemed to slow down. The world passes in front of his gaze at the speed of ... writing. This was the key thing about the text, whether writing or reading (but remember it took Lee a whole lot longer to write the book than it took anyone, other than me, to read it): it forced you to slow down. It made you, of necessity, more meditative.

Lee always maintained that the way to understand Reacher was as a primitive who has accidentally been parachuted into modernity: he was a nomadic hunter-gatherer type at heart, pre-agriculture, pre-urbanization, and definitely pre-internet. Pre-just about anything you can think of. Cro-Magnon man, with a toothbrush. A 'gorilla who can paint', as he nicely put it. Kind of archaeological or palaeontological, an archetype who reaches right back into the origins of human history, like he was 100,000 years old, or 200,000, or a million, still roaming about the savanna, efficiently dealing with any wild beasts who make the mistake of crossing his path. A palaeo-empiricist at work.

I guess he ought to know, what with having written it and all.

But that was the point: he had *written* it. He hadn't told a story around the camp-fire. He hadn't spoken it into a recording device and relied on someone else to write it out for him. He had spent a year squirrelled away in his office slowly cranking it out. He was a paragon of slowness. The fast was slow and the slow was also slow. Everything was slow because he was thinking about it and typing it out, slowly, with only two fingers. That was how he worked. It wasn't like you were pressing a button and it all popped up on the screen. It was the same with reading. Can you sit there for four or five hours at a stretch just reading? He could. It made all the difference.

'Psychosocial acceleration theory' has always seemed to me a bit of a misnomer. It should be called 'Psychosocial *deceleration* theory'. Jules Verne was always raving on about how everything was speeding up: now you could go around the world in *eighty days*! Time and space were tending towards zero. But he forgot about how things had also slowed down a lot. Psychosocial acceleration theory hinged on a shift in human history from fast to slow. God, for example, would always have all the time in the world. Eternity, in fact. When the immediate environment was harsh and dangerous, we used to do everything fast, if we had any sense at all – eat fast, drink fast, make love fast. The message was contained in the title, oddly enough, of one of Joel's books: *Kill Kill Faster Faster*. The faster you were, the longer you were liable to live. As soon as you started slowing down, someone faster would annihilate you. You were just baggage as far as the rest of the herd was concerned. A liability. But then the environment changed. It became, overall, with a lot of exceptions to the rule and endless variability, safer, healthier, more comfortable. For the first time in human history, it was possible, at last, to slow down, just a little bit, if you were lucky.

An experiment had been carried out in Newcastle, in the UK. Two groups had to play the same video game, called *Dictator*. You got to kill people or forgive them, depending. One group lived in one part of town, a rough neighbourhood, a quintessentially stressful environment, depressed, unemployed, broke, parentally dysfunctional, prematurely pregnant, socioeconomically speaking way down in the nether regions; the other group was in the more affluent part of town, with a higher income and better nutrition, education, literacy, manners, where people lived longer and teenage girls preferred to go to college. It will surprise no one that there was a marked difference between the two groups: Group 1 did a lot of killing; Group 2 was more forgiving, more altruistic. The term that the social scientists used was 'agreeableness': the Group 2 people were measurably more agreeable. More cooperative and trusting. Less *unpleasant*. The surprising thing was that the contrast between the two groups, separated by only a few miles at most, was greater than that between a city in the United States and the Hadza, hunter-gatherers in Tanzania. (How anyone got them to sit down and play a computer game I have no idea.)

Now project the same difference along the axis of time. The fast people started to give way to the slow people. Think of all those cave paintings – you didn't knock those off in a jiffy. And you had to prepare the paints – they weren't ready to go in tubes. Slowness became a virtue. The whole ecology had changed. You didn't have sabretooths and crocs and assorted carnivores waiting to snap you up around every corner. Within the last few thousand years – a blip in geological time – we started to write things down. Agriculture was taking off and we had to keep track of all those bags of grain. Religions were invariably associated with sacred texts. Painting is myth, writing is religion. Wheat and God – it could all be encompassed by the scribe. Didn't matter whether it was being dictated by the archangel Gabriel or Moses or Allah or Brahman or the Pharaoh, everything was susceptible to being written. Because we had more time. We lived longer, we had time, space, and tools, and the extra brain power to go with it. It was a breakthrough in civilization. Maybe it was even the basis of civilization, civility: slowness. After you; No, after *you*. No rush, relax, take your foot off the pedal, and so on.

The fast guys wanted gratification right here, right now; the slow guys were willing to hold back, to be reasonable, to defer gratification till tomorrow, or the next day. Further ado was OK by them. The slow guys were less violent (turn the other cheek), they could forgive and forget (well, maybe not forget), they could be good Samaritans, not just instantaneous avengers. They were closer to godliness.

It was the question at the core of *Never Go Back*: did Reacher once kill a guy, randomly? And did he, again lacking in restraint, father a child in some far-off place? Neither proposition was impossible or even improbable, but it came down to an argument between fast and slow. Old palaeo-instincts or new civility? Now he has to behave himself, Major Turner insists on it, so we have the one novel in which Reacher kills nobody.

As Elsa said: Reacher has calmness, composure. He can go slow. He doesn't have to be fast. Unlike Tom, he is no fan of car chases.

Reacher is not palaeo-man; he is rather a product of our more recent archaeology. He is an exemplar of slowness. Of writing. Which is why he is no fan of hyperspace or the smartphone or rush hour. Nor of instant coffee. He doesn't expect instant results. He hates the get-rich-quick guys (which is nearly everyone). His paramount value is … patience. And perseverance. *Die Trying*, for example. Or *The Hard Way*.

No *Kill Kill Faster Faster*. With Reacher it was more, 'I'm going to count to three …' Even if he tended to demolish his adversary on 'two', just to be on the safe side. At least it wasn't 'one' or 'zero'. So Reacher is on the side of the angels. The defender of slow.

54

WHILE REACHER SLEEPS

Exhibit A: the works of Jude Hardin.

Jude was an experienced and successful writer, living in Florida. He had already produced several series of novels. And then he discovered Reacher, a few years back.

Lest we forget: writers are also readers. They only become writers because they start off as readers. Would anyone even have the idea of writing a novel unless there were novels already in abundance? Every novel is a string of citations. Jude was just more explicit about it than most. The later works of Jude Hardin sprang up out of the works of Lee Child. He wrote to Lee and asked, politely, if he could make use of the 'Reacher universe' (such is the phrase). Lee nicely said he could, with only one stipulation: Reacher can be referred to, he can leave traces, but he cannot actually be seen. Reacher himself, like some kind of fictional God, must remain invisible, even though his works can be witnessed.

Jude's novel *Velocity* is an ironic exegesis of *Make Me*. The title itself hints – no, it more than hints, it shouts it out – that this is the one thing missing from the Child novel: speed. What is Reacher doing? Answer: snoozing on the job. It's fair comment: he often does. The true action hero shouldn't be fast asleep while everything is happening. If he is sleeping, he has to be sleeping *with* somebody, not just plain old sleeping. *Come on, Reacher! Snap it up! Ten'shun!* It's psychosocial acceleration in practice.

Jude Hardin does for *Make Me* what Tom Stoppard did for Hamlet in *Rosencrantz and Guildenstern Are Dead*: *Velocity* tells you what everyone else is getting up to behind the scenes, or rather on stage, but when the protagonist himself is off. It's the story that Lee Child forgot to tell. Everything that Reacher fails to notice. I have said that Reacher notices things that other people miss. I may have to take that back. In the case of *Make Me*, for example, he fails to spot that there is a nuclear missile right under Mother's Rest. *Reacher, how could you miss that?* The Hardin novel covers or uncovers all of Reacher's blind spots. It inhabits the margins and the crevices and the unperceived.

Nicholas Colt, moreover, is given a simple mission: assassinate Reacher. It shouldn't be that hard. After all, he is snoozing soundly. All you have to do is creep up on him and ... *Whammo!* Curtains for Reacher. On the face of it, these are orders coming from The Circle, the secret agency that covertly oversees the security of the nation and perceives Reacher as a threat, a subversive, a potential terrorist with a bad habit of going about bumping people off. It seems only fair to get rid of him. It is our sacred duty. There are (it is said) documents that conclusively demonstrate he really deserves killing. And Colt is given the job. But his heart is not in it.

I had come across the attitude before. I could even sympathize with it myself to some extent. Even Lee Child could sympathize with it. *Reacher! I'm going to get rid of him one of these days! I'm just working out how.* That sort of thing. He was just too damn successful, he was so good it was just a little bit depressing. Wouldn't the world be better without him? It was logical. I had come across a stray comment online by another writer, who had posted his thoughts on *The Hard Way*. The eleventh in the series, after all. *Surely he would be running out of steam by now,* this reader reasoned. So he reads the book, confident that he will find signs of decline, the waning of inspiration, a certain staleness creeping into the characterization, merely mechanical plotting ... But no! A curse on him, he's still right up there. There's no falling away. He hasn't lost it ... yet. Maybe the next one. The writer/reader concludes: 'It doesn't make you feel good about your own writing, not a little bit.'

Hence the temptation to eliminate Reacher. It was a question of site clearance before you could start to build something new. Unless you got rid of him, he was very solidly planted right there, smack in the way of your bulldozers and backhoes. How could you ever get anything done? Seriously. On the other hand, everybody loves Reacher. It's a dilemma. Colt likes his coffee black too.

Velocity is all about the ambivalence. To be or not to be. Viva Reacher – or RIP? 'Jack Reacher is a rogue vigilante with ties to terrorist organizations.' The Circle doesn't say what organizations. He doesn't look like a jihadi on the rampage, but it could just be a cunning disguise. And we know it's never going to come to court. The time has come for some extra-judicial initiative. Colt has no option, not if he ever wants to see his family again. Unlike Reacher he has a family, a wife, an adopted daughter, and a baby boy he has never seen. And he has a drug cartel on his trail to boot. Caught between a rock and a hard place.

Jude subtly recalls the opening page of *Make Me* by invoking the relatively unusual word 'nothingness': 'I drove through twenty miles of nothingness before I finally came to a sign that said WELCOME TO MOTHER'S REST.' Colt positions himself on top of one of the giant silos, sets up his infrared video camera and the sniper rifle with telescopic lens, and waits for Reacher to stick his nose out of the motel door, looking for a diner. It's the middle of the night. Reacher is in there with Michelle Chang, the PI (in separate rooms). The guy in the plastic chair is outside, keeping half an eye on him. In a way it's already curtains. First sleep, in room 106, then the Big Sleep. The orders are clear: 'Reacher is to be eliminated as soon as he steps out of his motel door.' There is even a clean-up crew waiting to load the body into a van 'and wipe down any blood and tissue splatters'.

But there is another organization in play (yet another that Reacher, still fast asleep, is blissfully unaware of). And these guys are gunning for Nicholas Colt. Colt is wounded but escapes, barely managing to slide down the ladder of the silo. A remote-control device is about to set off the live nuke which, he has recently discovered, is located right beneath the silo and will destroy everything within a hundred-mile radius or maybe set off World War III. Unless, that is, Colt can drive like the devil, with the bullets flying, and the smoke choking, and the helicopter landing, and … I have to stop there. It would be unfair to give it all away. Suffice to say that Reacher survives – he has to if the rest of *Make Me* is going to unfold. But for nearly the entire duration of

Velocity, in the midst of violent mayhem and potentially world-shattering conflict, Reacher's velocity is exactly zero.

Reacher is like one of the guys in that Hemingway short story, 'A Clean, Well-Lighted Place', going on about *nada*. *Nada* this, *nada* that. Reacher not only said nothing, but did nothing. He is a master of inaction. A man at rest in a room.

Until he isn't.

Like a slumbering giant, he only bestirs himself if he really has to.

In *Velocity*, Reacher doesn't get out of bed. Tucked up like a baby. Or a Child. Biding his time, going slow, not doing anything very much at all, almost nothing.

Finally. The light has gone on in his room. He is about to get up. *Make Me* is back.

55

FANMAIL

He doesn't have to 'intuit' everything: sometimes, if he wants to know what people in the world at large are thinking, he just uses plain old email, the way most people do.

```
to: LeeChild
from: infantrycaptain@hotmail.com
subject: We can kick Reacher's ass
```

That was how it had all started. Practically anyone could *say* that they could kick Reacher's ass. This was one of those rare occasions where the claim sounded almost plausible (always supposing that a fictional hero has some kind of ass to kick). *They*, in this case, were an infantry unit embattled and besieged somewhere in Afghanistan. Therefore reasonably tough well-trained warriors, with several tours of duty under their belts, and conceivably on a par with Reacher. Maybe.

Lee had a simple reply. 'Reacher can kick all of your asses. Guaranteed.'

They had bantered on like this for a while, hard-man writer to a bunch of real hard men. They were fans of Reacher and they wanted to fight Reacher. It was normal. They would just be better at it than most.

In Afghanistan, if you weren't actually getting blown to pieces by a car bomb or an IED, there was time for a lot of reading. The works of Lee Child were a great popular favourite. Everyone is reachable, if you try hard enough. Lee Child is no different to anyone else in that regard. His computer is not cut off from the outside world and stored in a safe overnight. He can be contacted, so these guys contacted him, and he replied and they exchanged emails, the thriller writer and the front-line real-world heroes. The ones who were still alive and in one piece.

And then eventually it got serious. Lee asked them what they thought about being in Afghanistan. None of them were all that crazy about it. Few of them had any idea what they were supposed to be doing there. Aside from wanting to take on Reacher, they told him how they felt about their mission impossible. Lee, for anyone who does not know this, has never served in the American army. He has never served in any kind of army. He doesn't have a whole bunch of guns sitting around in his apartment in Manhattan (maybe a few books about firearms, admittedly). But, just as he was capable of thinking or dreaming his way into the secret life of Lydia Lair, so too, in his quasi-mystic, alchemical, Jungian style, he is capable of burrowing into the collective unconscious of the military. And getting the feeling right. As far as the infantry were concerned, he was one of them. They were virtual blood brothers. Which is why they could communicate so openly and plainly, Lee to Delta Force and Delta Force to Lee. Like comrades in arms: no secrets. Copy that.

Lee is an opportunistic writer: magpie-style, he will pick up and use anything to build his novel. Words, ideas, images, sounds, arguments, events, people, history, music, noises, all get thrown into the mix, randomly, involuntarily. In this case, in a spirit of verisimilitude, but also respect, he felt a definite obligation to try to capture the mood and the mentality of actual serving soldiers. So he took one of the emails, from the Captain of Infantry, and put it, almost unedited, into the mouth of Jack Reacher. Here is Reacher in *Nothing to Lose*. He is sympathetic to deserters from a war they couldn't win. At the same time it is the real deal, straight from the front line, direct to Lee: apart from one or two proper names thrown in for good measure, this is all verbatim, unvarnished and unreconstructed:

I went where they told me. I followed orders. I did everything they asked, and I watched ten thousand guys do the same. And we were happy to, deep down. I mean, we bitched and pissed and moaned, like soldiers always do. But we bought the deal. Because duty is a transaction, Vaughan. It's a two-way street. We owe them, they

225

owe us. And what they owe us is a solemn promise to risk our lives and limbs if and only if there's a damn good reason. Most of the time they're wrong anyway, but we like to feel some kind of good faith somewhere. At least a little bit. And that's all gone now. Now it's all about political vanity and electioneering. That's all. And guys know that. You can try, but you can't bullshit a soldier. *They* blew it, not us. They pulled out the big card at the bottom of the house and the whole thing fell down. And guys like Anderson and Crawford are over there watching their friends getting killed and maimed and they're thinking, why? Why should we do this shit? (pages 475–6)

Of course, it was entirely down to Lee that, on top of the above, the Mr Big presiding over the aptly named town of Despair is an evangelical Christian desirous of Apocalypse. And that Reacher says to him, 'We're all atheists. You don't believe in Zeus or Thor or Neptune or Augustus Caesar or Mars or Venus or Sun Ra. You reject a thousand gods. Why should it bother you if someone else rejects a thousand and one?' I don't think he got that from the Captain.

Perhaps (as I have suggested) Lee is inventing nothing and all his fiction is only a permutation and reconfiguring of truth. But in this case there was nothing in the least hypothetical or chimerical about Reacher's speech. It was not something Lee had intuited, smoking his pipe towards enlightenment. Rather it was pure quotation, from a reliable source. There was nothing tentative or tenuous or sketchy about Reacher's perspective. It was all 100% pure and solid and authentic, hammered straight out of the coal-face.

So of course not everyone liked that. They didn't want truth; they wanted the lie. They wanted fiction, which is why they had bought the novel in the first place, and now they were getting fact. And they didn't like it, didn't believe it, were determined to deny it. Didn't want to know about the real human cost of war. The empirical side of the equation. (Vaughan's husband, for example, is brain-dead, lying in a clinic.) Lee was bombarded by emails and letters of complaint. He was denounced as a cheese-eating surrender monkey. Coward, traitor, gay, spineless, rat, anti-American, anti-Christ. An avalanche of hate mail. Specifically coming from people who were supposed to love the American army and yet who, when the American army had something to say for themselves, turned out to hate them. The offending pages were torn out time and again, graffitied, had messages (unfavourable) scrawled over them in big fat red marker pen. Some sheets appeared to have been used as toilet paper. White feathers would have been less of a health hazard. It all came straight through his letter box in Manhattan. The mail office at Random House, in those days, would just send it all on to the author, without any preliminary sorting or checking. He got the lot.

The irony was not lost on Lee. So long as he made it up, everyone was happy, they were ecstatic; if he happened upon the truth, it caused an outcry. As T. S. Eliot said, humankind cannot bear very much reality.

Spring

56

THE FORTUNE COOKIE

Lee had plenty of fans among gaolbirds. He had gone into prisons, from time to time, even one in New Zealand, to do readings and signings and so forth. Just with an even more captive audience than usual. But there was one reader – Kirk Bloodsworth – who became, in turn, the subject of one of his stories. Almost like Lydia, but he didn't have to pay a cent, even to a charity. It was a true story. Lee wasn't lying on his sofa and communing with the collective unconscious. For a change, he had done the kind of thing I tended to do all the time: go and see a guy and have a chat with him (Kirk wanted to call him Reacher), take some notes, and try to get the story down straight. Which was all part of the 'Exoneration Project'.

Kirk had read the beginning of *Killing Floor* ('I was arrested in Eno's Diner') and had the opportunity to reflect that he and Reacher had quite a lot in common: Kirk, like Reacher, was innocent. Post-conviction DNA testing had finally saved his bacon. But until the case was revisited, and relatively new forensic procedures were brought to bear, he spent many years on Death Row. Where he got to hang out with rapists and murderers, who tried to treat him as one of their own. But he wasn't having any of it. He maintained his innocence, right to the end, and repulsed all overtures from fellow inmates. He had to stuff his ears at night with toilet paper to stop the roaches creeping in, and during the day it was similar, with convicts in place of actual roaches.

Rewind to the trial. The jury found him guilty in a couple of hours flat and the courtroom exploded in applause and cheering. The prosecution had eye-witness testimony, but the testimony depended entirely on his face having been all over the television and the newspapers on account of the police identifying him as their number one suspect. There was a dead nine-year-old girl a couple of miles away. They thought he had done it because somebody had to have done it. And they were under pressure to come up with a conviction. And one of his neighbours suggested he was a likely-looking candidate. There was no real evidence as such, but an awful lot of testifying. The neighbours didn't like him on account of his wife and the flophouse. He had married Wanda because she made him feel good and he missed her when she was away, but there was no denying she was never going to win any popularity contests. Before that he had been in the Marines and had been trained to survive captivity in god-forsaken hellholes. He was honourably discharged, but joining up had probably been a mistake too: he wasn't sure he necessarily wanted to kill anyone, which might help to explain why he ended up punching his own lieutenant in the head. And he had started out as a crab fisherman and party animal, with a fondness (like Lee) for smoking weed. But he had been brought up by his parents to do the right thing. And he had never done anything he was ashamed of. He had been a discus champion. A childhood like a Norman Rockwell painting, with gardens, and fences, and bicycles.

But there's always a point in everyone's narrative where you might have gone in another direction. The 'if-only' moment. Kirk was no exception. He had a big, fat chance to go another way. And he had received a clear message, up there in neon lights, straight from the gods. Like nearly everyone who receives a message from the gods, he hadn't taken it seriously enough at the time. Jung would call it 'meaningful coincidence'. The kind of thing that sensible souls would not tolerate in narrative. And yet there it was, all over everyday life, every second of the day. The world was full of meaningful coincidences, and it took an effort of the will and imagination to drain the meaning and coincidence out completely. It was impossible to eradicate synchronicity and alchemical conjunctions. Least of all in the case of Kirk.

It happened in 1984, in April, when he was driving to his wedding. Of course, it was this marriage that had set him off down the road that led to Death Row. A few people – perhaps with premonitions of how it could all go badly pear-shaped for young Kirk – had already told him to rethink. But he was a headstrong sort of guy and he knew what he felt for her and had no doubts. Life would be good, so he thought. So he hops in the car and drives off. But the drive takes a while and he is hungry as he crosses the bridge over the Chesapeake, taking you from Maryland to Baltimore. It's 11.30 and the wedding isn't until 1. So he searches around amid the clutter of his car for a snack of some kind, an uneaten bag of chips perhaps or a packet of crackers. Which is when he comes across the fortune cookie.

He recalls he had been given it as a parting gift at a Chinese restaurant, but he had already eaten so he wasn't hungry right then and had just chucked it in the back of the car. He knew it would come in handy some day. Today is just that day. So he picks it up, takes the wrapping off, shoves it in his mouth, and chucks the wrapping on the floor. But the traffic on the bridge has stalled and he chances to look down – pure afterthought – at the small piece of paper on which the fortune foreseen for him by his fortune cookie has been written. It is like the voice of the Delphic Oracle. But better, because there is nothing in the least enigmatic or ambiguous about the message. It is as plain as they come.

TURN AROUND

Just two words. Nothing fancy. Short and sweet. But an imperative, addressed specifically to this reader and no other. Kirk looks at it once, considers for a moment. He could indeed turn around right then and there, as per the recommended course of action. But he has a ring in his pocket bought from a pawnshop for $25. He doesn't want to turn around. It's like getting orders from the dumb lieutenant. He doesn't really believe the fortune cookie. No rational being would. He smiles and keeps on driving, over the bridge, following the signs for Baltimore and the absurd destiny that lies in wait for him there. But now, many years later, having emerged from Death Row, he believed. He looked back and wished he had taken the cookie seriously.

They got the right man in the end, thanks to the DNA database. The nine-year-old girl got justice and Kirk was released and even became something of a celebrity. But another strange coincidence: he had actually been in prison with the very guy who had raped and murdered the girl. Kirk could understand now why the killer – who was in for another offence – was 'squirrelly' and tended to shy away from him. Coincidence upon coincidence.

Life – at least after the dominion of the self-replicating amoeba – relied 100% on the alchemical conjunction of divergent beings. And now, in the form of the 'Fortune Cookie' chapter in a book that did not yet exist, there was another coincidence, between writer and reader. Kirk, the exoneree, had read the stories of Lee Child and now Lee Child was hearing his story and writing about it. And Kirk was reading his own story, retold, mediated through the Child keyboard. Beyond their meeting and their conversation, there was a perfect circle turning around and binding them together. Maybe that was all Lee was ever doing: writing down the lives of his readers.

TURN AROUND

Kirk had failed to turn around, but now Lee was turning around for him, opening up the quantum door in the prison-house of life and showing all those other roads you could drive down, if you should choose. If you *could* choose.

57

FEAR AND FIREARMS IN LAS VEGAS

'So you're Lee Child?' He was looking askance at the name emblazoned on the badge that hung around my neck like an Olympic medal.

'That's me,' I said, trying hard to look every bit a tall, slim, *New York Times* best-selling author, half-poet half-pirate.

'Welcome to Shotshow, Mr Child.'

It wasn't just the security guy I was worried about either. The Shotshow (technically, SHOTshow, Shooting, Hunting, Outdoor, Trade) is the firearms industry's 'Greatest Show on Earth' and there were several thousand wannabe Dirty Harry types roaming about the aisles desperate for any excuse to whip out their weapons. Lee Child had been signing books there the day before and I purloined his pass in a feeling-lucky-punk kind of way. What the hell, I was in.

They say there are more guns in America than human beings, and most of them were in Las Vegas, at the Venetian complex. The Shotshow occupied several floors of a building roughly the size of Wembley Stadium, wedged between a couple of casinos. I was (it said so on my badge) an 'exhibitor' on stand number 13612. And the numbers went way beyond that. I had a notion, in a spirit of scientific inquiry, of counting the number of guns on display, but it was like counting grains of sand on the beach or stars in the sky. I gave up after 100 million or so.

Enough research, I was more into the romance. In thrall to the thriller and the western and the film noir, how could I not be bewitched by the sheer poetry of names such as Winchester, Springfield, Walther ('Bond, James Bond'), Beretta, Smith & Wesson ('the most powerful handgun in the world'), Sig Sauer, Mossberg, Heckler & Koch, and the like? Not to mention the nostalgia of tucking a classic Colt six-shooter or two in my belt. Or – Che in the jungle now – how could I not go and ogle the Kalashnikov, conspiratorially morphed, in a way every decent thriller writer will understand, into Kalashnikov *USA* ('Russian tradition, American innovation')? Like a kleptomaniac at Harrods, I didn't know which way to turn. But I kept going back to the Glock, the Jack Reacher handgun of choice, light but powerful, with no less than seventeen bullets per clip.

Maybe it was the smell of powder or gun oil, but there was definitely an aphrodisiac quality to Shotshow. I kid you not when I say that a higher than normal proportion of the women there struck up a conversation with me. They weren't all trying to sell me extra ammo either. Nor were they in thrall to the name badge. 'Honey, if I had hair like yours, I'd be a real bitch,' said one smoking gun-toter. But the truth is I only had eyes for Amanda Lynn Mayhew. Can you still say 'huntress', à la Diana? OK, hunter, then, and fitness fanatic. (She owns a magazine called *Fytness Fanatik* and is in training for a body-building competition, moreover. 'Doing a lot of tightening and toning.')

She was making a guest appearance at the '5.11 Tactical' stand. 5.11 Tactical don't sell guns, only the kind of clothes you might want to wear if you happen to be carrying a gun. Rugged but cool. For decades they have been supplying the FBI and the CIA. Now they are kitting out the cast of *Never Go Back* (and possibly Lee too). But I think I can guarantee that Tom Cruise will never look half as good as Amanda Lynn in her 'Range Tights'.

She worked out that I was not in fact Lee Child. She had been hoping to meet Lee, have a chat with him, get his autograph, and so on. So, in all honesty, she was just a little disappointed I was only a guy pretending to be Lee Child. But she kindly promised not to give me up and have me legally shot to pieces by the well-armed security people. She works for the Department of Natural Resources in Canada and regularly shoots moose and deer and bear in northern Ontario. Anything with antlers or horns or even just paws is asking for it on the North American continent, I realized, as I watched all the promotional movies with people creeping up behind assorted critters and getting themselves YouTubed grinning their heads off in a warm embrace with their dying victims. Amanda Lynn Mayhew made a pretty good case for the necessity of doing this sort of thing, with a view to stopping deer from taking over the world. OK, but I still found myself crying out, from time to time, 'Come on, you pathetic bastards, at least leave the bloody buffalo alone!' Or bison, whatever.

So I guess that rules me out of going on any kind of hunting expedition in the wilderness with Amanda Lynn Mayhew. Pity. But liking the feel of a handgun and a semi-automatic (so light!), I fancy I could definitely take a pop at 'hostiles' (i.e. fellow beings, similarly equipped) and stop them taking over the world. But there is an interesting split here in the gun-owning community. The hunters are a little bit wary of the urban cowboys. Amanda Lynn Mayhew insisted she only uses a rifle, a Weatherby Vanguard, not a pistol. And Lee, who wrote a convincing home invasion scene in *Make Me*, which I was obviously replaying in my head, similarly poured scorn when I spoke to him later. 'All the FBI guys point out that civilians with guns never succeed in seeing off home invaders. They're always too groggy, or they forget where the gun is.' Lee was appearing at a gun show, was photographed cradling an enormous semi-automatic weapon in his arms, and was wearing Tactical 5.11 pants, but at the same time he was no fan of unlimited gun-play.

Jack Reacher, although an expert marksman (sniper-level), is no kind of trigger-happy hero. If the gun-lovers who queued around the block to buy a signed copy of *Make Me* read the book carefully, they will discover that its protagonist never reaches for a gun unless he really has to. He only carries a folding toothbrush, for goodness' sake. As a rule he prefers to hospitalize bad guys with his elbows, or just head-butt them to death.

Trigger-happy heroes were, however, in attendance over at the vast NRA enclave. A lot of them. They were all constitutional experts, although they had a tendency to zero in specifically on the Second Amendment. They didn't like Hillary Clinton much. It was almost as if it was an act of treason not to bear arms. I came within a whisker of signing up. Well, there was a special deal on. And they were throwing in a free subscription to *American Rifle*. I too wanted to 'Stand and Fight' (as their slogan has it) – is that so bad?

Lee scoffed when I mentioned my near-miss. 'Right-wing politics in the USA has lost any connection with reality,' he said. '*If everyone had guns in their pockets, then there would be no more mass shootings* – it's cobblers. No one has ever stopped one of these mass shootings. It's all just toys for boys. Or fashion accessories.'

I couldn't even find my way out of Shotshow, I had to ask somebody. Maybe there is no way out. Shotshow is a microcosm of a locked-and-loaded nation, with the safety off. As the ad says, this is 'Remington Country'. The simple fact that even I, a rank amateur, could go and kit myself out like Rambo – and I was seriously tempted by the multiple-grenade launcher – is testimony to the militarization of an entire society. Something like Sparta. I am sympathetic to the neo-frontier spirit. I want to be a hero too, of course. I get the whole will-to-power/hell-is-other-people/ kill-Bill thing, I really do. It was exactly what Lee was there for: not the hardware but the software, the mentality, that was driving it all. The gun-toters buying his books thought they were getting something from him, and all along he was getting something from them.

As I strolled up the Strip in the sun, I was courted by Elvis and Mickey Mouse and Scooby-Doo and Darth Vader. At the Venetian complex, I could take a gondola along the 'Grand Canal'. Or, further up the street, go and eat at the Eiffel Tower. Everything in Las Vegas is fake. Even the sky is a lie (a *trompe l'oeil* concoction straight out of David Copperfield's box of tricks). It makes you want to reach for a gun.

There would be a shooting on this very street just a few hours later, outside the Bellagio hotel/casino. Nobody batted an eyelid: a cop car and an ambulance came and went. Maybe the gun in America is the last refuge of truth. It's an exercise in hardcore empirical epistemology: like Dr Johnson kicking a stone, when you get hit by a bullet, you really know it, there's no more room for doubt. Maybe dousing myself in elk urine (I could buy a bottle at the show, 'with enhanced estrous') and climbing a tree with a crossbow over my shoulder would make me feel more real for a while in a land of dreams and delusions and semi-naked 'police-women' with big truncheons. I was passing myself off as Lee

Child, but they were all passing themselves off as Jack Reacher or John Wayne or Amanda Lynn Mayhew.

Lee had flown off to some gig in Palm Springs. He was riding around in a new Rolls-Royce at the time (and it had to be 'new' – it was specified in the contract). I was stuck at the airport on account of a blizzard in New York. So I called him up and thanked him for the use of the ID. 'Ha!' he said. 'I guess we're interchangeable now.' Manifestly we weren't: he was in the back of a Rolls, I was stuck in an airport lounge. And yet …

It came to me when I was hanging around at Houston International the next day, leafing through a *Make Me* at the airport bookstore: Lee thought of himself as a reader when he was writing, but, conversely, we readers imagined ourselves as Lee Child while we were reading. We picked up someone else's badge. For a brief hour of bliss, we became interchangeable.

58

THE LETTERS PAGES OF THE
LONDON REVIEW OF BOOKS

4 March 2016
Get real
Christopher Tayler quotes Jack Reacher, in one of Lee Child's novels, claiming that he doesn't work out, and that his 'extreme mesomorph physique, with a six-pack like a cobbled city street', is 'genetic' (*LRB*, 4 February). Nonsense. Six-packs are not genetic, except in the sense that we are all originally endowed with them, more or less. But most of us lose them as adults, owing to bad diet and lack of exercise. It is physically impossible that Reacher could have a 'natural' six-pack with his diet and lifestyle. Even in fiction some minimum of realism is necessary.
J. P. Roos
Helsinki

11 March 2016
Ex-body-builder Montana Sam responds (unpublished)
So the question is, could a make-believe character, given his imaginary diet (he doesn't actually eat, since he's imaginary to begin with), have 'real' abs?

Already, this is problematic.

The good news for those who want Reacher to have abs is he 'drinks' an unbelievable amount of coffee and he does not cloud the coffee with problematic fats, like cream, dairy creamer, milk, or, pause for effect, sugar.

The bad news for those who want Reacher to have visible abs is he doesn't tan (except when he's digging holes with a spade in the Florida Keys with his shirt off – women, and some men, swoon here), and abs don't visibly shout out at you without the highlight of a tan (because different shades of brown are more visible than different shades of white).

Now, let's get to Reacher's diet, which is the crux of the matter. He seems to pile it in, yet he seems to eat sporadically. Diner food is noted for too much sodium, which will not help visible ab definition. Reacher does not seem fond of rice cakes, boiled chicken or fish, baked potatoes without butter, salad without dressing, or, the secret recourse of fashion models, cocaine.

Reacher lives an interesting dualism of highly sedentary (all those Greyhound bus rides) activity (or non-activity) combined with extreme physical action.

One would think killing people would add to the stress level, which might keep the bodyfat content low, but, then again, Reacher is not bothered by the body count.

Other query: does Reacher shave his abdominals and chest to highlight their definition?

Absolutely not.

Lee Child makes it clear in every novel that Reacher's appearance before a mirror is only a minor facilitator to allow him a glimpse of 'using the fingers of his hand as a comb'.

No mention of a loving and admiring swipe down his pecs to his abs.

If Reacher is 'manly' enough to have chest/ab hair, how much does he have, because this would interfere with the view, if not the existence, of his abs?

On the whole, I'm not sure delving into the minutiae of an imaginary creature's musculature is a healthy pursuit.

59

A BLONDE WALKS THROUGH THE DOOR WITH A GUN IN HER HAND

Carl had been memorizing the American presidents.

Inevitably Lee Child got in there. Not as a president, but representing one in some complicated Swedish way. Carl visualized Lee sitting on a sofa, holding a child on his lap. On closer inspection that child turns out to be a car (a small one). At the same time he is smoking weed. 'Now guess which president this is,' he said.

I had no idea. In fact to say I had no idea is an exaggeration. I had as many ideas as a bowlful of porridge.

'He comes after Ulysses S. Grant,' Carl said, as if that was going to help.

I pressed my hands to my temples. Still nothing. Less than nothing. I was fairly sure it couldn't be George Washington. 'Carl, I'm going to need a lot more coffee before I can figure that one out.' We were in New York, sitting on one of the benches in La Colombe, on Vandam, across the street from Mae Mae. 'Or maybe a dose of one of those drugs you're on.'

'Come on!' says he, frustrated. 'It's obvious, isn't it? Rutherford Hayes.'

'Oh yeah,' says I, smacking my forehead. (Just to be clear, this was ironic.)

'What is the name of Lee's daughter?'

'Ruth ... OK, the child, so that's the first syllable.'

'What kind of car? It's a ...'

'Ford. OK. I get it.'

'And then he is smoking ...'

'Thus producing a "haze".'

'I told you it was obvious,' he said, triumphantly.

Just then President Haze himself appeared outside the café, like a huge genie conjured up by this obscure incantation ritual, in a cloud of smoke. Probably legal. He stubbed out the cigarette in a way that, strictly speaking, could be considered ecologically unfriendly. He plonked himself down on a stool, peeling off about ten layers, until he became really quite svelte all over again.

Which almost saved me from Carl explaining how it was that he remembered that Ashgabat is the capital of Turkmenistan. (If you want to know, you are going to have to ask him. I forget.)

'I've come to a definite conclusion,' Lee announced, picking up the steaming mug of coffee. (We were all drinking it black – we had to if we wanted to be in the Child gang.) 'Philip Seymour Hoffman died on account of *not taking enough* drugs.' Hoffman had lived just around the corner in West Village.

Carl, who had studied the matter with forensic rigour, demurred. 'But apart from the heroin, they found traces of cocaine, benzodiazepines, and amphetamines in his bloodstream.'

Lee looked around the café. 'You'll be hard put to find anybody here who doesn't. It's West Village for chrissake.'

'Then,' Carl said, calling his bluff, 'there is the small matter of the fifty envelopes of heroin in his apartment.'

'Exactly!' Lee said. 'The idiot had stopped taking drugs for seven or eight years. Went clean. Then he goes back and he doesn't realize how the purity has increased while he's been gone. It used to be three parts out of four talcum powder. Now it's three parts pure. Supply and demand. It was *not* doing drugs for so long that killed him. Stopping is worse than starting.'

'Why would you *not* want to kill yourself?' Carl asked.

'You don't want to kill yourself,' Lee said, 'because you don't want to miss what's going on. You want knowledge. About your grandchildren. Or whoever. But really what do you know about any of it? Looked at over the long term, the lifetime of the planet, you basically know nothing anyway. So what's the difference? What difference would it make, seriously? At a certain point, the pain of dying and the pain of living are equivalent, so it all evens out.'

Carl wanted to know about *Night School*. How was it going?

'Sometimes I think it's crap,' Lee said. He was tearing a chocolate croissant in two. It seemed to help. They're good at La

243

Colombe. (I think they come from City Bakery, if you want to know.) 'Other times I reckon it's not too bad.'

'Is it as good as *Make Me*?' Carl asked.

'I don't know,' Lee said. 'It's different, that's for sure. I mean, at some level it's the same, it's got to have Reacher in it, obviously. But, secretly, I'm trying to make it as different as possible.' Stuffed in the other half of croissant. 'The last one, that was a real novel. Almost classical. Detailed description of locale, for example. Novelistic all the way through. Patient build-up. I probably had to do that with the mad professor here leaning on me. On my best behaviour.'

'Metonymic,' I said. I often slip that word in. Nobody really knows what I'm going on about.

'Whereas this one is more like a movie. Not a script. But it's faster. No one is gradually piecing anything together. It relies on *revealed exposition*. A cop drives up, gives you the information you've been looking for, then drives off again. Speeds things up no end.'

'More metaphoric,' I said.

Carl was laughing at the letter to the *London Review of Books* about Reacher's abs. 'It's a serious issue,' Lee said. 'It's like a monument. Architecture. You can't pull it down. It'd be an act of vandalism.'

I listed all the techniques Montana Sam had mentioned with a view to showcasing the ripped musculature. Tanning. Shaving. Low sodium. All neglected by Reacher.

'See,' said Lee, 'that's just it. Reacher doesn't care. But he has great abs all the same. Without caring.'

But, and this has to be remembered, Lee Child is not Jack Reacher. He did care. Maybe not too much about the abs as such. He was thinking more about the 20% of readers on Amazon who 'hated' him, did nothing but bitch about the last one. 'Do you think I should care?' he asked. He wasn't sure whether to engage or remain aloof.

Carl went on about his friend Tom McCarthy, who never read a single one of the reviews of *Remainder*.

Lee said he didn't read *all* of them. There were (at that moment) about 2,000 on Amazon (and they keep on multiplying). Who could read them all? 'The professional critics at least try to overcome whatever mood they're in at the time. The amateurs – it's all a mood thing. They can be … fickle.' He was quoting a 5-star review when Jessica Lehrman walked in and sat down next to us.

(She isn't blonde and she didn't have a gun in her hand, but otherwise it was similar.)

60

THE END OF THAT CONVERSATION, IN WHICH LEE COMPARES HIMSELF TO HOMER

Maybe it was the Jessica Lehrman effect, I don't know, but Carl was boasting about his next challenge: memorizing the whole of Baudelaire's *Les Fleurs du mal*.

'How long are you allowing for this?' I said. 'It would take me a couple of days to remember one poem.'

'I thought maybe a week would do it,' he said. He was due to have dinner with a French woman back in Stockholm and he wanted to impress her. It had to be in the original French, naturally.

'How about just the sonnets?' I suggested. 'Or the whole of the *Tableaux parisiens* section. Fewer than twenty poems. Wouldn't that be enough?'

Carl didn't want to scale down, though. He wanted to scale up. 'Maybe it should be ... the *Odyssey*?' I don't know if he was talking about the Ancient Greek original or not.

Lee was interested by the idea of trying to memorize Baudelaire. He had a second-to-none velcro memory, but he didn't usually go out of his way to memorize in any methodical fashion. 'How do you think you would go about it? Would it be the rhyme scheme? Or would you treat it as a narrative, try to get it all into some kind of order?'

Carl said he had been in touch recently with a guy who could memorize a string of random numbers, up to around 200. Like pi to 200 decimal places. So Baudelaire shouldn't be too hard, he thought. (The guy asked flat out *not* to be contacted by Carl ever again, please: he was too busy memorizing stuff to be bothered by any actual communication as such from whomever.)

'Everything before Homer,' I said, 'it was all mnemonics. You couldn't write anything down. You had to have a way of remembering it. I think if you got it wrong, reciting the story, you were ceremonially sacrificed. I bet that helped the memory no end.'

Lee thought about it. 'Everything after Homer too. Including *Make Me*. It's all mnemonics. Little memory triggers all the way through. So it sticks in your head.'

Jessica and I went to the counter to get in yet another round of coffees. We were talking about a rap artist called Killer Mike. She showed me some of the photos she had taken of him on tour. When we got back Lee was telling Carl one of his great secrets. Carl was planning to write a Scandi noir thriller. He had this idea of sitting in his office on September 1 and 'stealing' some of his inspiration, like osmosis, and then writing it in a month. Maybe just replace Jack Reacher with Jackie Reacher or something like that. Lee was fine with that. He approved of stealing.

'Lee, you know lots of old stuff in the field,' I said. 'John D. MacDonald and all that. Can't Carl just steal one of those?'

Lee nodded thoughtfully. He referenced one writer who had simply glued together chapters from different books. The composite work was published but nobody even noticed it was a pure rip-off until the author pointed it out himself. Lee vowed to find some old mystery story that Carl could simply purloin, rebrand, update, or maybe collage. 'Everybody is stealing from everybody else,' he said. 'So nobody is. Andy, you would know the word for that.'

I rubbed my chin. 'Mass kleptomania?'

'Yeah, but literary.'

'Plagiarism? Intertextuality? Collective unconscious?'

'Sort of thing. Nothing new under the sun.'

We all nodded sagely. Including Jessica. She was kind of shocked, though, you could tell. She was used to hanging out with rappers, who respected artistic integrity. Next thing Lee was suggesting writing a blurb right then and there before Carl had even written a word. Pure scam, of course. Or maybe the collective unconscious at work. What he liked about Carl was that he wasn't thinking like a writer any more. He wasn't making a big deal out of it, or saying, in the manner of Martin Amis, 'Hey, Ma, look, I'm writing!' He was thinking more like a pragmatist or a bank robber. Or a pirate. Which is how he thought of himself.

But he had one more piece of advice, relevant even to pirates. I had been talking about this story I was writing about a writer who comes up with a hero bigger and stronger than he is, but it turns out he is plagiarizing some other writer. Unless it is the other way around. I was still tweaking it. 'You have to think like a reader,' he said. 'Ask yourself what you would like to happen if you were reading the story.'

Carl asked for an example.

'What about *Gone Tomorrow*?' I asked. Set in New York. 'The mad subway scene at the beginning.' I knew it was often used in creative writing classes as an example of how to kick off a novel.

I don't know if it had anything to do with Jessica or not, but he didn't zero in on the subway scene. Great opening, but then he got stuck, didn't know what was coming next. Then he had an idea. A blonde walks through the door holding ... a knife and other weapons. 'I introduce this beautiful, mysterious woman,' he said. 'I started out thinking: I want my hero to go to bed with her. And then I thought: hold on, isn't the reader going to be asking, *What if she is ... bad?*'

Carl was leaving, he had a dinner to go to. So did Lee. 'A lot can hinge on a single letter,' he said, putting his coat back on. 'From *bed* to *bad*.'

61

TWEETS

@LeeChildReacher @AVFCOfficial I'm STILL pissed about Cruise playing Reacher, I feel betrayed by you Mister Child.

@LeeChildReacher I tried watching the Reacher movie, being a fan I couldn't get thru 20 mins. Cruise is not Reacher, never will be.

@LeeChildReacher @andymartinink Still feel betrayed by Cruise playing Reacher, way to f*ck over your fans for a paycheck Child, burn in hell

Every time I read a #JackReacher book I think @TomCruise are u frickin kidding me! He's about as #JackReacher as my nan!!!

Tom Cruise returns as Jack Reacher: Never Go Back. They got that title because he should Never Go Back to that role.

@SiobhanMoloney1 he was cast because he bought the movie rights! #miscast

Watching Jack Reacher as I love the books. No no no no no flipping no Tom Cruise is not him. Liam Neeson is Jack Reacher WTF no no no

@popsmac I would hope @LeeChildReacher was forced to comply — no one in their right mind would cast that role with cruise @TheRealBookSpy

@dongranger @LeeChildReacher Tom Cruise playing Reacher has to be the worst casting in the history of movie making.

Loving #KillingFloor but the overuse of 'shrugged' is killing me @LeeChildReacher

Reading a Lee Child book at the moment, but must say, the he said, she said does get on my nerves a bit

The author I'm reading must get paid by period, but who am I to say he has numerous books published, better shut up or Jack Reacher 🥃

Huge lee child fan, however the motivation behind the bad guys plans in 'without fail' was disappointingly weak. 'Persuader' next

Don't like the Jack Reacher books. I've tried but I find them really slow and un-gripping.

There are a lot of bad lines in Jack Reacher but chief among them is, 'you think I'm a hero? I'm a drifter with nothing to lose.'

If Amazon bookshops reduce the number of Jack Reacher thrillers clogging up the world, I'm all for them.

Lee Child talking some sense for once (instead of writing a load of boilerplate, cryptofascist, chestwig bollocks ...)

Damn you Hollywood!! Jack Reacher is 6'5" and Tom Cruise 5'7". You lied to me Hollywood!! you lied and ruined my life. Damn you to hell!!

@thisgreyspirit EVERYONE loves Lee Child. Except those that haven't read him.

@thisqreyspirit @paraicodonnell who? Lee Child? Oh my God I read my first one last year they're like crack. I don't know how he does it.

And Lee Child. Lee fucking Child. Jack Reacher is my life belt. Imagine. Well, I did say.

@albertocairo @LeeChildReacher read every single one of them my friend! You're hooked now, they're like literary crack!

@LeeChildReacher Thanks a lot for Jack Reacher man. Ur books have helped me find the JR in me, the mysterious free spirited guy. God bless!

Finishing my 6th Jack Reacher's book. Awesome. @LeeChildReacher, Brilliant histories. Brilliant main character. Thanks for those books.

Really enjoying this Lee Child thriller. Jack Reacher sure knows how to methodically kick down a door. Also he's like really tall

Just once it would be nice to see a thread about how great Lee Child books are without anyone making reference to the films.

@mygoditsraining Also the Reacher novels are stupidly entertaining. Samey but goddamn Lee Child can write the shit out of that idea.

Can believe it: 'Lee Child's Reacher thrillers were statistically certified as the most addictive novels in commercial fiction'

@LeeChildReacher in bed reading Echo Burning I am addicted I can't put it down. I love Jack Reacher xxx

@LadyKirsty1982 you delved into Lee Child's Jack Reacher books? I just picked up The Affair. They. Are. Awesome (and plentiful)!

@DanSmithAuthor He'd be too cool for school, Lee Child. With his semi-automatic weapon and his Benson and Hedges.

@vancerains loved 'Make Me' by Lee Child. I'm crazy about the whole Reacher series

I am addicted to the Jack Reacher novels. There, I said it. #JackReacher #LeeChild

I'm flying through these Jack Reacher books, they are awesome #jackreacher #leechild

@LeeChildReacher's latest Reacher is amazing! With each instalment, the writing gets better, the dialogs sharper, the story more captivating

There were 51 people ahead of me when I reserved the new Lee Child book with @WiltsLibraries — and now it is my turn #reacher

Need to sleep, but ... #JackReacher
@LeeChildReacher

#BooksWeLove Is anyone today writing complex
novels in style of John Le Carre? @LeeChildReacher
is in that level, but I've got/read all his

@LeeChildReacher Make me. Best one ever. Chilling
and awesome. Won't sleep tonight.

How good is @LeeChildReacher #makeme loving it.

Right, I'm outta here. My Kindle is calling and
so is #JackReacher #LeeChild

I love Lee Child. With the same depth of passion
which I hate Nicholas Sparks, I love Lee Child.

@LeeChildReacher Loving Reading my first Reacher
novel Killing Floor. Hooked. Can't put it down!!

I love the #JackReacher books just when you think
you've got it ... You're wrong. @LeeChildReacher
you're one very talented clever guy #ThankU

Make Me ... another fantastic Jack Reacher
thriller 😢. A superb cerebral page turner from
Lee Child, yet again 👌

The more I read crime fiction from around the
globe, the more I realise Lee Child has no peer.
He really is in a class of his own as a writer

@andymartinink @LeeChildReacher have recommended
to a friend who said Lee Child books are his sole
'literary indulgence'

On page 166 of 420 of Echo Burning, by Lee Child:
Holy crap this is good!

@LeeChildReacher Hi lee, I love the reacher
books. I hear the next one will be the last?
Please don't kill him off.

62

300 PAGES, ONE INSIGHT

'I've got nothing!' he said. 'Nothing.'

Just in case I missed it the first time. Emphatic.

Lee had been bragging about how he once won the Writers' Police Academy shooting competition. A bit like Will Smith in *Men in Black*, he managed to take down all the bad guys, avoid shooting little girls and old ladies, and finally kill the suicide bomber before he blew everyone to pieces. He could have been a G-man or PI, had he been that way inclined, or more likely the Mr Big of some criminal network. Professor Moriarty. If his readers ever desert him, watch out for a new crime wave, of the non-fictional variety. He made coffee, then we left for the conversation ('The Craft of Fiction') at the Center for Fiction on 52nd Street. He ran a hand through his hair in the mirror on the way out and tried to straighten his crumpled t-shirt. He was going, as usual, for the unshaven, disreputable look.

Maybe it was something to do with the subway. A suspicion of the inferno below the sunlit surface. Even on 86th Street. In fact, especially on 86th, because if you are going downtown, you have to burrow down another level to find the right train. Down and down again. And then downtown. You can't say that the New York subway system is one of the circles of hell (well, not any more) but, on the other hand, there is something about it that inspires thoughts of sinners and suffering, even without the rats skittering about.

'You know,' he said, while we were standing on the downtown platform, waiting for the 'B' train, 'you do have one insight in *Reacher Said Nothing*.'

'Good to know,' I said. I don't want to sound grudging here. It really was good to know, but in truth it was only a few months before that he had said there were two insights in the book. One was to do with the musical side (onomatopoeia and the voice and all that) and the other was how Reacher was capable of a lot of *inaction* (contemplation, ratiocination, inwardness) alongside the more manifest action scenes. So you could say my stock had gone down by 50%. But I guess if you add it all up, it's more like three insights. But anyway, it was just the one that Lee was conscious of on this particular day. On account of the subway, and the Writers' Police Academy, but also the writing of *Night School*.

'Do you remember when I gave you the big reveal?'

'Middle of January, last year.'

'That's right. Central Park was still frozen. And you said something like, "You evil mastermind."'

'*Evil mastermind bastard*, in fact.'

'Yeah, all that. I was a bit shocked, to be honest.'

'What!' Now it was my turn to be shocked. He was a hard guy to shock.

'I'd never thought about it before. You said I was all the bad guys I had ever dreamed up. All rolled up into one.'

'True.'

'That's the insight.' We were looking along the tunnel, uptown. Not total darkness. You couldn't see the headlamps of the 'B' train yet, but there was a suggestive cone of light bending around a curve. Lee said, 'I'd always thought of myself as more like Reacher till then.'

'Another psychopathic killer, of course.'

'But in a good way.'

Lee Child/Jack Reacher: it was an easy mistake to make. A naïve reading, but not unreasonable. The author is most like his hero. The hero is simply a more muscular avatar of the writer. An inch or two taller, a solid 70 lbs heavier, a degree or two more lethal. But the reality that we all tended to shy away from was that Lee Child was also the abominable Hook Hobie, the monstrous Little Joey, the gorgeous and seductive (but also hideously sadistic) Lila Hoth. They were all his alter egos. He was not just puppet master, he was his puppets. He was not just Hitchcock, he was the psycho in the shower too. All those evil schemes, they were his evil schemes. He was responsible for constructing them, even if it was Reacher's job to deconstruct them all over again.

Now the headlamps were visible down the tunnel. 'I guess it all cancels out,' I said. 'The good and the bad, I mean. You come out even, by the end.'

'I think that's why *Night School* is different.'

'You mean your speeded-up movie style?'

He made a kind of moaning noise and said he had woken up that morning with a great idea for how to develop the story. But then it had only lasted for a couple of paragraphs, because of his accelerated style. Which is where his 'I've got nothing!' line came in: his feeling, despite being three-quarters of the way through the book, of nevertheless being right back at square one every single day. But at least he had (a) Reacher and (b) an antagonist, the anti-Reacher. And the key point that struck me in what he was saying was that he had toned down the polarity between them on account of the single solitary insight in *Reacher Said Nothing*. (Which is not necessarily a great claim to fame, because he gets swung around, equally, by the maid with her bucket and the construction workers making a racket next door.)

'The thing about the bad guy,' he said. 'He's not quite so bad this time around. I mean, you kind of understand why he would be doing what he is doing. He has a background.'

'Does he have a name?' The hog farmers with some very bad habits in *Make Me* didn't even have names. It was always 'the guy with the jeans and the hair' and so on.

'Wiley. Horace Wiley.'

'Wile E. Coyote,' I said.

Lee ignored that. This was *Night School*, not Looney Tunes. 'He has a history, in the army, it makes sense that he would react that way. Even if Reacher has to go in and sort him out. Maybe it's what Reacher could have become, in other circumstances.'

The building noise, the rattling of the tracks, the rush of air, then the train slowing down.

'The sympathetic bad guy?' I said.

'There's more of a balance,' he said. 'It's not such a stark contrast.'

'And Reacher is going about beating up Germans.'

The doors were opening and people were getting out.

'That was one reason why I was worried about having you around,' he said.

'What?' I said. 'You beating people up all the time?'

'I was worried you were going to be disappointed in me.' That line of his kind of killed me. 'Everyone is always disappointed by authors. They can never be as good as they're cracked up to be.'

We hopped on the 'B' train. A disembodied voice. 'STAND CLEAR OF THE CLOSING DOORS.' We looked for something to cling on to.

63

THE FUNCTION OF CRIME

Fir trees. An icy river. Clumps of snow looking like punctuation marks against black rocks. Nordic noir in the spring. As I took the bus from Rygge Airport into Oslo, I thought of some of the writers who had reconstructed Scandinavia, exploring the dark underworld of the social democratic dream. David Lagercrantz, Stieg Larsson, Henning Mankell, and Maj Sjöwall and Per Wahlöö (*The Laughing Policeman*, the Beck series). Something is rotten in the state of Denmark ... or Sweden, or Norway: Jo Nesbø, with the great (yet flawed) Harry Hole roaming around town, tripping over mad serial killers. With bonus sadism.

But I was going to see Ben. We had met up in London a couple of months before and compared notes on the novels of Lee Child. He was a recent convert. Had read and loved *Make Me*.

Ben had once been a student of mine at Cambridge. He is a tall, broad-shouldered guy with iron-grey hair, a stubbly jaw, and the hint of a Scottish accent. Hadn't changed too much in twenty-five years. And he has a good memory. 'I can remember something you taught me,' he said cheerfully, while we were sipping cappuccinos somewhere in his neighbourhood.

'Really!' I said, genuinely amazed. 'What was it?'

'You put a red ring around one of my dashes and wrote next to it, "Not too many of these please."'

I was kind of annoyed at my former self. 'What the hell was I worrying about?'

He insisted it was good advice. 'It made me think. It stopped me overdoing everything, spraying punctuation around like confetti.'

Thus equipped for a brilliant career, Ben had since done many things. Worked as a television producer at the BBC, rather like

Lee. Then again, like Lee, had dropped out and become a writer. I had read his book, *A Line of Blood*, and thought it was really fine. No more red ink from me. It was original, with a distinctive voice and great characters. But dark. Some of his family used to worry about what he was writing, especially because it was in the first person and the narrator was deeply ambiguous. Ben had to keep pointing out to them the truth that the author and the narrator were not one and the same. They were not entirely convinced or reassured.

And now he was married to a Norwegian woman and they had two young boys.

But it took Anders Breivik and his massacre of sixty-nine young people on the island of Utøya on 22 July 2011 before he felt truly Norwegian. Which also explained why he had chosen a life of crime.

Ben had once made a study of human sacrifices. Some scholars had argued that the idea of sacrifice was another myth, mere semiotics, but to Ben sacrifice was anything but a metaphor or fairy tale. Years before, he had gone to South America and seen some of the bodies himself, thousands of years old, preserved in mud, ritually sacrificed. It had probably started with animals then, when that didn't work, humans. El Niño laid waste to farming communities and this was the Aztec attempt to appease the gods, to rectify the climate, anything – no matter how desperate – to fix the world. It was a sweeping symbolic gesture that achieved nothing. But one that we could never quite relinquish. If it isn't El Niño, it's something else. Sacrifice is an exercise in the *apotropaic* – the warding off of evil spirits. (I'll try not to use the '–' too much.) The logic is still in place, even if it isn't logical.

Ben had never intended to write a thriller. He had started a book about a family breaking apart a few years before. But he'd only written a chapter or two. He was telling me this as we wandered around Oslo and then came across the district, with buildings still boarded up, where Breivik had parked his home-made car bomb five years earlier. Oddly enough it was Ben's wedding anniversary on the day one man declared war. The couple had been having lunch a few blocks away and they thought the sound of the explosion was a clap of thunder. Which is when Breivik was setting out for Utøya to start systematically shooting the teenagers who were there at summer camp.

The massacre itself was horrific. But the response of the police was infuriating. 'For once you could legitimately use the adjective "bumbling",' Ben said. It was stock vocabulary to describe the incompetent policeman in mysteries (Conan Doyle's Inspector Lestrade and others). But maybe *bumbling* was too kind. They had been criminally irresponsible, amateurish. One very determined, highly efficient, coolly calculating killer on the loose, and a whole bunch of the Norwegian branch of the Keystone Cops chasing him. No Harry Hole in evidence.

Both of the two helicopter pilots in Oslo were on holiday at the same time. Therefore no helicopter.

While Breivik was on the island carrying out his plan, two policemen were cowering behind a dumpster ... on the mainland. They had to consider 'health and safety'.

The first boat – an inflatable – the police took to reach the island started to sink, so they turned around and went back to harbour again.

For three hours there was a post-it on the desk at police headquarters with the details of the perpetrator and the licence number of his vehicle (reported by a concerned citizen). Ignored.

Twice Breivik phoned to give himself up. The first time the police switchboard operator put the phone down because he wasn't speaking clearly enough. The second time it was dismissed as a prank call.

Only one policeman had ever lost his job in the wake of this catastrophe.

Norwegian police didn't take the possibility of evil seriously enough. They 'were in a massive state of unpreparedness'. According to Ben they still don't have a specified response time.

I recalled that Amy Winehouse had killed herself the day after (or at least had colluded in her own death). To her way of thinking she didn't measure up to the impossible standards she set for herself. She didn't fit in. Breivik killed seventy-seven people because he didn't think Norway measured up to the mythic standards he had dreamed up for an entire country. Maybe he didn't fit in either, but everyone ought to fit in with him. He had achieved some kind of record as the greatest Norwegian solo killer in history.

In Ben's first novel the child's point of view was pervasive and there was a prevailing sense that the adult world is mysterious and terrifying and does not always mean what it says. In the book he was working on now, *This Is Not America*, he was trying to write about what happens to a family who go to Norway from the US in search of a low-crime society – and then duly lose a daughter in a massacre. On an island like Utøya, she is shot first in the shoulder and then again through the head as she tries to swim away. The father was reasonably satisfied with the judicial process; the mother wanted revenge as soon as she got over the grief.

'I'm trying to make it less about Breivik,' Ben said. We went into the courthouse where the trial had been held and that Ben had attended every day for a couple of months. The verdict took seven hours to read out because each one of the murders was treated as a singular and separate crime. Breivik was ruled criminally responsible. Not insane. He had been too meticulous and prepared and systematic to be mad. Or if he was mad, then it was a kind of madness that was all too common. It had a logic, it had a rationale, as he tried to explain to the court. He had even written a manifesto or testament, published online, explaining his thinking, a compendium of hatred, hardcore video games (notably *Call of Duty: Modern Warfare 2*), and *The Lord of the Rings*, identifying himself as one of the 'Knights Templar', or OMA (One-Man Army). Someone had compared him to Gollum, constantly interrogating himself. He saw himself as a Crusader and was known by some as 'Commander Breivik'. There was, he claimed, a plot to dilute and corrupt Norwegian manhood. He hated all immigrants. He blamed the Norwegian government for letting them in and planned to wipe out the next generation of potential politicians (the children of members of the Labour Party had their summer camp on Utøya). This was his 'defence'.

At one point in the trial, Ben recalled, Breivik had caught the eye of a woman sitting in the courtroom. 'You are a beautiful and elegant Norwegian woman,' he said, addressing himself to her. 'I did what I did for you – you should be thanking me for it.'

Ben came out of the courtroom at the end of the trial

feeling more fully Norwegian than he had ever felt before. 'I felt I belonged,' he said. Because Breivik's murders were an attack on Norway itself. Norway was inclusive; Breivik wanted it to be exclusive. Ben gave up commuting to London and settled in Oslo full-time. And went back to the book. He'd got into the habit of writing – he was reporting on the trial for a newspaper – so he just kept on going.

'The worst thing is when children die. It's the most horrendous thing I can imagine,' Ben said as we walked along the waterfront. 'And that's exactly what I find myself describing.'

We gazed across the water at an island which still had snow on its upper slopes. In the summer, people from Oslo would take a ferry and go to their cabins by the sea. Or go sailing. In the spring, Ben told me, they tended to commit suicide a lot. Not in the middle of the very long and cold winter but more when darkness finally gave way to light again. That was when the suicide statistics spiked.

Which made me think of Émile Durkheim. He wrote his book about suicide in the early years of the twentieth century, following another financial crisis in which higher numbers of people had been jumping out of high windows. Part of his explanation had to do with 'anomie', that state of normlessness in which the individual floats free from the codes of society. But, in a way, it was like the opposite of normlessness: not a deficit but an overload, hypernomia, an exaggerated sense of normativeness, which causes you to feel insufficiently normative yourself (like Amy Winehouse, perhaps) or to sense that everyone else is insufficiently normative (as Breivik thought) and that they therefore need to be taught a lesson.

What is the 'function' of suicide? Durkheim asked himself. (The answer is not as obvious as you might think.)

But he also asked: what is the function of crime?

There was another line of mine that Ben remembered when we were roaming around Oslo. 'Didn't you used to say something about a society of saints?'

'That the amount of crime would remain the same. Yes.'

It was a good line, right up there with my lessons in punctuation, but I had to admit that I had stolen it from Durkheim. His point was that, even in a society of saints, the ratio of crime to virtue would remain unchanged because the standards would go up. The Sartrean rule that hell is other people still applied, even among saints. And even in Oslo. The Norwegian police should really have been reading up on Durkheim.

The next day I followed Ben along a street of houses with Icelandic dragonheads sprouting from their roofs like TV aerials. 'I try to think I'm going to work,' Ben said. Finally we walked into the 'Litteraturhuset', at the rear of the Royal Palace. Ben worked there every morning, from about 9 or 9.30. There was one of those wonderful Norwegian compound words on the door of the quiet room where several writers were quietly tapping at keyboards. This was the *Skribentarbeidsplasser*. Ben started writing at precisely 9.24. I sat in a chair about a yard to the right of him, but I couldn't ask him any questions. I couldn't ask anyone any questions. The atmosphere was too *pietistik* – tranquil, but with a definite hint of 'pious' too, as if something sacred was taking place. So I sat at my own desk and wondered what they were writing about.

Perhaps all of them were complicit in Nordic noir. They were, just like Lee, making up crimes of all kinds, massacres, in which children were being killed again and again, vast infernal conspiracies, human trafficking networks, sexual exploitation, robbery, rape, and murder, on a quiet, *pietistik*, but semi-industrial scale. I had to hope that there would be a Jack Reacher or a Lisbeth Salander or a Harry Hole to restore the cosmic balance.

But of course they were not making anything up. It was impossible to imagine anything that was worse than what actual human beings were capable of doing to one another. Nordic noir was simply infinite variations on palaeo-empiricism, a fresh iteration of a grand murderous tradition.

I was in the noir factory.

But, as Durkheim would say, what was its function? He argued that crime had a simple function. Although the manifest point of crime was to steal things away, it gave back far more than it took: it created a whole society of law-abiding citizens who became able to recognize one another as law-abiders by virtue (and it was a virtue) of the bad behaviour of the law-breaker. Transgression created conformity. Crime was a deviation from a norm that helped to establish that there was a norm. Crime generated the laws required to contain crime. As Ben said, 'We [Norway] are a country governed by laws.' The biggest celebration of the year is 'Constitution Day' on 17 May. At the same time, precisely because it was so unified, Norway created outsiders, deviants, and foreigners were seen as threatening.

The writers in the 'Litteraturhuset', like people standing on the edge of a cliff in the suicide season, were poised between the light and the dark. Norwegian even has a word for it: *Påskekrim* (Eastercrime) – a form of literature bestriding both sacrifice and resurrection. It wasn't just popular at Easter, it was like Easter all-year round. Maybe the Saturday between Good Friday and Easter Sunday, with a prevailing sense of 'Why hast thou forsaken me?'

The Breivik massacre had been recorded in the crime statistics as an asterisk, an anomaly in a separate category all of its own. It wasn't exactly normal by Norwegian standards. I heard while I was in Oslo that the number of murders was in fact going down. At the same time, the number of Eastercrime books was going up if the 'Litteraturhuset' was anything to go by. There were more Nordic noir murders than ever. More 'crime', less crime.

We were all making human sacrifices, in fictional form, to ward off evil. That was our function, as writers. Maybe it was working. Jorge Luis Borges has one of his protagonists imagine his own death in various horrific ways and in extreme detail. Fictional deaths, but realistic all the same. With the notion that, having once narrated or conceived death with enough clarity, then it would be impossible to die in just this way. It would already have happened and could not be repeated.

I gave Ben a comradely hug and headed down the hill towards the station. Outside the Royal Palace two identical sentries, as immaculate as toy soldiers, were marching up and down, symmetrically, with extreme precision, rifles over their shoulders.

The sun was shining, the snow was melting.

64

CRIMETHRILLERGIRL

Lee Child in Cambridge. Queens' College Old Combination Room (or 'OCR', as they say). Classic ancient oak-panelled hall, walls hung with portraits of distinguished past Masters of the college, going back centuries. A current master (of fiction) with academic masters smiling (well, not exactly smiling) down upon the writer. The author of the Jack Reacher novels breaking bread with the dons.

That is how it was supposed to be. But this is non-fiction. It didn't happen quite like that.

Maybe he should have been riding a bicycle in an academic gown and mortar board too. As it was he just rocked up in a sporty red Jaguar and parked on the forecourt at King's. And he did go to dinner at the St John's Chop House. Maybe that was more his style. I expect his next novel will be about a very large axe murderer who carries off his victims to a place called the Chop House. Or maybe a bunch of farmers in Nebraska who take their butchering skills up to the next level. Until Reacher steps off the train.

He couldn't stick around for the big formal college feast the following day. He ducked out, had something going on in some other part of the country. Which he really did, but it was more like playing truant. Going AWOL. Drifting off, in classic vigilante style. Like a ghost, or a dream, vanishing as soon as you had a proper look at him in the light.

In the OCR I ended up sitting next to a German guy called Gunther who had once been a student of André Brink's in Cape Town. And therefore knew Karina (who took 'Jack' to bed with her). And now he too had succumbed to the works of Lee Child. I told him I preferred Jonathan Franzen. That riled him. I was tempted to mention that in *Night School* Reacher was going about beating up Germans just for fun. And that the ball really had crossed the line too. Only the spirit of European Union camaraderie held me back.

'What happened to Lee?' asked Kasia, knocking back the claret.

'He had to run,' I said, making him sound like a fugitive from justice. Which he in fact is.

She nobly swallowed her disappointment. She had booked the OCR just for Lee, of course. In his honour. 'Who was that "Alex or Justin" anyway?' she said. 'The snooty one in your book.' She was referring to the guy in the English faculty who had in bygone days come back with a disdainful and dismissive response to my notion that Lee ought to come and talk at Cambridge. 'He's not quite one of us, is he, old man?' was the gist. Kasia was of the more permissive, laissez-faire, open-minded tendency within the faculty who tended to see Lee and everything else as part of a vast continuum of textuality, in which mere literary snobbery had no part. She had also written a book about boxing, so she was naturally on the side of Jack Reacher. She wanted to track Alex or Justin down and kick his arse for him.

Everything had turned on its head in the Academy. The barbarians were at the gates and we had just lowered the drawbridge. And now they were driving over it in their red Jags. A Child in Cambridge. He was there to speak about 'Books in the Making', on the cusp between a literary festival and an academic symposium. At the university that had rejected him forty-odd years before. And he got a massive audience at the biggest lecture theatre in town, where Jacques Derrida and Camille Paglia had once spoken. He said something about how he saw his readers as being like the Rings of Saturn: hardcore centre, maybe flaky and more spaced-out around the periphery.

But it was CrimeThrillerGirl – as we walked through King's one afternoon in spring, amid daffodils and students – who cranked up the argument. The one between Lee and me and Quiller (Christ Church graduate, devotee of the works of Adam Hall, stubble, crewcut, bit of a football hooligan look about him). CrimeThrillerGirl had come to Cambridge for the day to interview me about 'crime' and Lee and all that, and attend the talk. She was a blonde-haired horsewoman who had once worked as a bounty hunter in California and blogged about all things noir. And she had a début novel coming out as well: *Deep Down Dead*, with a kick-ass female protagonist, Lori Anderson. Which explains how this all got started.

Something to do with her and Lee and dead bodies, lots of them. So we were walking through Front Court, past the Chapel, and over the bridge, Lee, Quiller, mc, and CTG, in the general direction of Lady Mitchell Hall, and she starts wondering out loud what we thought we were all doing exactly, including her, making up stories about wicked serial killers, and axe murderers, and murderous farmers, and snuff film aficionados, and then coming up with some kind of fictional sticking plaster for the immense wounds we were inflicting on ourselves.

Fair question. I should mention, in a spirit of honest declaration, that all three guys here were just a little in awe of CTG, on account of her being so young and enthusiastic and cheerful and having the great moniker. And she was funny too. But I like to think that all that had almost nothing to do with her getting our full attention. In truth we really wanted to know what the hell everyone was doing, just as she did.

Nobody really knew anything, it turned out, but everybody had theories. There was only one actual fact that everyone pretty much agreed on. Crime was going down, but 'crime' was going up, statistically speaking. (Of course it is perfectly possible that you have been mugged and robbed and beaten to a pulp without ever reading a thriller in your life. I speak here only of the collective.) So there was a mystery to do with mysteries. Why were they so darn successful? How come Lee Child had a couple of hundred people turning up to hear him speak, one grey night in Cambridge, when they could have been going to Evensong and listening to choirboys?

Lee thought he knew. 'It's a low-crime environment now. You can't have crime writing in a high-crime society. You're too busy fending off bad guys to read about Reacher or Harry Bosch going about solving crimes. You wouldn't even take it seriously. It must be some kind of nostalgia. For the bad old days. When we really were killing one another all the time.'

CTG wasn't fully convinced. Weren't we still killing one another? Wasn't Lee striking too optimistic a note?

'I mean, come on,' persisted Lee. 'Think of the Vikings. It was all rape and pillage around here. Or war. Not too many Agatha Christies or Dorothy L. Sayers then, were there?' He had been writing a foreword to a new edition of Lord Peter Wimsey stories, so Sayers was on his mind. 'Maybe we're winning. Jack Reacher and Hercule Poirot are actually deterring crime.'

Quiller thought Lee could have had a brilliant career as a criminal. 'Now,' he argued, 'all the criminals are becoming writers. They realize there is more money in "crime" than crime. And you generally don't have to go to prison for it either. You end up giving lectures at Cambridge.'

'There's a few who ought to be banged up!' said Lee, with feeling. He was probably thinking of Baldacci. We went out of the back gate and crossed over the Backs and up West Road. The sky was overcast, with a threat of rain, and it was getting dark.

'There's a fundamental philosophical question,' I said. I would say that, in the land of Wittgenstein, but there was. '"How do you know the sun is going to rise tomorrow?" It's the problem of induction. But the answer is, you don't!'

'Another mad theory,' said Lee.

'I know,' I said. 'But it's really one of yours. It's right there in *Make Me*. You bury Keever with a backhoe, but you're digging him out again by the end, bringing him up to the light even, if not quite resurrecting him. Rescuing him from the darkness, right?'

'Ha!' he said, helpfully.

'Reacher arrives in the middle of the night. Then chapter 52 – you spend pages on describing the sun coming up. Lyrical and poetic. That's the whole point. Rewind the clock in your head a couple of million years. You're crouching in a cave at night. Nocturnal animals all around, roaring at you in the darkness. You're praying for the safety of dawn. That's why Nordic noir is so big. They don't have enough light up there in the Arctic Circle. A night that lasts for months. So you need a lot of prayers to make up for it. Let there be light and all that. You see, it's not even about fear of what other humans are getting up to. It's a basic astronomical anxiety. Our redeemer liveth.'

We had stopped to shelter from the rain amid the arches of the Raised Faculty Building. 'Have I got time for a fag?' Lee asked.

'Let there be light,' I said.

It was inevitable that it would come up at the Chop House. About how he wanted to die. Or, preferably, be killed. There's something about the word 'chop'. Also I had been saying, to the guy across the table, that I would probably have to kill off the great Master one fine day. Maybe, I speculated, in some Oedipal way, all readers secretly wanted to kill off the author. Overhearing, Lee chips in, 'I wish you would! Go on, you'd be doing me a favour! I'm glad you're going to Montana to learn to shoot – that could come in handy.'

It all started with this story I had heard about Lucius Wilmerding. True story. Ninety-something-year-old. But still driving. And he had parked his car outside a convenience store in Princeton. Where a stick-up happened to be taking place. And the gunman had come running out in classic style, and leapt in the back of Mr Wilmerding's car, held a gun to his head, and said, as was standard in these circumstances, 'Drive or I'll blow your fuckin' brains out!' Normally, you just drive. Drive and pray. But Mr Wilmerding was no ordinary man. He was, after all, ninety-something, and afflicted with several painful ailments of the kind that ninety-somethings are susceptible to, and spending half his time in hospital getting treatment, none of it pleasant. So he turns to the gunman and says, 'Go on then, shoot. Please shoot. You'll be doing me a favour.' The robber was so flummoxed by the old man's composure that he ran off and was duly arrested.

'I'm like that old guy,' Lee was saying, 'Kill me, please, somebody, anybody.'

He couldn't believe that he had just signed a new three-book deal with his publishers and they hadn't insisted on a medical. He thought he could drop dead at any time so he had got the payments front-loaded, with a notion of collecting before he conked out. Or some young punk puts a bullet through his brain.

So the author isn't quite dead yet, although he wouldn't mind dying, preferably heroically if possible. He hoped he would have the composure, when someone finally stuck a gun to his head, to say, 'Go on then, pull the trigger, you'll be doing everybody a big favour.'

He also had this idea that maybe Alex/Justin had been right and he never should have been invited to Cambridge. 'I'm the rabble,' he said. 'I don't belong here. They were right to reject me. I was stoned most of the time. From about 1970 onwards.'

65

THE END OF THE NOVEL

I mentioned that Kafka story. The one about a man who is trying to get through a door and he can't. So he waits outside, he never leaves the door, year after year, his entire life. Then, just as he is about to die, and can't even crawl through it, the doorman finally slams it shut, saying, 'This door was just for you.'

He said, 'I would just say, "Fuck you and your door! Who gives a shit anyway!"' Or, I like to imagine, he would give the doorman a good kicking. Lee Child chooses to be an outsider: he doesn't want to be admitted to any sacred temple, he doesn't want to be a member of any club that would have him as a member. He would rather be a barbarian at the gates than one of the cosy insiders. He prefers to remain 'Grievous', as he was known at school – aggrieved, aggressive. He doesn't want anyone pinning a medal to his chest.

We were back in New York. On Spring Street. Evening. Walking to the subway. *Night School* was in the hands of the publishers. Done and dusted. More than ever he wanted to pick a fight with somebody, anybody. 'You can't say "the hoi polloi". The masses, the mob. "Hoi polloi" already contains "the". So it's like saying "the the polloi".'

'But Lee....'

'Oh bollocks!'

Fundamentally, he was a stickler for correctness. Maybe the bad guys have to be killed off in his books on account of bad grammar. They stood accused of murdering the language. Maybe this was why Reacher often said nothing. Just to be on the safe side.

Maybe this also explained why the *New Yorker* had commissioned him to write 800 words on what he would un-invent. At least he wouldn't un-invent grammar. And it couldn't be something sensible but impossible like un-inventing nuclear bombs, or poverty. This was his big idea: 'I'm going to un-invent *fiction*,' he said. 'Kill off the novel. We'll all be better off without it.'

I grappled with the vision for a moment. It was a warm and pleasant evening in the Village. But it was like Lee Child had just wiped out a significant portion of the planet. 'What?! Hold on a second. No more ... James Joyce? No more Marcel Proust? No more ... Lee Child?!' I was reeling. Literature holocaust. Madame Bovary and Anna Karenina were dead, again.

'I'm going to eradicate all the airport bookstores at a stroke,' he said, gleefully. Chuckling, like some sinister Mr Big. He reminded me just a little, at that moment, of the great French utopian thinker Charles Fourier, who predicted that the libraries would crumble in the phalanstery of the future, because he had pretty much said it all. The argument was over. 'You'd have the truth, finally, and nothing but the truth.'

'But Lee ...' I'm sorry. This was all I could come up with before he cut across me, impatiently.

'I don't want to rule the world,' he said.

Not as if I had asked him whether he wanted to rule the world. But the possibility of it had clearly been on his mind. What with going around un-inventing stuff.

'Look at this street. It's a mess.'

I thought Spring Street was looking really quite good in the evening sun. Thriving, throbbing, pulsating. I'd definitely seen worse.

'I couldn't even organize the garbage collection!' Lee was envisaging what it would be like trying to rule the world. 'You want to know the worst job in the world? Mayor of New York! It's impossible. Do you want to be Mayor of the World?'

'Er ...'

'No of course you bloody don't. Who would? Do you want to know what I really want to do?'

'Sure.'

'I want to put my feet up for a change. I want to be completely irresponsible. I don't want to have to *do* anything. I'm going to find a beach somewhere and park my deckchair on it, put my shades on, and read a good book.'

'OK,' I said. Just trying to get the picture into focus. 'So you're reading a book.'

'Lots of books, a whole stack of them. No e-reader, thanks. Just the good old books.'

'And you would be reading ... what, exactly?'

'God, I don't know, everything, anything, the usual, a good novel, maybe a history, or a science book or something.'

'But,' says I, 'you've just un-invented fiction. So there wouldn't be any good novels to read. You'd only have the books about rust and air-conditioning and dinosaurs. Is that enough?'

You have to give this to Lee. He thinks about things. He really does. My question stopped him in his tracks. At least I think it did, unless it was just he was about to cross Spring Street and take the 'C' train uptown and wanted to check for traffic.

'All right then. Default setting. Delete the *un*-invent. *Re*-invent. But just let Connelly do his thing. I don't want to have to write any more. I've officially retired.'

'Baldacci will take over.'

'Let him! See if I care.'

'What about Reacher?' I said. 'No more Reacher books? You're going to disappoint an awful lot of readers.'

'Somebody else can do it for me,' he said. 'What about *you*?'

AFTER

IN CASE YOU WANTED TO KNOW WHAT HAPPENED TO THAT ROMANCE WITH CHANG

Chapter 1, THE MIDNIGHT LINE (November 2017)

Jack Reacher and Michelle Chang spent three days in Milwaukee. On the fourth morning she was gone.

MARTIN: Not quite a one-night stand. A three-night stand. Roughly par for the course for Reacher. The end of the romance initiated in *Make Me*. But more importantly, look how precise this is. It's all about the timing. Reacher has the uncanny ability to know what the time is without checking. The clock is always accessible in his head. You could say that Reacher embodies time. He is a walking, talking (well, not much of that), head-butting principle of temporality. He determines how long bad guys are going to spend in hospital – or possibly eternity. And then consider your titles – *Gone Tomorrow*, *61 Hours* – now *The Midnight Line*. And your next one, the one you just started: *Past Tense*. Everything is timing.

CHILD: Well, it's a chronological art form, propelling the reader through the story a beat, an hour, a day at a time. So a sense of beats, hours, and days passing is important. It grounds the reader against a scale. At this stage, it's all about postponement. I don't want to give anything away yet. Really, if Reacher was as smart as some people think he is, the novel would be over on page 2 because he would have worked it all out.

MARTIN: The farewell note on the pillow. The text within the text. Reacher as reader. It's interesting how often he really is just that, a reader (he's also a bit of a mind-reader). And he registers, in an almost literary critical way, that Chang uses not a metaphor, but a 'simile'. Not too many tough-guy vigilante drifters would bother with that distinction.

CHILD: He likes precision. Words have meanings, and he likes to know them. In general, people like the contrast between his enormous physicality and his delight at small intellectual diversions.

MARTIN: And Reacher is compared to New York. Big enough perhaps. Space as well as time. Isn't his ultimate geographical goal to encompass the whole of the United States? In *Make Me* he gets off a train to kick-start the novel. This time it's the bus. Reacher's trajectory is like a game of hopscotch.

CHILD: And he's noticing one person after another telling him his lifestyle is odd. There's a little introspection in this novel, largely because of Chang. But mostly he's happy. He enjoys small pleasures. I think you once called it the 'infra-ordinary' – not the extraordinary – that's what he's into.

MARTIN: He picks up the toothbrush. Can't leave that behind! It's about the only thing he carries on him, right? One of these days he ought to use it as a weapon, you know, poke someone's eye out or something.

CHILD: See, this is the trouble with literary critic types – they're fundamentally violent. They love to rip people to shreds. Reacher wouldn't dream of poking anyone's eye out with his toothbrush. He would use his thumbs for that.

MARTIN: You like to start with an 'end' (the 'end of several things') and an 'end-of-the-line'. Then it turns out it isn't. I assume your denial of 'denial' and Reacher's having no 'secret' thoughts is your critique of Freudian psychology. There is no unconscious, everything is out there, visible, audible, nothing is hidden, if you're only aware enough. And then we have it – the ring, the magic ring. You went to the same school as Tolkien – is this your take on *Lord of the Rings*? Or did you have Wagner in mind? You set *Night School* in Germany, after all. Or none of the above?

CHILD: I don't want to upset any *Lord of the Rings* fans – or the old school – but I never really read Tolkien. Don't like Wagner – preposterously overblown. The story is a simple quest narrative, and the ring is the trigger.

MARTIN: This is not a magic ring. A pawn shop 'on a run-down street beyond the restroom block'. What could be more prosaic? And it's very small, almost insignificant. And yet here we have the mysterious text which has to be deciphered. Reacher's exegetical skills being brought to bear. 'S.R.S. 2005'. Quite close to S.O.S.

CHILD: Reacher deduces from the size that it's a woman's ring, and he knows what she went through to get it. His instincts kick in ... as always, is he helping the little guy, or assuming the presence of a sinister 'big guy', who needs taking down? Some challenges intrigue him.

MARTIN: I know your alter ego is rock star. Or rock star manqué. The fifth Beatle. So here the crucial thing is really the music. You mention songs on the radio. And the guitars. 'Dreams, unfulfilled.' Is that you? Lots of short sentences (only three one-worders, though). A montage or collage technique. There is not much dialogue until Reacher gets into the pawn shop. But maybe the secret is that there is a lot of implied dialogue, going on in the head of Reacher. Internalized.

CHILD: Yeah, it's all about questions at this stage. I don't know any of the answers.

MARTIN: I feel I ought to do a proper interview, you know, your whole life in a nutshell, your opinions on everything. Would you like to summarize your thoughts on this and that? Art, life, love, Tom Cruise ...

CHILD: I'm with Kafka – the meaning of life is that it ends.

ACKNOWLEDGEMENTS

'Lee Child and the Readers': back in the day that might have been the name of a small yet groovy (and highly literate) band, known only to a few fanatically devoted cognoscenti. Now it feels more like a Cecil B. de Mille movie, with a cast of thousands (or, in fact, millions).

Nearly all of the loyal readers of the Reacher novels must remain, of necessity, uncredited. But I am glad to be able to spotlight a few select names. You are right up there in the credits, and I really am extremely grateful to all of you, whether you were involved in production or more like stunt doubles: Kirk Bloodsworth, Kasia Boddy, Stephanie Broadribb, Sharon Carr, Carl Cederström, Suzanne Chazin, Joy Connolly, Tom Cruise, Whitney Dangerfield, Jonathan Este, Elsa Fischer, Will Frears, Sam Fussell, Jude Hardin, Stephen King, Laura Kipnis, David Lagercrantz, Lydia Lair, Jessica Lehrman, Sam Leith, Heather Martin, Janet Maslin, Amanda Lynn Mayhew, Ben McPherson, Helen Moffett, Dan O'Hara, Karen Rinaldi, Joel Rose, Karen Slaughter, Henry Sutton, Karina Szczurek, Linda Taylor, John Thompson, Scott Veale, David Winters, Ivan Zatkovich. With heartfelt thanks also to those mighty institutions, Cambridge University, City University New York, *The Conversation*, *The Independent*, the *London Review of Books*, *The Iowa Review*, *The New York Times*, *The Spectator*, and the Stockholm Business School, for extending a platform to the Reacher creatures.